SCARCITY IN

The Built Environment and the Eco

Contents

3

Urban Systems - current status

4

Scenarios - into the future

Foreword

Jeremy Till

It was the colour of the ground he remembered most. Black. Spewed out from deep down below, it had flowed, and then frozen, into a delta of deep dark discomfort. Elsewhere they had thrown themselves into the cushions of moss that had formed in the crevices of this hard ground, but here the surface could cut eyes with its sharpness.

Closer to the houses the rock had been crushed into a stony mulch. Between the houses the government had laid a strip of black road, unnatural in its smoothness and bereft of any markings.

'It was the bankers,' said the woman, 'their eyes were bigger than their heads.' Her normally active face creased up at the thought of such stupidity. 'Idiots.'

'What happened?' he asked.

'They grew beyond their means, and accumulated a toppling mountain of foreign debt, but the money flowing through the system made so much noise it drowned out their senses. Idiots.'

'And then?'

'And then,' she looked at him despairingly, 'and then, this.' And she spun round, hand outstretched, silently remonstrating with the scene before them.

It was like a freeze frame from an instructional video *How to Build a House.* First you do this and at the end you have this. Houses were scattered seemingly randomly across the black ground, all in various states of completion. A concrete frame with expectant reinforced bars perched next to a fully complete house, curtains drawn against the nightmarish vision beyond. In other parts of the country he had seen houses hunkered down into the folds of the landscape, working with what was given, but here the buildings just sat on top, at the same time fragile and disdainful.

However, this was much worse than a frozen video scene, because there were signs of life in the midst of the building site. In the middle were half-completed houses where the owners had filled the concrete frame with haphazard windows and doors bought from the DIY store, and strapped them together with plastic tape and stretched polythene that flapped in the wind. Behind that they had strung up blankets as curtains, just as he had seen in squats in London. And all around lay the detritus of construction. Piles of insulation blown apart by the weather, cranes lying on their sides like dead animals, rusting dumper trucks settling down on deflated tyres, concrete mixers cradling their lumpy loads, clutches of wires disgorging from the ground. In other parts of the world these abandoned parts would have been scavenged, but here the collapse was so complete that they had no further purpose to serve. There was nothing more to build, not just because there was no money to build with, but also because there was nothing to build for; it appeared that the country had already gone far past its limits.

'The money stopped. The work stopped. Instantly.' said the woman curtly.

The owners were left stranded at the precise point that the construction programme had progressed to; trapped by the burden of cheap money, which was now worth nothing, all they had were these partial fragments of the dreams the bankers had sold them. He did not know whom to feel more sorry for. The people in the completed houses who had invested most and so lost most, and were now perpetually reminded of the folly of the moment, hence the drawn curtains behind which they could live out a semblance of a refined life. Or those in the half-finished buildings; those people existed in a state of suspension, on the one hand living out the pioneering vision of the wild west, on the other hand restricted in their means to reach completion. Or should he feel most sorry for those who owned the useless empty frames, which held out no hope of ever being completed?

In reality, he should have placed his concern everywhere in equal measure. All of them had a share of abundance and a share of scarcity. All had something to show but lacked something else. The owners of the completed houses at least had windows and warmth, but lacked the perfect wholeness they had been promised. The half-finished had a sense they might get there through their own ingenuity, a certain control over where they were going, even though they lacked the immediate means to get there. And the ones who had barely started at least had the comfort that they had not invested too much, even though they lacked anything to show for their dream of a better life. Scarcity and abundance flipped around, relative to what was measuring them and who experienced them.

'This is a landscape of pure scarcity,' he blurted out, pleased with the phrase, thinking it might work as a chapter heading.

'There's no such thing as pure scarcity,' she replied quickly, words tumbling together, 'it's always on the move, always constructed, always affecting someone.'

As if on cue, a young woman appeared around the corner, struggling with a pushchair as it bounced around on the crushed rock where a pavement should have been. In his eyes it was strange that she avoided the smooth road, but she was conditioned to protect her child from the merest hint of traffic. Eventually she reached a bus stop, a pole stuck in the black ground with a mess of concrete spilling around the edges.

'Surely there can't be buses here!' he said.

'Oh yes there are, the municipality promised to provide infrastructure, including a regular bus service, and are now fearful of breaking that agreement. Idiots.'

Sure enough a bus came, empty but on time, and the young woman leant down to lift up her heavy load, wanting for a pavement to be installed to bring her up to the level of the bus, wanting for more marks of civilisation to cover the harshness of the underlying scene.

'One day nature will come and take this back,' the first woman said, 'but nature works on a different clock here.'

It would be a long time, beyond their lives, before they could throw themselves into the moss again.

'In the meantime, there is work to do.'

To unpick the constructions of scarcity. To find new forms of abundance.

Introduction

Arna Mathiesen

Why This Book?

In October 2008 Icelandic dreams of prosperity and global eminence turned into nightmares of economic ruin and international embarrassment. After a period of extraordinary economic growth at the beginning of the century, the economy of Iceland collapsed into a rapid and deep fiscal crisis, when in one perilous week three of the country's major banks went bust. This was the end of a five-year period of building activity, on a scale previously unseen in the country. The problems were not merely economic. They were also social, spatial and environmental.

The crash in Iceland was an inherent part of the global economic decline that began in 2007. At the same time it was quite unique. Icelandic households turned out to have had some of the largest contractions in private consumption of any medium-to-high-income countries, and their debt was deeper.

Many homes, initially built as shelters and as signs of prosperity, turned into immense burdens. The economic growth had come at a high cost firmly intertwined with the built environment and spatial practices. Within six years the footprint of the Reykjavík Capital Area, where two-thirds of the population lives, was enlarged by 25%, posing diverse spatial challenges for the inhabitants.

In this book the crash and its aftermath in Iceland is viewed as an opportunity to understand how ecological and manmade systems are related to one another. It reflects on how alternative ways of wiring those systems might lead to better local solutions. While seeing the challenges and opportunities through the lens of scarcity, and by applying ecological approaches to design, the case of the Reykjavík Capital Area may inform a new spirit of development in various cultures and climates.

This is a book for people who are interested in the built environment, the challenges it poses and the opportunities it offers when it comes to crisis point.

The several books already published on the subject of the economic meltdown in Iceland focus primarily on the state of the economy. The most serious attempt to understand the processes leading to the collapse, a report in excess of 2,400 pages initiated by the Icelandic parliament for investigating the fall of the Icelandic banks, makes for an interesting read, but not a single word is devoted to the built environment. This despite the fact that the banks were major players in the building bubble, as generous lenders of money to pay for construction and to finance building companies, some of which were even run from the banks' premises. Many large companies in the building industry went bankrupt along with the banks, and some have now resumed practice with new registration numbers and no debt.

The primary goal of economics is ostensibly to keep scarcity at bay. Here architecture and design can be helpful, as a preoccupation through the ages has indeed been economising with space, and determining how to get the optimal value out of the location and the materials at hand.

This book has been initiated and edited by architects and urbanists, and it is the only one to date which relates the economic crisis in Iceland to the built environment in particular.

Some of the contributors to this book are local scholars. Others are practitioners, artists, photographers and/or activists who have investigated the situation through action on the ground, both before and after the crash. Still more come from outside Iceland, bringing their different perspectives and observations. All are contributing their reflections on the built environment in the context of the dramatic incidence and future scenarios are explored through workshops with students of architecture, urbanism and planning. The result is an anthology; a multiplicity of voices that together reveal links between the crash and the built environment.

The Reykajvík Capital Area is on the south-west coast of Iceland; an independent country on an outpost island on the edge of Europe.

It is the kind of book that the reader can dip in and out of, not necessarily being interested in all the subjects it covers. It offers insights, for a range of different professionals, students and anyone wanting to learn more about the wide range of subjects it contains. The reader can jump back and forth in the book and find thought-provoking observations in the text or the rich array of images.

Despite a global connection via the internet, and through financial and ecological systems, Iceland is a self-contained unit inasmuch as it is an independent legislative enclave, and the territory is separated from others by several hundred kilometres of ocean. This makes it easy to achieve a certain overview of the situation, making it an advantageous research object for comprehensive analysis. The geographical features of the country are also appropriate for demonstrating frugality through urban processes, since every decision involving the transport of materials for sustenance from other territories involves even more expense, and more CO_2 emissions, than elsewhere.

The Reykjavík Capital Area falls into a common category as regards its size, with a population that has just exceeded 200,000. Small cities (those with less than 500,000 inhabitants) are home to 52% of the world's urban population (World Urbanization Prospects).

The book can therefore deliver valuable insights applicable to many other urban contexts across the globe, hit by a shrunken economy.

The Structure of the Book

The layers of a case study on the Reykjavík Capital Area which April Arkitekter, a Norwegian-Icelandic architecture firm based in Oslo, conducted on behalf of the Oslo School of Architecture (AHO) are reflected in the four-part structure of this publication.

The range of contributors and material represented in the book reflects the lengthy process of search and investigation of the project which, through workshops and seminars, led to a series of new and interesting connections and findings. The foreword of the book was written by Jeremy Till, Head of Central Saint Martins College in London. He was the initiator and leader of 'Scarcity and Creativity in the Built Environment' (SCIBE), a research project exploring both conceptually and empirically the relation between scarcity and creativity in the context of the built environment.

1. Urban Transformations - before the crash

Part one begins with a chapter (by me, Arna Mathiesen) about the expansion of the Reykjavík Capital Area, and reflects on its connection to the expansion of the banking system which so memorably crashed in October 2008.

A study led by Ásdís Hlökk Theodórsdóttir, a planner and educator, who recently became the leader of The Icelandic National Planning Agency, is introduced by her and Salvör Jónsdóttir, who was previously the planning director of Reykjavík City. The study examines how municipalities in the south-west corner of Iceland deliberately misinterpreted the stipulated population growth, in order to justify their plans for the largest developments possible during the boom.

My photo essay describing the upscaling across the categories of the built environment in the capital area during the boom, from the perspective of an Icelandic architect living abroad, is then presented.

Massimo Santanicchia, an Italian architect and urbanist, active member of the so-called 'Pots and Pans Revolution' in Iceland, and teacher at the Icelandic architecture programme, analyses the urban developments in the built environment in the same period, from the perspective of justice.

This is followed by my chapter on the resources of Iceland and how they can be seen in relation to the built environment.

The art trio 'Silliness' (Kjánska) write about one of their works 'Groundbreakings', which took place in different villages on the coast of Iceland in 2007 and was a comment on the spirit of entrepreneurship that was in the air just before the crash.

An outside perspective of the pre-crash culture comes from Thomas Forget, an American designer and critic who participated in the 2007 International Planning Competition for the Vatnsmýri area of Reykjavík.

Finally, artist Ásmundur Ásmundsson's work from 2007, as presented by Valur Antonsson, emerges as a monument to the culture of finance and its literal concretisation.

2. Agents of Change - after the crash

This part opens with my reflections on a work by 'The Art Nurses' (Listhjúkkur), a collaboration between the artists Ósk Vilhjálmsdóttir and Anna Hallin. It explores the confusion triggered by the crash, and the new attitudes which then emerged, pointing towards fresh and more basic practices. The setting of the work was the site of the eruption of Eyjafjallajökull, and a giant half-built concert hall in Reykjavík.

Emanuel Giannotti is an Italian architect. His research has covered the interrelation between how the less wealthy organise themselves to create housing options, and how the governments react to their agendas regarding the housing problems. He visited Iceland, accompanied by a group of students from abroad who took part in the workshops. Giannotti and I contributed a chapter on how top down and bottom up approaches are evolving in Iceland, and how this relationship could be remoulded in the light of the crash.

Turf houses have acquired a rather uncertain status in the course of the debates about local resource management. Hannes Lárusson is an artist who grew up in a turf house, and is in the process of establishing a centre around such constructions. He writes a chapter about the Icelandic vernacular architecture.

The ambivalent relationship between creativity and labour in the context of the crash, experienced by the 'creative worker', is the angle explored by artist Bryndís Björnsdóttir and anthropologist Tinna Grétarsdóttir. As with all the authors, they donate their work for this book, contributing to a shared understanding.

Artist Margrét H. Blöndal presents her project Dyndilyndi which involved children in the designing of public and private spaces, accommodating different kinds of organisms and their social activities. Artists then further developed the material, and the results were presented and performed with people from different professions in a festival at The National Gallery of Iceland.

Hildigunnur Sverrisdóttir, an architect and educator, writes about the sociopolitical role of architects. The chapter includes a diagram, by April Arkitekter, reflecting how the roles of the architect relate to scarcity and abundance.

What follows is a chapter about a number of practitioners who have adopted alternative approaches to the built environment, and from whom we sought inspiration when undertaking student workshops with future scenarios in mind.

The second part of the book ends with architect Magnús Jensson's description of an ongoing participative project: The New City, with people coming together weekly to talk about the planning of a new, alternative city, knowing how painstakingly resource craving it can be to change the existing cities. The project may be a reminder of the Icelandic spirit which got the settlers to the country and into the current predicament, however, building up a new visionary society might be the Icelandic contribution to new urban thought that challenges the ruling model of the existing city of growth, seemingly out of control.

3. Urban Systems - current status
Part three aims to achieve a more systematic mapping of the urban systems for tackling new design challenges, and establishing knowledge as a base for new scenarios in the future. It provides a concise overview of how the systems in the Reykjavík Capital Area function, identifies the problems that need to be tackled and suggests opportunities that can be exploited.

Kristín Vala Ragnarsdóttir is professor of sustainability science at the Institute of Earth Sciences and Institute for Sustainability Studies at the University of Iceland. She writes about the geology.

Ursula Zuehlke is a German electrical engineer who studies Environmental Science and Natural Resource Management in Reykjavík. She writes about the water system.

Sigríður Kristjánsdóttir is the director of the Master of Planning programme at the Agricultural University of Iceland; which hosted a SCIBE design workshop in 2012. She writes here about the Icelandic planning system.

Lúðvík Elíasson, an economist at the Central Bank of Iceland, writes about the financial system.

I write about housing from the perspective of an Icelandic architect and urbanist running an independent architectural practice and research unit in Oslo, specialising in housing and urban development.

Salvör Jónsdóttir, a co-author in part one, writes on the food system.

The section ends with my conversation with Hildigunnur Sverrisdóttir, on the subject of communication.

It became very clear, while compiling these contributions, how much one depends on the pool of people around a city as to which chapters get developed at the end of the day, and what kind of approaches are taken. What people stand for, where they come from, and what hat(s) they wear, or have worn, will of course always colour a narrative one way or another.

4. Scenarios - into the future
The last part of the book shows how an ecological design approach can be used as a tool to produce knowledge about future scenarios for increased resilience, using the Reykajvik Capital Area as a case study.

Sybrand Tjallingii is Professor Emeritus from Delft University of Technology in Holland. Tjallingii's chapter introduces ecological approaches to planning and urbanism, and is an excellent introduction to the student projects produced during workshops in Reykjavík where such approaches were applied.

Giambattista Zaccariotto is an architect, urbanist and educator. Zaccariotto and I write about the workshops in Reykjavik in autumn 2011 and spring 2012, reflecting on research by design: how design processes can produce new knowledge which can help us to find better solutions through developing the built environment. The design briefs and selected subjects from the workshops are presented - four residential areas chosen for close study, with the focus on four themes: water, food, dwelling and mobility. Ecologically speaking, these case study sites were located on vastly dissimilar terrains: on a lava, on a landfill, on tundra and on fertile soil. Reconceptualising these areas in the light of a new set of principles, and imagining future transformations that fit within the ecological potential of the local landscapes, helps envision potential future roles for people and spaces. Themes such as central versus dispersed solutions, and ways to encourage local initiatives through urban design, were explored.

The student projects were carried out by pupils from an undergraduate programme of architecture at the Icelandic Academy of the Arts (the only architecture department in Iceland), the Master of Planning programme at the Agricultural University of Iceland and the post-professional European Master of Urbanism (EMU). Zaccariotto has made a selection and put the material together for a coherent presentation.

The editors reflections on policy implications, and conclusions drawn from the project, are included.

Increased awareness amongst the public since the crash, exacerbating an ongoing controversy about resource management in Iceland, is reflected in the diverse selection of contributions in the book. After all, it is composed of the voices of many people with different political convictions, from a variety of disciplines and from many strands of society, with their own expressions, lingo and culture. As such they don't necessarily represent the opinions of the editors. They are, however, all describing the same phenomenon, the built environment in the Reykjavík Capital Area. In this respect the content of the book mimics the way in which matters are managed in the smaller versions of 'small cities', where there is usually only one of each type of specialist... if that.

SCIBE was a collaboration between the Technical University of Vienna, The Oslo School of Architecture and Design, and the University of Westminster, based on the analysis of urban processes in four European cities: London, Oslo, Reykjavík, and Vienna (www.scibe.eu). The Reykjavík case study 'From Abundance to Scarcity' is the counter case to 'From Scarcity to Abundance' on 'the capital city of Oslo before and after the oil'. This contribution to SCIBE from The Oslo School of Architecture was carried out under the leadership of Professor Christian Hermansen.

April Arkitekter initiated and coordinated this book which far exceeds the scope of the original case study.

1.

Urban Transformations before the crash

In 2007, the French *Le Figaro* described the "Icelandic miracle":

'With a gross domestic product of 40,000€ per capita, Icelanders have, according to the UN, the world's highest standard of living, just after Norwegians. Unemployment almost doesn't exist, and over the past ten years, the economic development grew by 4.5% per year on average. At this time, the prime minister of Iceland, Geir Haarde, said: 'Our greatest pride is to have improved the general standard of living of the population since 1994, the average disposable income of households after tax increased by 75%!'

The Expansion

Arna Mathiesen

0   5   10   15

The urban transformations

Between 2002 and 2008, the capital area of Iceland was upscaled by 25%. New residential and industrial areas, as well as highway constructions, make up most of the expansion of the territory. The Reykjavík Capital Area (RCA), where two-thirds of the population live, consists of seven municipalities (there were eight before two of them merged in 2013).

This was the culmination of an expansion of a city, whose density had declined from 120 inhabitants per hectare in the 1940s to 36 inhabitants per hectare in 2005.[1] The developments under construction in the six years immediately before the crash are mostly located on the fringe where the city most clearly meets the natural elements.

During the eight years preceding the crash, 0.7 apartments were built per each new inhabitant in the country ('The Housing', part 3), and the units were large, 350m³ of residential space being allocated per each new citizen.[2]

About half of the population growth in the boom years was due to immigration from abroad.[3] Among the foreign workers in Iceland in 2007 and 2008, 36% were employed in the construction sector,[4] contributing to the transformation of the built environment. Poles are by far the largest group - 43% of all the immigrants. Most of the immigrants, now amounting to 8% of the total population (3% before the boom), are still in Iceland. The vast majority of them are not planning to leave despite being unemployed since the crash.[5]

If one didn't know better, it might be tempting to conclude that the rationale for the urban development in this period was to supply enough housing for immigrants, but at the end of the day insufficient numbers turned up. However the picture is actually more complex, with mass emigration of Icelanders who were looking for better living conditions elsewhere after the crash. The moves fit neatly into economic theories that stress the value of 'labour mobility', considering people as 'mobile populations', even though the architecture is moulded in immovable concrete.

In a global context, the built environment is responsible for:

40% of global energy consumption
30% of greenhouse gas emissions
3 billion tonnes of raw materials used annually
20% of global water usage[6]

20   25 Km

In Iceland many, if not all, of the problems that emerged after the crash are intrinsically entangled with the environment produced in the boom years:

Economic
- The increase in the number of households in financial distress from 12.5 % in early 2007 to 23.5% in autumn 2008, on the eve of the banking collapse.[7]
- The rise in negative equity among homeowners, from approximately 6% in 2007 to 37% by the end of 2010.[8]
- The proportion of homeowners simultaneously in financial distress and suffering from negative equity, rising steeply from approximately 1% to 14% during the crash (this figure had declined again to 10% by the end of 2010).[9]
- Bankruptcy in the building industry, among the big entrepreneurs and the producers of building materials – in some cases, the only ones on the island.
- Municipalities, and energy companies owned by them, on the brink of bankruptcy because of infrastructure ventures during the boom.
- The scarcity of affordable space, rented or bought.
- The rise in the cost of infrastructure maintenance due to the ever decreasing housing units in relation to new road constructions.

Social
- Loss of jobs.
- A brain drain.
- By the close of 2010, the parents of every fifth child in Iceland unable to pay their debts.[10]
- Austerity measures affecting public services.

Spatial
- Challenges to everyday physical mobility within the city as a result of recent urban transformations.
- The combination of urban morphology and local weather exacerbating problems – extreme winds around new high-rise buildings have resulted in injuries.
- Damage to structures because of excessively fast building.
- Loss of historical culture caused by the pressure on the older areas in the centre.
- The scarcity of customers reducing the usage of newly built commercial spaces even before those structures had been completed.
- The abundance of empty houses.

Environmental
- Soil sealing, soil erosion and the loss of agricultural soil.
- Increased pollution within the city and in the surrounding area, with a higher volume of CO_2 emissions from cars, geothermal ventures and the upgrade of an aluminium plant.
- The unsustainable exploitation of building materials and energy which are finite resources.
- The multiplication of construction waste.

Lack of a Vision for the Future
- A dearth of role models for a sustainable environment.
- An absence of pilot projects pointing the way for good practices in the future.

This is an incomplete list.

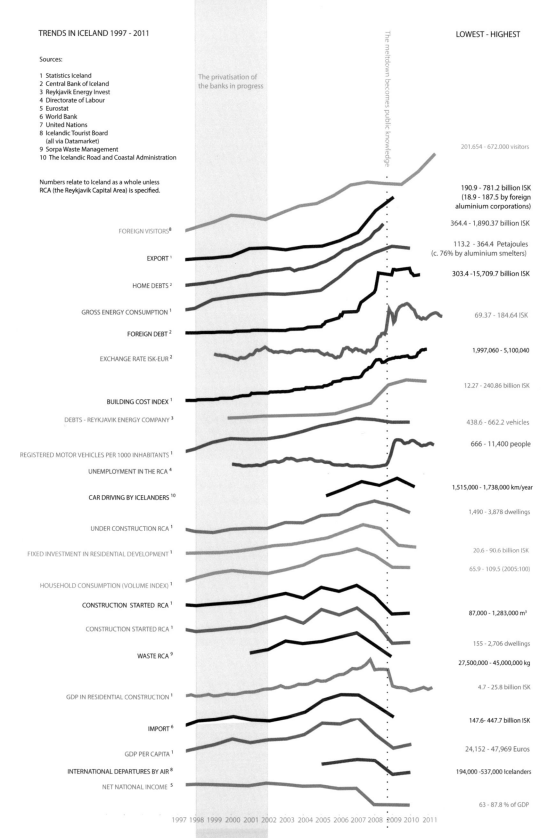

TRENDS IN ICELAND 1997 - 2011

LOWEST - HIGHEST

Sources:

1 Statistics Iceland
2 Central Bank of Iceland
3 Reykjavik Energy Invest
4 Directorate of Labour
5 Eurostat
6 World Bank
7 United Nations
8 Icelandic Tourist Board
   (all via Datamarket)
9 Sorpa Waste Management
10 The Icelandic Road and Coastal Administration

Numbers relate to Iceland as a whole unless
RCA (the Reykjavik Capital Area) is specified.

The privatisation of
the banks in progress

The meltdown becomes public knowledge

201.654 - 672.000 visitors

190.9 - 781.2 billion ISK
(18.9 - 187.5 by foreign
aluminium corporations)

FOREIGN VISITORS [8]   364.4 - 1,890.37 billion ISK

EXPORT [1]   113.2 - 364.4 Petajoules
                                        (c. 76% by aluminium smelters)

HOME DEBTS [2]   303.4 -15,709.7 billion ISK

GROSS ENERGY CONSUMPTION [1]

FOREIGN DEBT [2]   69.37 - 184.64 ISK

EXCHANGE RATE ISK-EUR [2]   1,997,060 - 5,100,040

BUILDING COST INDEX [1]   12.27 - 240.86 billion ISK

DEBTS - REYKJAVIK ENERGY COMPANY [3]   438.6 - 662.2 vehicles

                                        666 - 11,400 people
REGISTERED MOTOR VEHICLES PER 1000 INHABITANTS [1]

UNEMPLOYMENT IN THE RCA [4]

                                        1,515,000 - 1,738,000 km/year
CAR DRIVING BY ICELANDERS [10]

                                        1,490 - 3,878 dwellings
UNDER CONSTRUCTION RCA [1]

FIXED INVESTMENT IN RESIDENTIAL DEVELOPMENT [1]   20.6 - 90.6 billion ISK

                                        65.9 - 109.5 (2005:100)
HOUSEHOLD CONSUMPTION (VOLUME INDEX) [1]

CONSTRUCTION STARTED RCA [1]

CONSTRUCTION STARTED RCA [1]   87,000 - 1,283,000 m³

WASTE RCA [9]   155 - 2,706 dwellings

                                        27,500,000 - 45,000,000 kg

                                        4.7 - 25.8 billion ISK
GDP IN RESIDENTIAL CONSTRUCTION [1]

IMPORT [6]   147.6- 447.7 billion ISK

GDP PER CAPITA [1]   24,152 - 47,969 Euros

INTERNATIONAL DEPARTURES BY AIR [8]   194,000 -537,000 Icelanders

NET NATIONAL INCOME [5]

                                        63 - 87.8 % of GDP

1997 1998 1999 2000 2001 2002 2003 2004 2005 2006 2007 2008 2009 2010 2011

15

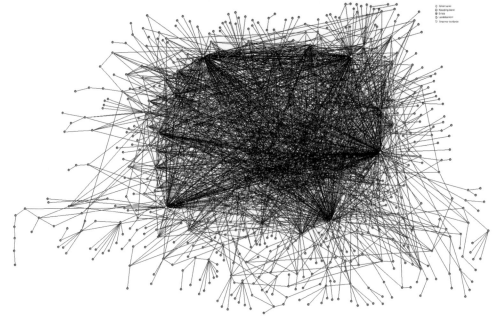

Ownership links between 1,307 companies with over 500 million ISK in assets in 2008.[11]

Urban Growth – Bigger Banks

The 'Flat Screen Theory', expounded by the most notorious tycoon involved in the boom, proposes that the banking system collapsed because of the general public's greed, buying too many flat screens (and all the other bits and pieces that were considered necessary requisites for a good life). It is true that Icelanders bought a very large number of flat screens, and of high-end quality. Flat screens use up a lot of resources in terms of materials necessary for their production, and buying lots of them certainly necessitates having plenty of disposable cash.

The expensive affair was to a large degree financed by bank loans. However, a close look at how many loans were taken out in the country shows that companies were borrowing on a much larger scale than homeowners. Their loans grew to almost ten times that of the latter.[13] The conditions that applied to those company loans were also different. An individual or a group that takes on a loan to finance a residence gets a sum of money that is linked to the property ie. a mortgage. Behind company loans, however, the people concerned have limited liability and consequently did not suffer, when the crash hit, to the same degree as the many households. A company can declare bankruptcy if the balance sheets are not showing profit, but the individuals running it are free from further obligations.

When a bank grants a loan, it issues a bond to finance the loan and puts the amount of

the loan into the lender's bank account. This means that the loan becomes both an asset (deposit) and a debt (bond) in the bank's financial statement. As the financial statement is in balance, the bank can continue to lend out money as long there is a demand for loans and bonds. The more loans the bank issues, the higher its interest earnings and thereby profits. The maps above show the ownership connections between Icelandic companies over a certain size. The banks are central actors, entangled in the complex maze.

In such a system, it seems fairly clear that it would be beneficial for the banks to support as many companies as possible that were involved with making something costly, thereby generating a continuous, and even accelerating, demand for loans and bonds. Building infrastructures, and everything else to do with the built environment, is expensive and some of the companies that swelled the size of the banks were in the building industry. Some building firms were even run from the premises of banks. Many were sustained by bullet loans (kúlulán), loans which were renewed by the time a payment was due.

When the municipalities had prepared plans for new building sites and sold them to local investors after a communal lottery, such a company could turn up the next day, and offer five times the original price. When asked what all that was about, they claimed there was more money in the building industry than in banking.[14]

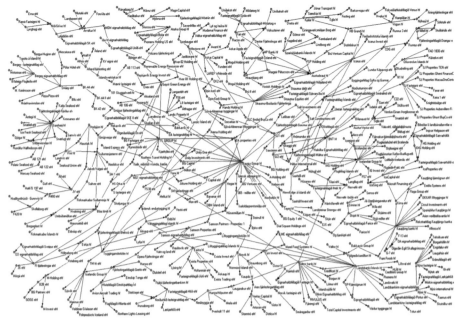

Ownership links between 453 companies with over 500 million ISK in assets, the minimum being a 10% connection, in 2008.[12]

It was difficult for traditional building firms to compete with the companies, of the kind described above. The atmosphere made people uncritical when it came to investment in building lots, property and infrastructure; it seemed as though it must be a good idea, when the 'ultra-successful' banks were thinking along those lines.

Four months before the meltdown of the banks, they constituted 14 times the size of the country's GNP.[15] The sum of debts owned by the Icelandic banks was a world record. The size of these banks was 80% of Northern Rock - in the US, only the banks Lehman Brothers and Washington Mutual were bigger. If the

collapse was transferred into other economies, it would be equivalent to almost 300 Lehman Brothers banks collapsing in the US, or 140 Northern Rock banks collapsing in the UK.[16]

After the financial meltdown, many of the insolvent companies were able to have their debts written off, while the homes, municipalities and the state took the risks and are still saddled with heavy debt. With the entanglement of the myriad companies as seen on the maps, it is difficult to trace whither all their profits from the boom disappeared.[17] According to the 'Flat Screen Theory' tycoon, they ended up in 'Money Heaven'. Islands in the Caribbean and the English Channel spring to mind.

1 Presented by Haraldur Sigurðsson from the Planning and Building department of Reykjavík at Nordisk regionplankonferens, 28-29 April 2008, Malmø/København.
2 See: Statistics Iceland (citing: National Economic Institute/Icelandic Property Registry). Residential Buildings in Iceland 1970-2012; Dwellings by Number of Rooms and Type of Dwellings 2000-2009 and Population - Key Figures 1703-2013. via DataMarket. http://bit.ly/1esaP1Y
3 Population by Origin and Citizenship. Reykjavík: Statistics Iceland. http://bit.ly/19HFMDa
4 Sigurðursson, Karl and Arnarson, Valur, Erlendir ríkisborgarar á íslenskum vinnumarkaði árin 2010. Veitt atvinnuleyfi, áætlað vinnuafl

og atvinnuleysi. [Foreign Citizens in Icelandic Labour Market 2010]. Reykjavík: Vinnumálastofnun, 2011. http://bit.ly/1iafiuv
5 http://mark.hi.is/sites/mark.hi.is/files/filepicker/17/wojtynska_skaptadottir_olafs_participation_of_immigrants.pdf
6 United Nations Environment Programme (UNEP). www.unep.org
7 Ólafsson, Þorvarður Tjörvi and Vignisdóttir, Karen Áslaug, Households Position in the Financial Crisis' in Iceland in: working paper No. 59. Reykjavík: Central Bank of Iceland, 2012, p 1. http://bit.ly/1e9hcac
8 ibid.
9 ibid.
10. ibid.
11 Bjarnadóttir, Margrét V. and Hanssen, Guðmundur A., 2010. 'Cross-

Ownership and Large Exposures; Analysis and Policy Recommendations' Report of the Special Investigation Commission, Volume 9, appendix 2.
12 ibid
13 Ólafsson, Stefán, 'Hverjir drekktu Íslandi í skuldum?' Eyjan, September 14, 2012. http://bit.ly/1gt1ais
14 Interview by Arna Mathiesen and Giambattista Zaccariotto, 4. 6. 2001 with Guðmundur Hreinsson, a former building contractor.
15 The Financial Supervisory Authority, Iceland, FME see: http://www.fme.is/media/frettir/12.03.2010.Hlutfoll-JEB.pdf
16 ibid
17 Johnsen, Gudrun. Bringing Down the Banking System: Lessons from Iceland. Palgrave Macmillan Publishers, 2013. p. 112.

Going for Growth

Ásdís Hlökk Theodórsdóttir and Salvör Jónsdóttir

Introduction

Here, the results of a study carried out by a research group on transport and planning at Reykjavik University in 2011 are presented. The study looked at planning and development in the greater capital region in Iceland, with emphasis on the first decade of this century. Nearly 80% of Iceland's population lives in the greater capital region, as it is defined in this study. It includes the eight municipalities[1] that make up the formal capital region, plus 11 surrounding municipalities that lie within the distance of 60 km from the capital Reykjavik. Population development, residential development, and growth of urban areas were analysed, and the planned future growth, according to approved municipal plans, was explored.

As the population of the greater capital region in Iceland is only around 250,000 the numbers dealt with in the study may not seem high in an international context. They are, however, significant in the local context, and the relative growth is believed to be of wider interest – this limited size of the society allows for a comprehensive analysis of a whole system which may give valuable insights into the underlying reasons, and the lessons to be learned.

Construction in the greater capital region was at a historical peak in the middle of the first decade of this century, and led to a substantial surplus of buildings and housing.[2] The construction boom has primarily been explained by increased and easy access to finance for investment in property. However, that aspect is not the focus of this study. Instead we aim to shed light on the role planning authorities and planning decisions have played ie. regarding

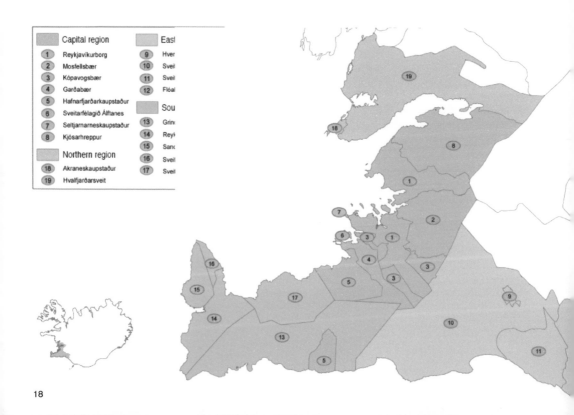

Capital region		East
1 Reykjavikurborg	9	Hver
2 Mosfellsbær	10	Svei
3 Kópavogsbær	11	Svei
4 Garðabær	12	Flóal
5 Hafnarfjarðarkaupstaður		
6 Sveitarfélagið Álftanes		Sou
7 Seltjarnarneskaupstaður	13	Grin
8 Kjósarhreppur	14	Reyi
	15	San
Northern region	16	Svei
18 Akraneskaupstaður	17	Svei
19 Hvalfjarðarsveit		

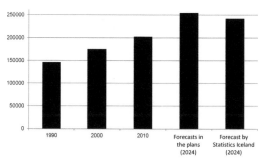

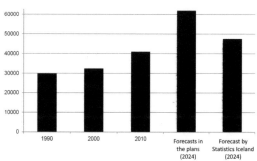

2 Population in the core capital region.[3]

3 Population in the fringe communities.[4]

played ie. regarding the scope of construction and development in the greater capital region of Iceland.

The following research questions led the study:

a) How have municipal plans guided regional development in the greater capital region?

b) To what extent was the property surplus developed in the first decade of the century created by the plans?

c) What needs to be addressed in the planning system and/or planning practice, to make planning more effective in this respect?

Methods and Scope of the Study

Planning decisions on housing construction were analysed, focusing on the first decade of this century. Statistics on population and construction in the region were examined, as well as statutory municipal plans prepared by the 19 local authorities in the study area and the regional plan for the formal capital region 2001-2024.[5]

Population and housing development were examined for the period 2000-2010 in comparison with the period 1990-2000. The projected population and planned development, according to statutory municipal plans, were also examined.[6]

Population

According to the Icelandic Planning Act, all construction development has to be consistent with previously approved plans. Local authorities shall adopt municipal development plans with a planning period of at least 12 years. There, they shall present their population forecast for the municipality and their decisions, based on the population forecast, on housing numbers and areas allocated for development in the planning period.

The population forecasts that local authorities present in their municipal plans are the key prerequisite for the housing numbers and allocation of land for development made in the plan. Therefore, the quality of the population forecasts is one of the most critical factors in these plans.

---

1 The greater capital region – sub-regions and municipalities. In the chapter the capital region is referred to as the core capital region and the other sub-regions are together referred to as Fringe communities.

The Icelandic National Planning Agency has published guidance to support local authorities in their work.[7] The guidance emphasises that local authorities should both look to the regional context and pay regard to national population forecasts and trends, when working on their population forecast. Handbooks and manuals on municipal planning, and the planning literature internationally, also deal with approaches to population forecasting as a basis for decision-making on housing numbers, social and physical infrastructure and land allocation.[8]

Statistics Iceland, the national centre for official statistics, publishes and regularly updates a population projection for the country as a whole, but the only population projections presented for individual regions and municipalities are those that local authorities present in their plans.

Over the past two decades the population growth in Iceland has largely occurred in and around the capital, while the population in smaller towns and rural areas around the country has been relatively stable. Statistics Iceland published its last national population projection in 2010. It predicted the population would grow by nearly 0.3% annually in the first years, rising to 0.9% in 2020, and then decrease again down to 0.4% by the end of the projection period, 2060.[9]

One of the core decisions, and a mandatory aspect, of municipal plans is the estimated need for residential units.[10] The forecasted population forms the basis for decisions on residential areas along with demographic factors such as average family size and age composition. Other factors, including age and quality of housing, availability and mortgage rates, have an impact on new housing development. Nevertheless, the most common practice when estimating the need for residential development in municipal planning in Iceland is to focus on the population forecast and the average number of residents per dwelling unit. Population projections made by Statistics Iceland, both for the country as a whole and those made by local authorities for planning purposes, are clearly the most important figures when it comes to making decisions on the allocation of housing units.

The Icelandic National Planning Agency supervises and guides local governments regarding land use planning. However, no guides related to assessments for housing needs have been published. The simple methods mentioned above are generally applied. As municipalities in Iceland are generally small, a more thorough demographic analysis has not been considered necessary.

Review of the municipal plans in the greater capital region indicates that a desire for growth has been the driving force, rather than an analysis of the actual demand for housing.

	Population increase	Housing unit increase
Greater capital region, total	**17%**	**29%**
Core capital region	16%	24%
Fringe regions:		
- Northern region	21%	37%
- Eastern region	28%	45%
- Southwest region	28%	76%

4 Comparison of increases in housing units and population in the greater capital region 2000-2010.

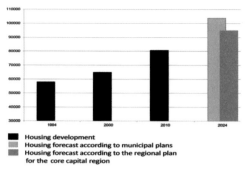

- ■ Housing development
- Housing forecast according to municipal plans
- Housing forecast according to the regional plan for the core capital region

5 Housing development and projections in the core capital region.[11]

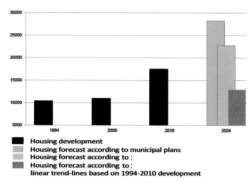

- ■ Housing development
- Housing forecast according to municipal plans
- Housing forecast according to :
- ■ Housing forecast according to : linear trend-lines based on 1994-2010 development

6 Housing development and projections in the fringe communities.

Discussion

a) How have municipal plans guided regional development in the greater capital region?

When the 19 municipalities that make up the greater capital region are studied together, it is clear that they allow for considerably more development than seems realistic, if compared to the population projection published by Statistics Iceland for the country as a whole, as well as linear extrapolation of development in recent decades in the region. Two factors seem to have the greatest impact. One, the amendments made to the regional plan for the core capital region which was initially adopted and approved in 2002. The other, the policy of the fringe communities to achieve considerable expansion.

In the core capital region, the eight municipalities had in 2002 settled on a common, well grounded regional plan. During the first decade of this century individual municipalities did however request a number of amendments to the plan, resulting in a 9% increase in the housing units established for the region. These amendments seem to have been primarily market driven – developers sought land to develop and municipalities competed for new residents and development.

In the fringe communities, the municipal plans generally projected considerable growth without examining the regional context or the actual need. They wanted to become fast-growing urban communities and part of an expanding capital region.

No common or coordinated planning policy had been formulated for the fringe communities, but instead the municipal plans presented growth, that was primarily based on marketing and image work carried out by individual local authorities, or even landowners and private developers. Difference in property prices and land values, between the core capital region and the fringe also created preferable conditions to realise these policies. The study has revealed that the combined housing projections presented in the municipal plans for the fringe communities seem to be an overestimate of as much as 118%; the precise figure depends on the baseline period used.

Another characteristic of the development in the greater capital region is the continuing suburban expansion, affecting the urban areas but also the rural ones. It occurs despite the fact that most of the municipalities have policies on densification in their municipal plans. Most of the fringe communities are promoting low density residential development in rural areas: it is a form of development relatively new in the Icelandic context but is well-known elsewhere, along with its negative impacts.

b) To what extent was the surplus in property, developed in the first decade of the century, created by the plans?

Two things must be present for a land use plan to be able to serve its role as an effective framework for development. Its policy must be based on realistic projections of population and the need for housing, and it must be accompanied by implementation plans and an institutional framework capable of implementing its policies. Looking at the municipal plans in the greater capital region, many examples can be seen of plans with unrealistic projections of numbers of housing units and land allocations for development. Moreover, there seems to be very little resistance within local governments to the pressure from market forces for more land for development, and for more housing units.

21

This suggests that the practice of municipal planning needs to be improved, not only with regard to policymaking and land allocations in the plans, but also the institutional framework and implementation of the plans.

The construction boom experienced during the last decade cannot be explained solely by the easy availability and low cost of housing; no houses can be built without allocation in plans and permits having been granted by planning authorities. The final decision about development lies with the local authorities, and therefore it is of outmost importance that they understand their role as planning authorities and have the tools to function accordingly.

c) What needs to be addressed in the planning system and/or planning practice, to make planning more effective in this respect?

A number of key lessons can be identified:

First, the approach to forecasting and projections applied in municipal planning in Iceland needs to be revised and improved. Although simple methods can still be used in forecasting for small communities, the baseline period must be carefully chosen and the regional context considered.

Second, planning statistics need to be more systematically collected and analysed by planning authorities. This needs to be the case for on-going development and current housing stock, as well as future provision.

Third, the study indicates the value of regional planning frameworks, be they made by regional or other strategic planning instruments such as a national planning framework. The study also highlights the importance of an institutional capacity to implement such policies. In the case of the core capital region, where the local authorities had agreed on a common framework for development, the institutional framework did not hold up to the pressure brought to bear, and as a result the individual, market-driven approach taken by individual municipalities held sway. The aforementioned regional plan was optional, but has since been made mandatory by the Planning Act of 2010. Along with the legal provision, a strong regional planning entity must be in place to implement and follow up on the policies made in the plan.

In terms of a shared vision and overall planning for the fringe communities, it can be expected that the first generation of a national planning policy, currently being developed, will address this important issue since spatial form and distribution of urban development are among the key themes.

Fourth, guidance available to local planning authorities, plus supervision and monitoring of local planning, seem not to have been effective to a satisfactory degree. Hopes may be put on the new national planning strategy in this respect too, since its responsibilities include regular reporting on the status and development of land use and planning in the country as well as a strategy on planning and development. Although the national planning strategy should add value to the Icelandic planning system, the role and practice of planning authorities need to be revised, at the local and national level. Policy and plan making for local communities needs to be based on a vision, coupled with realistic analysis of past trends, in the community itself and its regional surroundings. Amendments to the policy and/or the plan must be carried out with equal care. Small local governments in Iceland need guidance in this respect and it is the responsibility of national authorities to rise to the occasion, supported by academic and international research.

Acknowledgements

The study was partially financed by the Icelandic Housing Financing Fund's research fund. The authors want to thank Davíð Þór Guðmundsson and Grétar Már Hreggviðsson who worked as research assistants with the authors on data collection and analysis. The study's findings have been presented in a report in Icelandic, published by Reykjavik University in 2012[12] and at the annual conference of the Association of European Schools of Planning in 2012.

An aerial view over a development of ranches in Árborg.

1 Since this study was carried out, two out of these eight municipalities have merged, leaving seven municipalities which constitute the formal capital region.

2 See e.g. Runólfsson, A. and Þórisson, I.S. *Hvenær aukast framkvæmdir á nýjum íbúðum á höfuðborgarsvæðinu? Greining á fasteignamarkaðinum.* Reykjavik: The Landsbanki bank, 2009. http://j.l.is/Uploads/Maillist/Docs/fasteignamark-adurinn_okt09.pdf

3 The graph shows forecasts presented in municipal plans compared to the national forecast done by Statstics Iceland. Here the national forecast is projected onto the region in question.

4 Ibid.

5 Information on the municipal plans was acquired from a national plan database available online on the Icelandic National Planning Agency's website and from local authority websites.

6 Statistics Iceland website: Population statistics. Registers Iceland: *Statistics on construction 1994-2010* (data prior to 1994 was not available). Urban areas were mapped from municipal plans, Corine classification maps from the National Land Survey of Iceland and from Google EarthTM.

7 Elmarsdottir, M.K. and Theodórsdóttir, A.H. *Leiðbeiningar um gerð aðalskipulags - ferli og aðferðir.* Reykjavik: National Planning Agency, 2003.

8 See e.g. 'Population Projections' in: American Planning Association. *Planning and Urban Design Standards.* New Jersey: John Wiley & Sons, 2006, p 503-506, and Rayer, S., 'Population Forecast Errors: A Primer for Planners' in: *Journal of Planning Education and Research*, Summer 2008 vol. 27 no. 4, p 417-430.

9 *Spá um mannfjölda eftir kyni og aldri 2011-2060.* Reykjavík: Statistics Iceland, 2010. http://bit.ly/1cPBxjS

10 Ministry for the Environment. *Skipulagsreglugerð. Nr.400*, 1998.

11 The graph shows housing allocations in the regional plan as originally approved in 2002.

12 Theodórsdóttir, A.H., Jónsdóttir, S. Guðmundsson, D.Th. and Hreggviðsson, G.M. *Veðjað á vöxt, byggðaþróun á stór-höfuðborgarsvæðinu.* Reykjavík: Reykjavík University, 2012. http://rumsk.ru.is/index_files/gogn/vedjad2.pdf

The Upscaling

Arna Mathiesen

A hallmark of the years before the financial meltdown was upscaling - across all the scales of the built environment. Sizes of spaces and buildings increased, numbers of buildings multiplied and the functions expanded.

Building big, high and impressive had become the ideal, using the finest materials imported from around the world. Design and art were also sought after for finishing the impressive spaces. The upscaling did not relate in any meaningful way to the population growth in the same period (see 'The Expansion' and 'Going for Growth' in part 1 and 'The Housing' in part 3).

Myriads of architectural competitions were held across Reykjavik Capital Area. Dotted around the town, a few single towers popped up, with no apparent connection to the surrounding urban fabric or the features of the local landscape.

After the crash there was a scarcity of means to finish the plans and maintain buildings, public spaces and infrastructure, or indeed to use and inhabit the spaces produced.

Designers

In Iceland the concentration of architects is relatively high, with roughly one architect to every 1000 inhabitants[1] (this remains the case even though many of them have left the country due to a lack of job opportunities). This is above average for European countries.[2]

Icelandic architects have received their education from a worldwide spectrum of design schools, as education in that subject was only established in the country a few years ago, and there is still no graduate programme. Furthermore, many designers came from abroad to participate in the radical urban transformations of the boom period.

The activity of architects may have been at a peak during the boom, with very long working hours, but it didn't automatically follow that it was particularly economically beneficial for all those in the mainstream. New standards implemented in legal frameworks, as well as growing demand for Building Information Modelling (BIM)

'In only fifty years it went from being a lovely little harbour town to becoming a concrete monster tied up by motorways. Copenhagen was based on Paris, and still looks sort of like a Paris of red bricks, while Reykjavík looks like Rönne on Bornholm (a small village on an island in the Baltic Sea) surrounded by Los Angeles. I'm not kidding. Reykjavik is the most spread out city on the planet. It's one of the major achievements of modern city planning how they managed to make people who live in a city of 100,000 spend on average, one hour per day in their cars.'

Hallgrímur Helgason in a lecture at New Nordic, an exhibition showing Icelandic design at Louisiana Museum of Modern Art in Denmark, 2012.

Education

and extensive quality control systems, resulted in consolidation and industrialisation in the profession, rendering only a few offices capable of taking on the large jobs. The offices in question turned into one of the elements in a developer's package, as it were, making it difficult for other architects to compete for the jobs.

Large infrastructural projects were reported to be the most financially favourable for architects as so much money was involved in making them - the architectural fees, although high, were swallowed up within the huge budget.

Designers were instrumental in forming, and legitimising, the radical transformations of the boom by virtue of their drawings, and their signing of building and planning documents. They did not necessarily have an education as architects and planners, because other disciplines in Iceland (engineers and building technicians for example) also have the right to design, and sign the relevant documents.

The number of institutes of higher education and research increased, along with their respective sizes, across the region. This reflected an international trend, stressing the importance of education in strengthening economies. The largest school at university level, Reykjavík University, was built on a plot given by the city of Reykjavik in a green belt centrally located in town, on an attractive slope facing west by the shore. The venture was backed by tycoons, with this aspiration in mind: "Reykjavik arrives on the map as a European university city and the international expansion of Icelanders in the field of education begins".[3]

The location was adjacent to the University of Iceland and on the far side of wetland areas that were currently occupied by a local airport, but were envisioned as the home for a new mixed use area worthy of an international hub of finance. This location was considered an appropriate one for a competitive environment that would foster new synergies, but is just a little too far for easy pedestrian access to the other university across the valley. The ambition for the whole plan was to boost the gravitas of Reykjavik city, and transform it into a new local version of Silicon Valley, a vibrant habitat attracting the best creative talent.

Infrastructures of Energy and Water

In the new residential settlements from the boom most of the roads, hot and cold water pipes, electricity and sewage facilities have already been installed, to supply all the buildings that were planned for the total development area. Regardless of whether the neighbourhood is finished, half-finished, or has hardly any buildings so far, in order to serve the few, widely scattered inhabited dwellings, the newly built water system needs to be used at full pressure, just as it would be if serving the number of buildings originally planned for the whole area.

From the turn of the century, the energy production in Iceland has doubled. The bulk of the electricity (about 80%) services three aluminium plants and one ferro-silicon plant. An aluminium plant on the outskirts of the capital area was upgraded, and another one 50 km north of Reykjavik was planned in the boom period. A new greenfield aluminium plant was built in Reyðarfjörður, in the east of Iceland.

A public utility, owned by municipalities on the south-west corner of the country, went into the business of contributing to the electricity production by building Hellisheiðarvirkjun which is probably the largest geothermal power station in the world.[4] Excessive hot water (a side effect of the extensive drilling) is now being reinjected into the geothermal reservoir so as not to waste energy.

Unexpectedly, this procedure has caused fractures in the rock, generating earthquakes felt within a 45 km (28 mile) radius, putting the built structures under strain and spreading anxiety among the population. Some of the excessive hot water escapes and lies on top of the groundwater layer which is in danger of getting contaminated. A cloud of sulphur reaches the capital area, causes health problems and disturbs electrical equipment.

Resources - buildings, infrastructures, water and geothermal areas - are being sold off to finance the debt.

The many resource-intensive ventures, including its exclusive headquarters and bad financial deals, have pushed the publicly owned energy company to the brink of bankruptcy, triggering the privatisation of its assets.

500 BILLION ICELANDIC CROWNS (ISK)

400

300

200

100

2000 2001 2002 2003 2004 2005 2006 2007 2008 2009 2010 2011 2012

—— Municipal Debt in the RCA[5]　　　　　▪ ▪ Municipal Income in the RCA[6]

Public Buildings

Public institutions and administrative buildings were upgraded and redefined by their position in town, their scale and their symbolic role in the new, so-called sustainable Iceland that was under construction.

While many of the architectural competitions were in relation to schools and banks, many others were for public cultural buildings. One of them was a music hall of 150,000 m² standing half-finished when the economy crashed. In the first competition documents for the building, the plan was that the main hall would seat 1500 people. Despite experts having cautioned that the scarce population of Iceland could never afford to run such a large venue, the plans gradually grew and more concert halls were added within the building. When completed, the main music hall could seat 1800 people, with an additional seven venues in the building, for concerts, exhibitions and conferences.

After the crash, some declared that the building should not continue and should be demolished, as the nation simply could not afford it, while others thought it should to be finished and transformed into a prison for economic criminals who had led the nation into the financial abyss. But there were also those who viewed completion of the building as the only good solution for reconstructing the pride of the battered nation.

Despite the spiralling debt, the building was continued with the help of Deutsche Bank, and in May 2011 the biggest concert hall in Scandinavia was ready, with its outer walls fabricated from a work of art designed by a renowned star in the international art world. In April 2013 Harpa, a concert hall and conference centre, won the European Union Prize for Contemporary Architecture, the Mies van der Rohe Award.

A Portrait: The Little Toe of Ólafur Elíasson and I, work by Steinunn Gunnlaugsdóttir (shown in the photograph). Photographed (by a site worker) next to Elíasson's glass element on the building site of Harpa, spring 2008.

'I finished watching the Star Wars series with my daughter yesterday. I felt as though some of the recent buildings of Reykjavik were in the backdrop, e.g. the headquarters of Reykjavik Energy and the Harpa concert hall.'

The writer Unnur Jökulsdóttir on Facebook, October 2013.

Commercial Space

The eagerness of municipalities to attract retail businesses, in order to appeal to potential inhabitants and increase tax revenue during the boom, put private companies in the position of stipulating conditions regarding the way their premises were formed. If a municipality's ideas for the design of future amenities failed to correspond with the preferences of the company in question, that company would threaten to take its plans elsewhere.[7] Consequently, the planning and design of amenities relied on the premises of profitable retailers, entailing big parking areas, close to a major road. The resulting sprawl has made public transport expensive, and access to shopping and other services difficult for pedestrians.

During the boom Icelandic tycoons bought sizeable stakes in many of the largest shopping chains and other businesses in the UK and Denmark, such as French Connection, Hamleys, House of Fraser, Goldsmiths, Debenhams, Oasis, Karen Millen, Whistles, Whittard, Sterling, Magasin Du Nord and Woolworths.

Recently built residential areas, under construction from 2002 to 2008. With the new roads shown in grey, new motorways are in turquoise, and shopping areas in red.

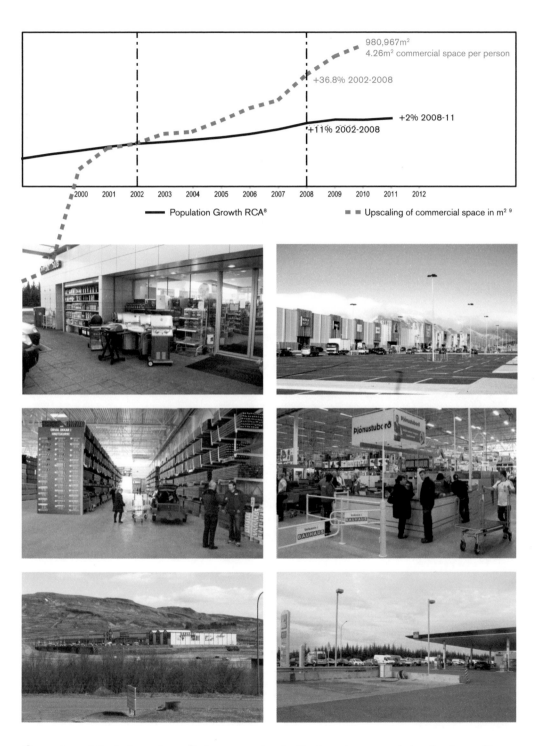

980,967m²
4.26m² commercial space per person

+36.8% 2002-2008

+2% 2008-11

+11% 2002-2008

2000 2001 2002 2003 2004 2005 2006 2007 2008 2009 2010 2011 2012

—— Population Growth RCA[8]   ▪ ▪ Upscaling of commercial space in m² [9]

'Supporters of the Independence Party are people who like to make money during the day and to barbeque in the evening. Leftists are people who think that you can solve some riddles of life by chatting, meetings and poetry readings.'

A professor of political science at the University of Iceland, Hannes Hólmsteinn Gissurarson, talking on national television, about the lifestyle of the supporters of the Independence Party, January 2008.

Mobility Infrastructure

Disparate parts of the individual municipal plans in the Reykjavík Capital Area are connected by main roads financed by the Icelandic state, not directly affecting the budgets of the municipalities. Larger roads are connected by means of cloverleaf interchanges, which each have a price tag similar to the cost of one new school. The road corridors often divide new residential areas into two, and usually separate them from the adjacent land uses.

The main roads built between 2002 and 2008 extend for 60.8 km (37.7 miles), minor roads for over 163 km (101.2 miles) and nine major cloverleaf interchanges were completed. In the same period, only 3 km of exclusive bicycle lanes were created.

From 2005 onwards, private companies became increasingly responsible for building infrastructure, as they were owners of whole developments.

Many cars were adapted with bigger tyres and body parts, making them more robust, for crossing ever more inaccessible landscapes.

New main roads, cloverleaf interchanges and smaller roads under construction from 2002 to 2008 shown in red.

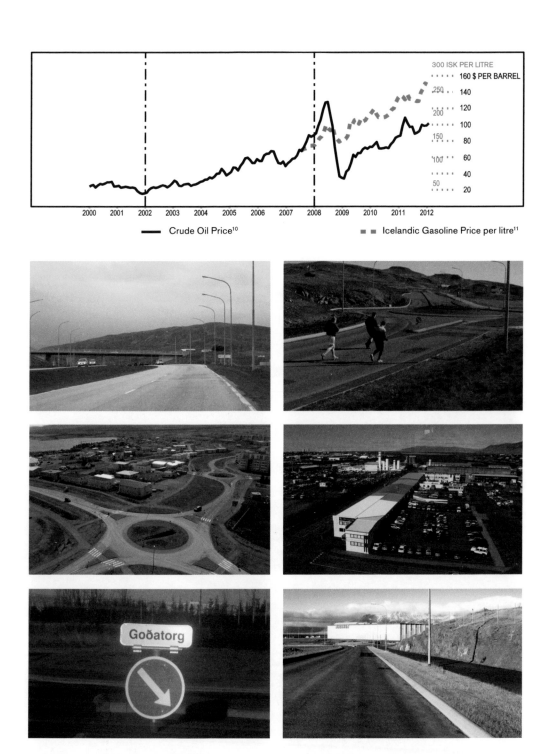

		300 ISK PER LITRE
		160 $ PER BARREL
	250	140
	200	120
		100
	150	80
	100	60
		40
	50	20

2000 2001 2002 2003 2004 2005 2006 2007 2008 2009 2010 2011 2012

—— Crude Oil Price[10]   ▪ ▪ Icelandic Gasoline Price per litre[11]

'I arrived from the US on a Friday and when I came to Reykjavík I saw all these huge vehicles lining up for a convoy on the way out of town. I thought this had to be some sort of military operation going on.'

An American tourist.

Spaces of Leisure

Spaces of leisure were upscaled in size, in number and in the range of functions. For instance, the basic supporting facilities for sports, such as the little coffee-making corner at horse stalls, became a luxurious second-floor entertainment lounge covering the same area as the whole stall, with exclusive views over the surrounding landscape. Full-size indoor football fields were built, with supplementary spaces for cinemas, ice skating, swimming, and other sports. Golf courses also increased in number and size.

The low level of participation in evidence on the photographs is best explained by demographics. There are far too few people to populate the facilities, the total number of the inhabitants in the RCA being around 200,000. Many of the ventures fell into bankruptcy and some facilities had to be taken over by the municipalities.

'We don't have trains in Iceland...
How do young people travel? I mean, if you don't have trains how do younger people travel?
People who don't have cars, how do they travel in Iceland?
Oh, young people drive cars. They have jeeps, that's the most common vehicle there is. Jeeps with a four-wheel drive.
You need it in Iceland?
Yeah, it's the biggest hobby... People go out at the weekends, and they drive into the unknown. And they go across glaciers and they might fall into cracks, and even die. And there are many of them together, and people in one jeep might have to rescue people in the other jeep. And then they come back and they have very good stories to tell...'

Artist Björk in a television interview in Germany, when asked why such a star would arrive on a train but not by plane.
http://www.youtube.com/watch?v=Q-dFRFsQKGQ

Financial District

During the boom years Icelandic politicians had the proclaimed goal to turn their country into a significant financial hub on the global arena. A massive development was underway for a financial district directly east of - and on a similar scale to - the whole of the old part of Reykjavik, which is still perceived as the centre of the capital area, and accommodates most of the administrative buildings. The main street of the financial district, Borgartún, can truly be considered to be the tenderloin of the city fabric, on the waterfront and facing Mount Esja. It was planned as the new Wall Street of Iceland, lined with shiny office buildings in a variety of shapes, in a sea of parking. Embedded in the very heart of the street, the public planning and building offices are contracted to rent space in a new complex where five skyscrapers were planned. Only one of them was actually built, and that has stood empty most of the time since the crash.

The old city centre

The financial district

Borgartún (Iceland's Wall Street)

Reykjavík Department of Environment and Planning

Chinese Embassy

The centre of Reykjavik contains most of the historical structures in the capital area. Only 0.36% of units in the RCA were built before 1900, and only 0.84% were built between 1900-1907. This map shows both historic and newer structures under threat of demolition.[12]

Buildings that could be demolished according to municipal plans accepted during the period 2002-2006 (included are structures built before 1918 and newer buildings, purchased with development in mind).

Buildings built before 1918 that are not protected by heritage conservation

In the years immediately before the crash a wall of high-rises was constructed between the old city fabric of Reykjavik and the seafront. The trend has started up again in year 2014 despite public protests over several years.

Fringe

New districts and landscapes, previously considered rather inhospitable environments such as windy and snowy heaths, were planned for residential use. When the financial crisis hit, these areas were in different stages of completion. Some buildings were finished but a large number were missing many of the parts one usually considers constituting a building. Long and winding roads created by abundant resources lead to these areas and usually the infrastructures of energy and water are ready for something to happen. The stunning views to the mountains and the ruptures in the landscape make for a mixed feeling. Will the holes in the ground wait for that lump of concrete they were initially made for? Will they be left to contribute to the tradition of manmade desertification or will they become shelter for a new habitat or a pond?

1 Association of Icelandic Architects website, http://ai.is/?page_id=135
2 Luca Molinari, 'Taking Sides in Italy.' *Volume #36*, July 2013. (Archis, Amsterdam)
3 Author's translation of a declaration on the university website at the day of the opening http://www.ru.is/haskolinn/frettir/nr/11746
4 Reykjavik Energy, http://www.or.is/um-or/frettir-og-tilkynningar/erin-di-forstjora-orkuveitunnar-vekur-athygli
5 Capacent, via Datamarket, see http://goo.gl/bbwFSA
6 ibid
7 Arna Mathiesen and Giambattista Zaccariotto's interview with architect Gunnlaugur Johnson, 4 June 2011.
8 Statistics Iceland
9 Statistics Iceland
10 U.S. Energy Information Administration, via Datamarket
11 Gíslason, Hjálmar (citing: Seðlabanki Íslands, Seiður ehf., Viðskiptaráð Íslands, Xignite) http://datamarket.com/data/set/1uu5/bensinverd-samsetning#!ds=1uu5!1w4a=2.3:1w-4b=1&display=columnstack
12 Hilmarsson, Snorri, et al. *101 Tækifæri*, Reykajvík: Torfusamtökin 2010.

Areas under construction from 2002 to 2008 shown in red in relation to the terrain.

Spatial Inequalities in Reykjavik

Massimo Santanicchia

The neoliberal experiment, which was undertaken in Iceland from the 1990s up to the financial collapse of 2008, generated unprecedented inequality, not just in the country's income distribution[1] but in the built environment as well. I intend to outline the spatial inequality that has emerged in the city of Reykjavik. Two urban artefacts are examined through Sennett's concept of 'The Open City',[2] which gives us the instrument to value their spatial definition.

Inequality

Equal is a word with multiple definitions. From the Collins English Dictionary we can read some of its meanings:

1. Having identical privileges: all men are equal before the law.

2. Proportioned, evenly balanced.

Equality therefore implies not only justice but also a state of coexistence and juxtaposition of different parts. Inequality, on the other hand, is a condition in which some people are more privileged than others, a condition that is out of balance. From the same source, inequality is also defined as: 'disparity, from the Latin 'disparare' meaning to divide or separate'. UN-Habitat defines various forms of inequality 'from different levels of human capabilities and opportunities, participation in political life, consumption and income, to disparities in living standards and access to resources, basic services and utilities'[3]. Inequality is therefore a division, a separation and a fracture. I define equality as the ability to connect people to opportunities, education, political life, social life, resources, nature and to other people; equality is about communication and understanding. Consequently spatial inequality is a fracture created by our city artefacts - buildings, infrastructures and neighbourhoods - that separate people from opportunities, nature and other people. Spatial inequality undermines a primary function embedded in public space: the connections. It is in the mingling present in our public spaces that we find the foundation of democracy.[4] Cities represent the most evident context in which spatial inequality can be studied, and this is not just because more than half of the world population lives in them today, increasing to nearly 70% by 2050,[5] but because cities represent the world that men have fabricated.[6]

The Global Report on Human Settlements states that 'Future urban planning in both developed and developing countries will be taking place in the context of inequality and poverty'[7]. If inequality is a shared condition, how can we plan for more equal cities? Planning is produced by us, in response to political, economic, environmental and social factors,[8] 'therefore when we think of planning we should think of it as part of the production and reproduction of the social relations of power'[9]. Planning is an ongoing process, a constant negotiation between different powers; between myself and others; between my needs and society's needs; between land as a private right and collective good.[10] Spatial inequality is the result of our political, economic and ideological structure; it is the result of the same forces that create the city and produce planning, urbanism and design. These forces are our choices. Urbanism plays a significant role in city-making because it is a political act and a form of governance.[11] Design is about making decisions and finding solutions that influence our society for the present and future generations. It is vital for everybody, especially planners, architects and designers, to be able to see the spaces of our city and read the connections between intended and produced space – the connections between project and reality.

'Mistakes were certainly made. The private banks failed, the supervisory system failed, the politics failed, the administration failed, the media failed, and the ideology of an unregulated free market utterly failed. This has called for a fundamental review of many elements of our society. In that respect, democracy, the rule of law and close international cooperation have been, and will continue to be, our strongest weapons.'

Prime Minister Jóhanna Sigurðardóttir reflecting on the Icelandic economic collapse, April 12, 2010.

'Thinking spatially means seeing the various politics and technologies of planning in the contextual place in society; they become examples of particular relations of power that constitute the conditions of freedom and dominance in the socially produced urban space.'[12]

Spatial inequality is determined by these relations of power.

Spatial inequality

The way we build our city determines, to a large extent, our quality of life for a very long period into the future. To appreciate quality of life I refer to the words of Peñalosa:

'The task is not simply to create a city that functions efficiently. It is to create an environment where the majority of people can be as happy as possible. Happiness is difficult to define and impossible to measure, but it is ultimately what all efforts, collective or individual, are about. [...] Although human happiness has many definitions and requirements, in terms of habitat it demands elements such as being able to walk and play; having contact with nature such as found in parks, trails and waterfront; being able to see and be with people; and feeling included and not inferior.'[13]

We need to look at how the built fabric can foster happiness, in the sense of 'producing' equality and therefore encourage connection and dialogue among people, increase social opportunities and connect us to nature. The concept of 'The Open City', discussed by Richard Sennett, represents the tool hereby adopted to comprehend and value our cities in terms of spatial equality. In 2008 Sennett wrote an essay entitled The Public Realm. In it he discusses the contrast between open and closed systems, and how this influences our way of thinking about the public realm, and as a consequence how we think about cities. An open space is described as one that can adapt and evolve; it is a vehicle of social expression. It acknowledges the diversities present in a city and promotes their dialogue. These spatial dialogues are endless and perpetual, and take place between the different artefacts (buildings, neighbourhoods and infrastructures) that constitute a city. Artefacts "talk" through their edges. In an open space the edges promote dialogues and connections; they are porous, absorbent and can host niches of life and diversity. These types of edges are borders, areas of connectivity and spatial equality.
In contrast, a closed space is one in which there is no terrain for negotiation or change, for adaption or evolution. When artefacts are so difficult to change they become weak and turn into obstacles and divisions in the city. A closed space does not connect but excludes, and therefore becomes an unequal space. The edges of the artefacts are impenetrable, repellent; they do not promote connection but separation and disparity. These types of edges are boundaries, areas of dis-connectivity and spatial inequality.

Skuggi and Vatnsendi

Following Sennett's logic of differentiating between a closed and an open space, the instruments of 'adaptability, diversity and borders and boundaries' will be used to describe and to analyse spatial inequality, in two case studies selected from the capital region's built environment repertoire of the last ten years: Skuggi and Vatnsendi. These represent two recurring urban artefacts in city-making: a residential complex located in a consolidated urban context, in this case the city centre of Reykjavík, and a new neighbourhood. The problematic spatial conditions that they generate are examined.

1 Map of the city centre of Reykjavík. The built space is shown in black, unbuilt space in white, and streets or car parks in red. Encircled in blue is the Skuggi development and in green Hallgrímskirkja. Frakkastígur Street is highlighted in yellow.

Skuggi (Shadow)

Skuggi lies on the north shore of Reykjavík city centre. It is a residential complex for approximately 800 people distributed in 250 luxury apartments.[14] Its construction started in 2003; today it stands unfinished with less than 200 occupants.

The Skuggi development started with the erasing of any connectivity with the past; the old sawmill Völundur, a fine example of Reykjavik's industrial legacy, was demolished along with some small timber houses. The justification was freedom of choice and 'growth', and if growth could be measured in height, this would be an illustrious example. The tallest tower reaches 16 floors, whilst the average height of buildings in the centre is three.

Skuggi has 'sold' the charm of the city centre and its view of nature – in this case Esja, the mountain most beloved by the Reykjavikians – with the people's consent. These elements were commercialised in the formula 'city-centre-luxury-flats-with-a-view'. The size of the Skuggi development creates a disconnection within the urban fabric: this is spatial inequality. As Susan Fainstein states, mega-projects (and Skuggi is surely an example in Reykjavik) 'produce a landscape dominated by bulky buildings that do not encourage urbanity, despite the claims of the project's developers'[15]. But it also created social tensions and resentments among the local residents, because it is really the expression that certain citizens have more rights than others. Skuggi is built exclusively as a luxury residential tower, with no allowance for other functions. This lack of 'layering of old and new, small and big, that gives central cities their ambiance and opportunities'[16] is essentially the malaise of this development.

The ground floor of the entire development is a blank wall that encloses the parking garage. The streets around are ignored, nothing happens in them except for the wind increasing as a result of the towers. The edges of Skuggi act as boundaries; there is no terrain for negotiation or adaptability, no space for the colonisation of the ground floor. The death of street life is implicit. We are in the heart of the city; historically this was a productive site that gave work and income to the people living around it. Now it is a mini enclave that excludes the very context that it claims as its key asset. The disconnection from the immediate surroundings and the existing street is total; the main access to the towers is from its own internal private plaza replete with CCTV that emphasises even more the separation

2 Skuggi's edges: Starting from corner A and moving anti-clock wise, this is what a pedestrian sees walking next to Skuggi

Corner A

Corner B

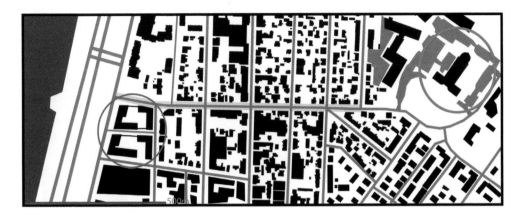

from the rest of the city. No space is left for negotiation, no way to engage the pedestrians walking around, no way to make them interact with the built form nor to enhance the street as a social place. There are no 'eyes on the street' as Jane Jacobs[17] would define the small shops and activities that are present along the city's pavements, and that are a characteristic of the city centre; nothing that might establish a human-social-physical connection between the inside and the outside of the buildings. There are no benches or any other activity that can be shared with the existing community. It is exactly in the design of the edges that the potential life of the city is embedded. It is through them that we feel accepted or rejected, and thus feel equal or not.

Changing Skuggi today is very difficult, if not impossible. Nevertheless we can learn a number of good lessons from it. Firstly, the importance of establishing a dialogue with our heritage, not just as a reliquary, but as an essential element that defines our spatial identity and recognises our past actions. It teaches us that when a building is built in a city centre the formalisation of its ground floor is vital. A ground floor, or at least a good percentage of it, should be thought of as a niche to host different activities (shops, restaurants, cafés); it should be considered an extension of the public life present in the surrounding pavements. It should be high enough not just to host public activities but to communicate and connect better with the outside world. The treatment of its surface should encourage a link between indoor and outdoor. Fenestration is therefore important, and numerous places of access will also guarantee an intense use of the street. Benches or steps also play a big role in articulating the extension and projection of a building onto the public realm. Skuggi also teaches us that a view is a public good that we must strive to protect for the interests of the community and not just the few. It can help us learn that an artefact produces a space, the unbuilt, which has an even higher value than the built one. As this space belongs to the community it becomes a public good, and a public good must prevail on private interest and this should be our guiding principle.[18] Finally, an artefact located in a community cannot be produced without the community's consent; spatial equality means dialogue between the people involved in the production of the city.

Corner D

3 Map of Vatnsendi. The built space is shown in black, unbuilt space in white, and the streets and car parks in red. Encircled in blue is the first development Sveit í borg, and in green the area assigned for reforestation but now destroyed by the new development.

Vatnsendi

'**Úthverfi**' is the Icelandic word for suburb and it literally means 'out areas'. Vatnsendi was developed during the 2000s. It was originally an area designated partly for 'Sveit í Borg', which means countryside-in-the-city, and partly, for reforestation. None of this has been executed today. The idea of 'Sveit í Borg' was to offer a country lifestyle at a modest distance from the city. The presence of the lake, a public good, created the perfect place for nature lovers to live. So the first people to move in were hardy citizens with either a passion for horses, or people who wanted to farm and grow vegetables. Connection to nature was the identity of the community that was established, but this changed when the area was developed in the years of the financial frenzy.

The neighbourhood created is a deeply fragmented area. It was marketed as a place of outstanding natural beauty with fantastic views over the lake and mountains, but it turned out to be a disordered mix of artefacts. Vatnsendi's streets are not places for socialisation but the realm of the car. Single houses are distanced from the street by the driveway and entrances to garages, whilst multi-storey buildings are surrounded by extensive car parks. Nature, that was supposed to be the unifying element, becomes instead something to be admired from a distance. The lake remains difficult to access and even the Scandinavian 'almannaréttur', the right of everyone to enjoy nature, is denied here.

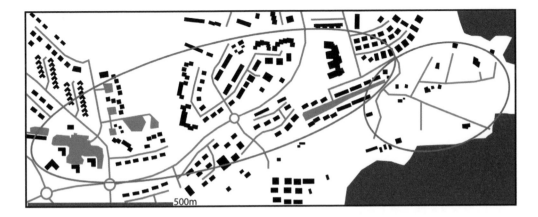

Developments like this one erase any spatial-social context (public streets, squares, plazas and nature) which for centuries has made possible the mingling of the different social groups. People no longer walk here because there is nothing to do. The moment I started walking in the area suspicious residents called the police. The layout of Vatnsendi forces us to drive, decreasing our chances of meeting people. The area has an exclusively residential purpose, with zoning in total operation, and the lack of any other activities makes us feel inappropriate users of the space. We feel like intruders and therefore unwelcome.

Places like this have sprung up all over Reykjavík. They grew fast, too fast, following the caprices of the financial market; they grew without value and without services. We can learn a great deal from neighbourhoods such as Vatnsendi. First and foremost that designing a street is an art, not just a science that responds to speed and capacity. The street in a neighbourhood should be imagined as a place of communication with active borders that facilitate social integration and connection among its neighbours and among its citizens. To reach this goal it is vital to think of the street (or at least some of them) as a place where mixed activities can happen, within shops, residences and libraries. Density is important, but even more important is the relationship of the artefacts to the street and to each other.

Conclusion

These case studies show different types of spatial inequality. In the city centre of Reykjavik, Skuggi severs the link with the built legacy by altering its scale. It cuts the connection to nature and creates tensions among the old and new residents. Vatnsendi's spatial inequality is evident in the disconnection which exists among its artefacts. They remain in fact an island in a sea of redundant roads, traffic calming measures, roundabouts and car parks. The lack of any other facilities, such as shops, condemns Vatnsendi residences to a reliance on private transportation for even their most basic needs; the rest of us feel like intruders for merely walking in the area.

As Prime Minister Jóhanna Sigurðardóttir said in the epitaph, 'mistakes were certainly made'. The design process also failed because it betrayed its investigative and critical nature - one which should look for new solutions, should question the established neo-liberal system, and should produce innovation, not simply stuff. When the word design is applied to the city, it acquires a new meaning too, and that is vision.

How we want to design our city equates with how we want to be.[19] Design therefore becomes politics, it is about what decisions we want to make. In this effort of imagination we need to ask ourselves what our priorities are, and this will help us to define a set of common policies. But city-design is not an abstract tool, it permeates the urban artefacts. It is about how many points of access a building should have, where they should be placed, how tall buildings should be, and for whom they should be built. City-design is architecture, 'aesthetic intention and the creation of better surroundings for life are the two permanent characteristics of architecture, these aspects emerge from any significant attempt to explain the city as a human creation'.[20] We need to have planning instruments that do not simply talk about quantities and traffic, but that are capable of building a better quality of life by improving public spaces, by protecting and enhancing the environment and, above all, by working towards social justice. 'Pursuit of social justice presupposes social solidarities, and a willingness to submerge individual wants, needs and desires in the cause of some more general struggle for, say, social equality or environmental justice.'[21] By redesigning the rules that produce the city we redesign ourselves, this is the constant process that is at the base of city-making.

5 A section along Frakkastigur Street, showing the incompatible height of Skuggi alongside the rest of the urban fabric.

1 Ólafsson, S. & Kristjánsson, A. S. (2010), *Income Inequality in a Bubble Economy – The Case of Iceland 1992-2008*, Reykjavík, University of Iceland

2 Sennett, R. (2008) 'The Public Realm', unpublished essay for *Quant*

3 UN-Habitat (2008), *The State of the World's Cities 2008/2009: Harmonious Cities*, London, Earthscan, p. 51

4 Sennett, R. (2008) 'The Public Realm', unpublished essay for *Quant*, Jacobs, A. and Appleyard, D. (1987) 'Towards an Urban Design Manifesto' in Larice, M. and Macdonald, E. (eds) (2007) *The Urban Design Reader.* London and New York: Routledge. pp. 98-108.

5 UN-Habitat 2008, p. 11

6 Harvey, D. (2008), 'The Right to the City', in *Social Justice and the City*, London, 2009, The University of Georgia Press

7 UN-Habitat (2009), *Global Report on Human Settlements 2009:*

Planning for Sustainable Cities, London, Earthscan, p. 6

8 UN-Habitat (2003), *Global Report on Human Settlements 2003: The Challenge of the Slums,* London, Earthscan

9 Foglesong, R.E. (1995), 'Planning the Capital City', in S. Campbell and S. Fainstein (eds) 1996 *Readings in Planning Theory*, Blackwell, p. 105)

10 Ibid.

11 Peñalosa, E. (2007), 'Politics, Power, Cities', in Burdett, R and Sudijc D. (eds) 2007 *The Endless City*, London, Phaidon.

12 Foglesong, R.E. (1995), 'Planning the Capital City', in S. Campbell and S. Fainstein (eds) 1996 *Readings in Planning Theory*, Blackwell, p. 105)

13 Peñalosa, E. (2007), 'Politics, Power, Cities', in Burdett, R and Sudijc D. (eds) 2007 *The Endless City*, London, Phaidon, p. 318.

14 http://www.101skuggi.is/

15 Fainstein, S. (2009), 'Mega-

projects in New York, London and Amsterdam', *International Journal of Urban and Regional Research*, DOI:10.1111/j.1468-2427.2008.00826.x, p. 783

16 Ibid, p. 783

17 Jacobs, J. (1961), *The Death and Life of Great American Cities*, New York, Penguin

18 Peñalosa, E. (2007), 'Politics, Power, Cities', in Burdett, R and Sudijc D. (eds) 2007 *The Endless City*, London, Phaidon

19 Harvey, D. (2008), 'The Right to the City', in *Social Justice and the City*, London, 2009, The University of Georgia Press

20 Rossi, A. (1984), *The Architecture of the City*, Cambridge, the MIT Press, p. 21

21 Harvey, D. (2005), *A Brief History of Neo-liberalism*, Oxford University Press, p. 41

Scarce or Abundant Resources?

Arna Mathiesen

The Territorial Implications of Resource Scarcity

Scarcity has territorial implications. In a discussion about the good life in Plato's *Republic*,[1] the idea of having more exotic foods at dinner parties, instead of eating perfectly delicious olives and other locally harvested (but possibly boring) foods, triggered the need for territorial expansion and the introduction of a whole new class in the state: soldiers for invading territories inhabited by others, and defending new frontiers, so paving the way for the safe collection of the foods of desire. On the other hand, the concept of post-scarcity - from the alternative worlds of science fiction - reflects on the spatial dimensions of resource scarcity: resource exhaustion on earth could theoretically be unproblematic for humans, if fresh assets could be found and harvested on new planets. Without access to other spheres, and with finite resources distributed unevenly around the globe, spatial interventions for exploiting resources unfold in geopolitical scenarios on this planet according to the options, needs, desires and social conscience of different individuals and groups.

The settlement of Iceland (the first emigrations westward from Europe) is a classic example of that described above. In a contemporary context however, the development of the urban landscape in Iceland during the last ten years illustrates how such scenarios can evolve in the present age of globalisation, in the local built environment in a developed country which has incorporated the rules of the European Union.

Understanding how the generous resources are managed is a key to capturing urbanisation in Iceland. It would seem fair to assume that habitation in this context was about being self-sustainable on that island far at sea. That concept would certainly seem to fit neatly into the principles of sustainable development: closing as many of the resource cycles as possible, as close to the source as possible, and preserving the resources to the greatest extent possible for future generations. In Iceland this has not always been successful. In virtually no other place in the world has habitation imprinted such a deep mark on a country in terms of vegetation cover that has been wiped out in large parts of the island, leaving lifeless deserts.[2]

A Brief History of Settlement

When the future Icelanders first left behind their origins in Norway, Scotland and Ireland, and started from scratch in a virgin country, they needed as a group to sustain themselves on an island, more or less independently of other territories. This was not easy on barren land at latitude 65° 00' N and longitude 18° 00' W, surrounded by the Atlantic Ocean. Until recently, the sea was a tremendous obstacle imposing many days of hazardous sailing to reach the nearest neighbours.

The Reykjavík Capital Area is on the south-west corner of the country. Smoky Bay is the translation of the Icelandic place name Reykjavik: the bay where the steam is. The first Norwegian settler came in the 9th century and he chose Reykjavik for his dwelling.[3] It was a place with hot springs and water, in a location by a creek; a sheltered space with fish in the sea, rivers and lakes.

Iceland was for centuries (1262-1918) under Norwegian and Danish rule. The economy during that period did not allow for many goods to be imported for the general public. During their first 900 years in the country, until the late 18th century, the inhabitants did not enjoy any notable progress in technical skills, unlike the rest of Europe.[4] Resourcefulness and hard work had to be applied, and buildings were constructed with local materials, earth, stone, driftwood and turf; this was a housing type that demanded continuous maintenance. Inequalities in the allocation of resources between the local people created a division between the better off and the poor who were often left starving, sometimes to death.

0		135		270 km

+ settlements
-- isoline
— coastline

The settlement pattern. Settlements line up along the coast of Iceland.

Urban History and Local Ecology

Urbanisation started to develop in earnest in the 19th century when, with population growth, resources became scarcer inland. Tiny villages formed where there were suitable natural conditions for harbours, facilitating transport, and usually some other benefits, such as sheltered landscape, proximity to fishing grounds, fresh water, peat for energy and so on. New technologies and larger fishing boats - steamboats, and later trawlers - also played an important role. Some other developments were in their early stages. Danish merchants started to establish durable warehouses in the late 18th century.[5]

When the Danish king wanted to implement reforms in his kingdom in the same period, a suitable place for developing domestic industry had to be found in Iceland too, where the Danish were rulers. Reykjavík was selected. Only two families were living there at that point, but it became the location for a textile industry, with several buildings springing up along one street. The textile venture was not entirely successful though, and only 301 people, distributed in 42 buildings, were living there in the year 1800.

There was hardly any town to speak of until the industrial revolution finally reached Iceland in the late 19th century, and by the turn of the century the inhabitants of Reykjavík numbered 6,000, constituting 8% of the country's population.[6]

Local ecology was still playing an important role in shaping the town. Turf was in short supply locally as a result of so many buildings being built in the same small area. In 1894 it was prohibited to build new turf houses in Reykjavík.[7] At the beginning of the 20th century the municipality bought plenty of land surrounding the village on which the inhabitants could graze their animals. Far into the 20th century urban life in Reykjavík was intertwined with agricultural practice, and buildings were not put on wetlands or windy heaths, unlike the more recent developments of nowadays.

Plans for the city were to a large extent created under the influence of the garden city movement, as promoted in a book by an Icelandic doctor in 1916,[8] establishing the areas which nowadays are considered by many to be the most attractive in the town.

The population growth in Reykjavík exploded during World War II, with an urgent need for a workforce that could build new infrastructures for the allied forces occupying Reykjavík. First the British came, then the Americans. New, and supposedly more effective, equipment such as bulldozers, brought by the army, was put to use for building airports, roads and other infrastructures. The Americans did not leave their permanent base (half an hour's drive from Reykjavík) until 2006. By that time the base had generated immense building activity across the country, laying the foundations for some of the largest building contractors.

A detailed urban master plan for Reykjavík was published in 1966.[9] It was ideological, the inhabitants should benefit by 'living closer to nature'. Cars had started to be a common sight around the country, about twenty years earlier, and they played a key role in the plan. It legitimised the expansion of residential areas onto the barren windy heaths around Reykjavík, at a distance of about 10 km from the centre of town, and accessed by cars along generous road corridors. Spatial separation between work and living space in this scheme made it necessary for almost all the workers living in these new territories to drive across town every day. Even though the intention was to tailor the plan for a local spirit, it was not made in a vacuum. In fact, it was made for Reykjavik City by a Danish team: an architect and a road designer.

The plan, often going under the name of the Danish plan, was criticised by some members of the architectural profession as soon as it appeared.[10] The critics proved right: a plan, depending on and giving much weight to the car, would produce many challenges, not only in new neighbourhoods but also in the existing city. Car-based lifestyles led to a reduction in green open space in the existing town, and an increase in noise and pollution. Vegetation was sacrificed in the push to allocate more space to roads and parking.

By the time the boom took off in the early nineties, the weakness of the 40-year-old plan was a well-known fact. Moreover, Local Agenda 21, aiming at sustainable goals, had been in existence for ten years and was adapted in legal frameworks from the start of the nineties. In addition, the city of Reykjavík launched at the turn of the century a series of public participation programmes, involving over 800 people, in an effort to prepare for a long-term policy for the city.[11]

However, all seven municipalities in the capital area contributed to a further expansion of the city fabric into the surrounding barren and windy heights, previously not considered an attractive proposition for habitation, and they made the population ever more dependent on vehicles for getting from one place to another. Since the plan drawn up in the sixties, the city has gradually become less and less dense. The urban tissue of Reykjavík has now merged together with the tissue of the neighbouring municipalities, making it radiate up to 25 km from the centre; a vast territory considering the population of just 200,000. Since the 1960s, new factors have emerged to exacerbate the use of the car even more. A greater number of women working outside the home, and a conglomeration of shopping into larger units located further away from the homes, have made the private car even more indispensable for a larger part of the population.

It is true that the Danish plan facilitated many people moving nearer to nature and away from the existing city fabric, as was its intention. And so did the ensuing development in the boom period. However, the developments on the outskirts look more or less exactly the same, containing the same housing typologies and relating to the ground in the same way, regardless of the natural terrain – whether it be tundra, fertile soil or lava. The type of dwelling in the urban context deviates in a number of other respects from traditional architecture that used local materials in auspicious locations, and turned its back against the harshest winds. The most striking change (one shared by many other places on the planet) is that, in the course of less than a century, everyone came to have totally separate private spaces, whereas in the past they had lived for the most part in a shared space, in which everyone on the farm completed the handicraft work, ate and slept... together.

For a more detailed account of the way in which Iceland was settled and planned in relation to its resources through the ages, see Trausti Valsson's Planning in Iceland: From the Settlement to Present Times.[12]

The recent history of hardship is vividly remembered by some of our grandparents who have personally passed on the information to us. With these memories fresh in mind it is easy to understand the dreams of a better life, and hopes that any progress would improve the economy and make life easier. The mere thought of homesteading survivalism sends shivers down the spine of many people.

The Earth Hut Thesis

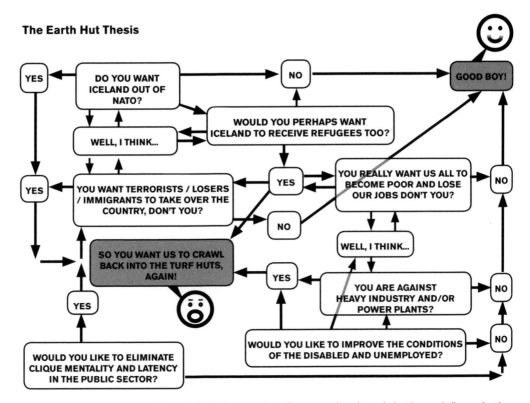

'The Icelanders used to live in earth huts. By faithfully supporting military operations, heavy industries, capitalism and nationalism, (so called) conservative governments managed to get the nation out of the earth huts. However, some individuals want nothing more than to go back to the earth hut stage. The diagram above is a useful tool to sort the sheep from the goats. The first aluminium plant in Iceland was established in 1969. By that time the Icelanders were not living in turf huts. Less than 10% of the Icelandic people lived in turf huts when Iceland joined NATO (The North Atlantic Treaty Organisation), an intergovernmental Military Alliance, 20 years earlier.

It was not the army, big industries or the hardship of the less well-to-do that got Icelanders out of the earth huts, and there is precisely no reason to think we are on the way back into them.' (from the Earth Hut Thesis by Eva Hauksdóttir)[13]

Comments such as 'we don't want to go back to the turf huts, do we?' effectively thwart discussions about sustainable solutions. Many former colonies, now 'emerging' economies, might identify with the sentiment.

Recently The Earth Hut Thesis was set forth, simply summarising the discourse. It shouldn't have the effect of scaring anyone from living in such huts though; they can be pleasant spaces, built with local materials found in great abundance and they can be constructed by anyone, with just a little know-how, some tools and using their bare hands ('A Hole in the Hill' in part 2).

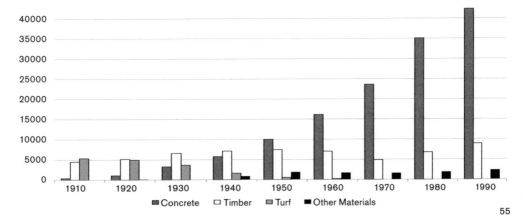

Resources per Day per Capita

Energy [14]
1422.5 KWH

Fish [15]
10.5 KG

Water [16]
1412 LITRES

**ENERGY FOR KEEPING 23,708
60 WATT LIGHTBULBS GOING 24/7**

49 DAILY PORTIONS OF FISH

**941 X 1.5 LITRE BOTTLES
A DAY**

ONE INHABITANT

**IN ADDITION THERE IS AN AREA OF 0.32KM² PER INHABITANT OF ICELAND
AND IN THE YEAR 2012, PER ONE INHABITANT OF ICELAND TOURISTS HAD NINE
OVERNIGHT STAYS (TOTALLING 2,889,000 AND GROWING) [17]
+ ALL THE WATER, ENERGY AND FISH NOT YET EXPLOITED**

Current Resource Management

Now, more than eleven centuries after settlement, Iceland is the most sparsely populated country in Europe with 1/3km² per capita, and there remains far more renewable fish, energy and clean water locally available than the small local population of approximately 300,000 could ever consume.

The Urban Implications, On a Country Scale

The resource management of Iceland - with technologies for faster and safer transport, exploitation of hydropower and more efficient fishing methods - has prompted radical urban transformations across the country. Holes are being drilled into the bedrock to harvest geothermal energy. Huge dams have been built inland, to make it possible to harness the power of falling water in the highlands, and to channel the energy along large power lines supported by pylons across seemingly untouched landscapes, all the way to the shore where it is put to use. Since most people in Iceland rely on getting jobs that have been created by others, the pattern of urban development, in terms of which towns grow and which towns shrink[18] in population size, is defined by the locations on the coast that fishery companies and smelters have chosen for their businesses.

The way in which the urban fabric relates to the features of the local landscape, and the resources at hand, is primarily a visual one: the fantastic views.

Each new plan for resource exploitation brings with it more infrastructures. The alternative to moving to places where work is generated along the coast, is moving to the capital area where the job market is more diverse. Never before has a larger proportion of the total population, or two-thirds, lived in the Reykjavík Capital Area (RCA).

Recent developments in Reyðarfjörður, a village in the countryside.

Empty blocks of flats, left over from the boom, rise up from the existing urban tissue, and a large percentage of the older and abandoned buildings lie in a state of decay. Brand new sports halls, donated by the owners of the new aluminium smelter nearby, defy the scale of the town. Temporary modular housing for guest-workers, imported for building the aluminium plant, lurk desolately on a heath midway between the town and the plant, keeping the guest workers at arm's length from the local population.

Considering the costly urban transformations the current resource management has triggered, and the fact that the resources have not been able to save Iceland from crisis, questions arise about the management of the remaining resources.

It is argued that exploitation of hydro and geothermal energy is to be encouraged because energy emits much less CO_2 than oil and coal and since there is such a quantum of resource per capita some people think that the Icelandic reserves are boundless and that exploiting them at will, for whatever purpose, could never be wasteful. That is far from the truth.

In fact, if all renewable energy in Iceland were to be harnessed (estimated 50-55 TWh as opposed to the current 17 TWh) it would be just a fraction of the 2200 TWh energy market of Europe.[19] Bear in mind that a 1000 MW submarine cable, which is currently under debate, could carry 6 TWh which would only satisfy 0.16% of the energy requirements of the UK. It should be noted that in the case of Iceland, geothermal and hydropower is not renewable over a longer perspective in the way that wind, solar and wave energy is. The reservoirs of the geothermal water get emptied gradually, taking hundreds of years to fill up again. The dams for creating hydropower gradually fill up with residue from the glacial rivers, making them redundant in the long run[20] and as soon as the glaciers have melted as a result of global warming the infrastructures will become useless.

Even if the way in which the exploitation is managed had no questionable urban consequences, environmental impacts are certainly a serious concern, and the economic profits for the local people are disputable.

Nowadays there are plenty of technologies to exploit the resources, but there are challenges when it comes to capitalising on them.

Much of the fish is exported as raw material, since the policies of the European Union make processed fish less profitable. However some fish from North Atlantic waters is shipped to China for processing, only to be shipped back again to be sold on American or European markets. Fish is, by law, a national property, but the right to fish for commercial purposes is actually held by just a few companies.

Transport of energy from Iceland to other countries is technically challenging. About 80% of the harnessed energy[21] is sold cheaply to international corporations (Rio Tinto, Becromal, Century Aluminium) and foreign states (China) who use it for feeding energy craving metal smelters (smelting aluminium and raw materials for the steel industries) located along the coast of Iceland. Deals are bound up for decades, and the price (kept out of the public eye) is linked to the aluminium price which has been declining since the crash.[22] Consequently the National Energy Company was operated with a deficit in 2013. It was even worse for the public utility owned by municipalities. Their newest energy venture, built during the boom, had a contracted energy price that was bound to the Icelandic currency, which was devalued by about 50% when the crash hit.

Not only does this mean that almost all the profit, if any, ends up serving the loans for paying for the infrastructures, but local producers of fruit and vegetables are denied the electricity at the same prices, which results in imported goods being cheaper than local produce.

There is a tug of war on how to exploit the resources, how to apply them and how to distribute any profits.

In an advisory referendum in October 2012, roughly 80% of the electorate voted in favour of Iceland making a declaration in the constitution that the natural resources (those not in private ownership) were national property. However, this has not passed through parliament.

Global issues and local challenges

The municipalities in the capital area have soaring debt stemming from their infrastructural ventures exploiting the energy in the vicinity. Their balance sheets provoke questions as to whether capital cities can declare themselves bankrupt like other cities (Detroit), and what that would entail. Solutions aimed at shifting the debts, or making them disappear one way or another, are tempting, and hopes are entertained that the fix will come from external sources. New building plans are being implemented and the devaluation of the Icelandic currency already attracts many tourists who bring foreign currency with them. In addition, steps are taken to attract investors and their cash. The bait is Icelandic resources; landscapes, water, energy and an economy allegedly recovering, with new banks, full of new funding (which incidentally is hard for local companies to get hold of).

It is a paradox that economic problems due to energy exploitation trigger yet more exploitation and a sale of the resources. Now exploitation is no longer limited to energy with relatively low CO_2 emissions. As the state issued permissions for oil to be sought and exploited in the Dragon Zone off northeast Iceland (to Icelandic and Norwegian companies, and the Chinese CNOOC) the prime minister stated:

'We can reap the potential economic benefits of extracting oil and gas and, at the same time, address the importance of long-term sustainability...'[23]

Environmentalists, however, draw attention to the environmental consequences on the Reykjanes peninsula and in the Highlands, which are considered to be one of the last great wildernesses in Europe with renowned and unparalleled geology and geomorphology, the highlands being a space one can currently journey through for days without seeing any apparent signs of human habitation bar a mud track:

'Despite the stated goals and policies of the Icelandic government for the protection of wilderness areas, these areas have consistently been under seige. A recent study at the University of Iceland shows that they decreased by 68% from 1936 to 2010. It is very important to stop this trend and protect those areas that are still unspoiled. Nevertheless, there are plans for power plants, paved roads and power lines in the region...'

From a petition site for nature preservation: http://heartoficeland.org/

Design finds itself in the intersection between these two perspectives. An Icelandic designer is 'told' that, the more that gets sold on the world market of one of the most blacklisted building materials available, and the less there will be left of the most stunning wilderness in Europe - the Icelandic Highlands - the better off he and his country will be... financially.

This time around, there aren't even any buyers on hand to buy the energy for the price needed to finance the venture. The price of aluminium is collapsing and stocks from production in China are piling up. On the other hand, some players in the field will profit while the operations are underway: There will be plenty of jobs for engineers at the National Power Company of Iceland, many entrepreneurs and engineering firms (most likely the biggest ones) will thrive, and the MPs

of the areas concerned will get backing. For the individuals involved, it will certainly be a win-win situation... financially.

A recent study reveals that the Icelanders have the largest ecological footprint per capita. At least seven planet earths would be necessary to sustain the global population if everyone behaved like the average Icelander; 27 planets in fact if the aluminium production and fisheries were included in the calculations.[24] The 'sustainability' to which the prime minister referred in his speech is an economic objective that sustains current living standards and disregards true ecological sustainability which would preserve precious resources for future generations.

Even though the National Power Company acknowledges that building new energy infrastructures triggers unsustainable economic growth, they claim there will be sustainable profits in the long run, e.g. Icelandic engineers' knowhow, exportable to other countries.[25]

Global warming, with the consequential ice melting in the Arctic, opens up transport routes, and thus facilitates shorter sailing journeys between China and Europe. This has expedited a gold rush in municipalities in north east Iceland, and new international alliances. Dreams of gainful scenarios have triggered new masterplans, aimed at establishing a deep sea port in Finnafjörður,[26] with German Bremenports as a promoter. The company runs the second largest harbour in Europe and has established an Icelandic company. The Chinese government is very interested in this project. A Chinese agent (a former director of the Chinese ministry of propaganda) has also attempted to buy the largest farm in Iceland (300km^2) with the most powerful waterfall in Europe, Dettifoss, running along its boundaries. Detailed knowledge has also been accumulated of ownership to property in central Reykjavík, and buildings have been purchased in strategic urban locations. Take for example the building rounding the corner into Borgartún (Reykjavík's financial district) on the end of the Skúlagata axis opposite the new music hall. With a perfect view over the Directorate of Internal Revenue, the National Commissioner of the Icelandic Police, Reykjavík Police Station and The Financial Supervisory Authority, this building has been transformed into a Chinese embassy with enough space to accommodate 450 employees.

The Arctic Sea Routes

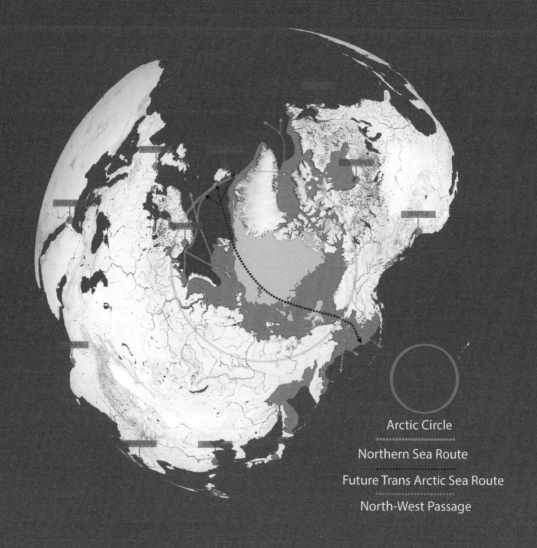

Arctic Circle

Northern Sea Route

Future Trans Arctic Sea Route

North-West Passage

The Icelandic Highlands

Areas marked in red, covering 35,000 km²,
are incorporated within a diverse legal framework
- masterplans and other regulations -
which aims to protect the Icelandic highlands from urban transformation.
The current government wants to lift those restrictions,
so making it possible to harvest more geothermal energy and hydropower.
This may have irreversible and wide-reaching
 consequences for the Icelandic highlands,
across water catchment basins and ecosystems,
and will drastically change the appearance of the area.

Nothern Sea Route VS Suez Canal
China - Europe

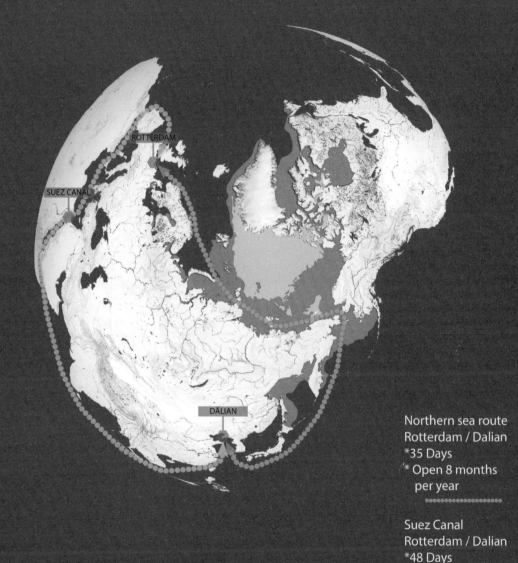

ROTTERDAM

SUEZ CANAL

DALIAN

Northern sea route
Rotterdam / Dalian
*35 Days
* Open 8 months
  per year

Suez Canal
Rotterdam / Dalian
*48 Days

Northern Sea Route
Size: 4,000-5,000 (TEU) Speed 19 Knots

2187.5t fuel used
Icebreaker Service : approx. 200,000 $

Suez Canal
Size: 4,000-5,000 (TEU) Speed 19 Knots

3000t fuel used
Service average 251,000 $

1 Plato, Grube, G. M. A. og Reeve, C.
D. C. *Plato: Republic*. Indianapolis:
Hackett Pub.Co.1992.
2 Þórhallsdóttir, Þóra Ellen,
'Ásýnd landsins'. Reykjavík: *Rit
Ráðanautafundar*, 2001, p 77-85.
3 Edwards, Paul, *The Book of
Settlements Landnámabók*. Winnipeg:
University of Manitoba Press, 2006.
http://bit.ly/1f8Lqfd
4 Erlu Valdimarsdóttir, Þórunn, "Skúli
fógeti gat Reykjavík með Friðriki
fimmta", *Skírnir,* vor 2013, pp. 141-160.
5 Reynarsson, Bjarni, 'The Planning of
Reykjavik, Iceland, Three ideological
waves. A historical overview':

"Planning Perspectives". Oxford:
Routledge, 1999, p.14 and p. 49-67.
https://borg.hi.is/pir.rtf
6 Ibid.
7 Erlu Valdimarsdóttir, Þórunn, *Sveitin
við sundin: búskapur í Reykjavík
1870-1950*. Reykjavík: Sögufélagið,
1986, p 3.
8 Hannesson, Guðmundur. *Um
skipulag bæja*. Reykjavík. 1916
9 *Master Plan for Reykjavik 1962
- 1983 / Adalskipulag Reykjavikur
1962 - 1983*. Reykjavik: the City of
Reykjavik, 1966.
10 Ólafsson, Björn. 'Er Aðalskipulag
Reykjavíkur Úrelt?' Reykjavík: *Birtingur,*

1 June 1968, p 30. http://bit.ly/1k6G5IU
11 Reynarsson, Bjarni, 'Reykjavík – the
Future City', a paper presented at the
conference: Area-based initiatives in
contemporary urban policy, Danish
building and Urban Research and
European Urban Research Association,
Copenhagen 17-19 May 2001, http://
www.sbi.dk/eura/workshops/papers/
workshop1/reynars.pdf
12 Valsson, Trausti, *Planning in Iceland:
From the Settlement to Present Times*.
Reykjavík: Univ. of Iceland Press,
2003. See: https://notendur.hi.is/~tv/
Planning%20in%20Iceland/BookV.pdf
13 Hauksdóttir, Eva,

Dynkur on the river Þjórsá is one of several waterfalls that will disappear if the current plans are realised.

'Moldarkofakenningin'. *Eyjan*, October 2013 8. http://bit.ly/1a1bXxp
14 Statistics Iceland (citing: Orkustofnun). *Raforkunotkun 1998-2012*. Reykjavík: DataMarket. http://bit.ly/1fbzPMu
15 Statistics Iceland. Author's calculations based on information from 'Catch, value and processing of catch 2011'. Reykjavík: *Hagtíðindi Statistical Series 97/26*, 2012:03. http://bit.ly/1k6uNUZ
16 Environment: Key Tables from OECD. Water abstractions. OECD iLibrary: http://bit.ly/1iGDsQa
17 Óladóttir, Oddný Þóra,

Ferðaþjónusta á Íslandi Í tölum, aprÍl 2013. *Reykjavík: Icelandic Tourist Board, 2013*. http://bit.ly/1dl8vCQ
18 Oswalt, Philipp (ed.) for the Kulturstiftung des Bundes. *Shrinking Cities, Volume 1*. Ostfildern-Ruit: Hatje Cantz Verlag, 2005.
19 Arnarsson, Hörður General Assembly at the National Power Company, on November 10, 2010.
20 http://goo.gl/H47IER
21 Statistics Iceland (citing: Orkustofnun). *Raforkunotkun 1998-2012*. Numbers from 2011. *Reykjavík: DataMarket*. http://bit.ly/1fbzPMu
22 RÚV–Kastljós – 17.10.2011,

Arnarsson, Hörður, in interview with Seljan, Helgi
23 http://eng.forsaetisraduneyti.is/minister/sdg-speeches/nr/7846
24 Jóhannesson, Sigurður Eyberg. *Vistspor Íslands*. Reykjavík: Háskóli Íslands, 2010, p. 68. http://goo.gl/jy7ZdE
25 Arnarsson, Hörður. General Assembly at the National Power Company, March 2013, http://goo.gl/zuMwec
26 News on RÚV (*National Television*) June 27th and 28th 2013, posted on Youtube by Einarsdóttir, Lára Hanna http://goo.gl/KojO9i

The Groundbreaking Tour (Skóflustungutúrinn)

Silliness (Kjánska)

The Groundbreaking Tour took place during the summer of 2008, a few months before the collapse of the Icelandic banking system that marked the beginning of the economic depression in Iceland. The Groundbreaking Tour was the last in a series of works that experimented with the possibility of making politically committed art during the high point of the neoliberal economic upswing that gave rise to the 2008 crisis.

The 'Silliness' collective was founded towards the end of 2006 by Anna Björk Einarsdóttir, Magnús Þór Snæbjörnsson and Steinunn Gunnlaugsdóttir. Its main goal was to make politically committed artwork that would traverse the fantasy of Icelandic nationalism and multinational capitalism. In so doing, the collective took an active stance against the domination of art for art's sake in the Icelandic art scene, and the merger of art with the banking system; during those times the latter served as the most visible sponsor of the arts in Iceland. The collective's main project was an experimental documentary, the little object a, that later became Political Cinema #1 as well as various performances such as The

Groundbreaking Tour. Political Cinema #1 sought to understand the society that gave rise not only to the massive industrial undertakings of the Icelandic state to provide electricity for the aluminium smelters in east Iceland, but also the banking bubble that burst around the same time as Political Cinema #1 was premiered. The collective strove to intervene in a society characterised by a booming economy at the height of the banking bubble. While the appearances of that society have changed to some extent, politically and economically very little changed. Silliness's goal was to create politically committed art despite, and in direct confrontation with, the common complaint that such art would always necessarily be naive and silly. In fact, the members of the collective embraced the utopianism of radical political movements of the twentieth century, while at the same time maintaining their sharp humour and jovial mood; they set about reinventing a twenty-first century parodic praxis.

The Groundbreaking Tour took place in six villages around Iceland. The project consisted of six groundbreakings for a variety of industries; they were intended to highlight employ-

ment opportunities that might save the decaying countryside. Adopting the rhetoric used to justify the massive state spending on the provision of cheap electricity for privately-run aluminium smelters for multinational corporations, Silliness presented villagers with various projects; they all involved innovative ideas on the use of natural and human resources to draw international investors to Iceland, while providing labour opportunities for the locals. Environmentally Friendly Weapons Factory was pronounced in Vopnafjörður. The ingenuity of the idea was to make a wanted product from the aluminium available locally in Alcoa, and thereby provide jobs for people in Vopnafjörður. A High Security Prison Camp for NATO was suggested to the residents of Hvammstangi. It would allow them to benefit from the expansion of the industrial prison complex, while putting Iceland's unique location at the service of NATO. A Pleasure Centre was announced in Raufarhöfn where business elites from Europe and the USA could indulge in carnal pleasures. The town would just be called upon to provide an international airport to service the centre. In Vík, it was a Nike Sweatshop. The labour

of under-achieving children from Reykjavik could be used to produce consumer goods that would otherwise have to be imported, thus countering global warming as well as creating the products Icelanders wanted. The Pan-European Concentration Camps for Illegal Immigrants in Búðardalur were meant to assist the European Community in tackling the problem of illegal immigration. If the labour power of the illegal immigrants was utilised to attract transnational corporations to produce goods, the concentration camps could be run at a profit. Lastly, a Nuclear Waste Storage Facility in Suðureyri was announced, which displayed a façade by the Danish-Icelandic corporate artist Ólafur Elíasson. As a result, the facility could act as a tourist attraction as well as benefiting the international art scene.

After each groundbreaking event, all including speeches, champagne and hand-shakes performed by only one person, Kjánska introduced the ideas to people in town by distributing detailed leaflets that explained the ingenuity of each operation. In just one week, Silliness managed to perform six groundbreak-ings all over Iceland, even in the most remote

corners of the island, thus demonstrating the wealth of underdeveloped and unexploited opportunities in Iceland. *The Groundbreaking Tour* received a warm welcome from local residents and was featured in local newspapers and online media. The groundbreaking for Environmentally Friendly Weapons Factory was made headline news by the Icelandic national broadcasting service (RÚV), and the municipal manager declared the activities to be of a serious nature as the Factory's pamphlets featured the logos of various official institutions and companies.

The performance took a clear stance against the exploitation of Iceland's natural resources and its population, for the benefits of international capital. The collective saw the absurdity of the situation, as represented in the building of the aluminium smelters in east Iceland, the massive hydroelectric power plant in Kárahnjúkar and plans underway to provide

further new aluminium smelters with cheap electricity. An inspiration for their project came from Helguvík where members of the local population, in spring 2008, took the first steps towards a groundbreaking project without even having the approval of the appropriate institutions. The same summer, locals in the Westfjords embraced proposals to build an oil refinery in Arnarfjörður. The collective had imagined that the prospect of building a nuclear waste storage centre would be considered outrageous, but in fact this idea had been proposed in the past, and some Icelanders had been open to exploring the idea. All of Silliness's groundbreakings in the summer of 2008 were aimed at addressing vital contemporary issues, the very worst kind of developments that showed no regard to human lives or nature, but merely focused on the possible profits that could ensue – and at a great cost to the local population and to the environment.

Big Plans / Small City

Thomas Forget

'Europe is absent… I can't quite picture your arrival. What was your impression of Reykjavík harbour? Is there any attempt to make the visitor feel that he is arriving at a capital city? Not much.'

W.H. Auden (1937)[1]

From the perspective of an outsider, the parameters of the 2007 International Competition to reimagine the Vatnsmýri area of Reykjavík seemed logical. The commissioners envisioned the project area, occupied primarily by a small domestic airport, as "a contemporary and robust urban fabric with the flexibility required for research, technology, and knowledge based enterprises mixed with significant housing, services, and residential forms."[2] They aspired to create a regional hub that would reorder the spatial logic of the Reykjavík Capital Area and repair the damage of rampant suburban sprawl that had begun in the late 1990s, as well as a global hub that would mediate the economic superpowers of Europe and North America. In another era, the enormous scale and ambition of the project in this tiny and remote nation would perhaps have seemed absurd, but not in the early twenty-first century. The "irrational exuberance" of the era, as well as the emergence of large-scale global hubs in Europe and Asia, such as Euralille and Pudong, rendered the premise of a North Atlantic hub plausible, if not rational.[3] In Iceland, as in other countries that sought to position themselves as leaders in the new global economy, national pride catalysed an already acute faith in economic growth and development. Historically, various global powers have taken practical and symbolic advantage of Iceland's location on the American-Eurasian continental rift. During the late medieval and early modern eras, Norway and Denmark maintained colonial settlements in Iceland that provided resources and trading opportunities. During World War II, Allied Forces occupied the nation and employed it as a strategic military base. During the Cold War, the nation (more willingly) provided a dramatic stage for a critical summit between Ronald Reagan and Mikhail Gorbachev. The recent proposal to redevelop Vatnsmýri suggested a new chapter in Iceland's participation in global affairs, a shift from that of a subordinate facilitator to a chief initiator in geopolitics.

As a foreign participant (with Jonathan F. Bell) in both the preliminary and the final stages of the Vatnsmýri design competition, I sensed the importance of national identity to the redevelopment project, and thereby attempted to update the "critical regionalism" agenda of the twentieth century - to integrate an Icelandic ethos into a globally oriented design solution.[4] Coincidently, two years before the competition, I had developed a conceptual understanding of the nation's built environment while on a tourist visit. On the periphery of the civilised world, I observed, space is different. Buildings and cities in Iceland may look like their peers in Europe and America, but they lack the aesthetic conviction of their precedents. In most countries, the built environment is a primary vehicle of cultural significance and political power. In Iceland, by contrast, nature is the primary generator of meaning. The aesthetic dimension of the built environment there resides not in architectural styles or planning principles, but rather in the ways in which buildings and cities occupy and/or resist the land. The result is an uncanny condition, especially for foreigners: everything looks familiar, but nothing is normal.

An especially vivid memory from my initial trip to Iceland is the national system of roadside signs that mark the boundaries of towns and cities in bold graphics: signs that mark an entrance into a town or city depict a black skyline (generic but somewhat reminiscent of Reykjavík's skyline) against a yellow sky; signs

that mark an exit from a town or city depict the same graphic with a red diagonal strip over it, recalling the internationally-known symbol for "no," as in "no entry" and "no smoking." In this case, the signs say "city" and "no city." The signs do not distinguish between cities and towns, perhaps because Iceland has only two areas (Reykjavík and Akureyri) that qualify as cities in the conventional sense. In most of the nation, the signs are useful (especially for foreigners) because of the elasticity of the concept of "city." What may appear to be just a cluster of houses or farms, or even an empty space, may in fact be a town. In the capital area, the seemingly random locations of the signs underscore the detrimental effects of sprawl on community identity, and the lack of connectedness between developments and their context. Meanwhile, signs in undeveloped areas, where no town seems to exist, remind us that even the vast expanse of nature is subject to political forces.

Against Paradigm

Austurvöllur, the oldest public square in Reykjavík, symbolises the precariousness of Iceland's participation in western architectural discourses. The general location of the square, in between the original coastal settlement of the Danish colony (chartered in 1786) and Tjörnin (a small lake), has accommodated various public functions throughout its history, most recently as a public demonstration site in the wake of the financial crisis. Throughout the first half of the nineteenth century, the city's first cathedral, Dómkirkjan (designed by Andreas J. Kirkerup in 1796), dominated the loosely defined borders of the irregular landscape of the area.[5] In 1874, the Danish-sponsored millennial celebration of the founding of Iceland motivated the formalisation of a portion of the area into a more conventional public square (in the European sense): planners defined a perfectly rectangular space, demarcated it with fences, created axial pathways through it,

and placed a self-portrait by Icelandic-Danish sculptor Bertel Thorvaldsen in the centre of it.[6] Dómkirkjan regulated the placement, but not the orientation, of the square. The square is not built around the church, but rather (and somewhat awkwardly) beside it. This misalignment is understandable, as the space adjacent to the cathedral already had the vague definition of a public square when the planning of Austurvöllur occurred, and as the space in front of the cathedral was too close to Tjörnin to accommodate a conventional public square. As in a typical medieval city, multiple forces (both physical and social) shape this public space, and the result is an idiosyncratic (and wholly Icelandic) urban condition that escapes the limiting vision of the nineteenth-century planning principles that inspired it.

Alþingishúsið, the colonial (and eventual national) parliament house designed by the Danish architect Ferdinand Meldahl, arose on the southern edge of Austurvöllur in 1881, directly adjacent to and in front of Dómkirkjan. Alþingishúsið is a soundly Northern European building that fulfills every expectation of its typology: solid, symmetrical, and imposing—an architectural object that commands respect. At the same time, its slight misalignment with respect to the central axis of the public square (caused by the close proximity of Dómkirkjan), and its awkward perpendicular alignment with respect to the cathedral, further distinguish Austurvöllur as a public space that simultaneously adheres to, and elides, the strict geometric order of nineteenth-century planning initiatives. Considering that Dómkirkjan and Alþingishúsið co-participate in an annual ceremony that marks the opening of the parliament session, their unusual geometric relationship is especially vital.[7] While the aesthetic expectations of European paradigms of planning and architecture are evident in the square and its buildings, the space reflects the unique formal and social conditions of its context. Geometric rigour and local contingencies coexist.

The history of the governmental architecture

of the City of Reykjavík reflects a similarly tenuous relationship to European paradigms. Until the opening of Ráðhúsið (the City Hall) in 1992, the city operated without a formal seat of government for over two centuries. It is inconceivable that another European capital could have hesitated for so long without succumbing to the lure of an architectural headquarters through which to exert its symbolic and political authority.[8] Reykjavík is different, and Ráðhúsið, designed by the Icelandic firm Studio Granda, wisely upholds the legacy of the municipal government's decentralised public identity. Ráðhúsið is irregular, permeable, and permissive. Its smooth concrete forms create an elegant, quasi-symmetrical composition that hovers over a corner of Tjörnin, and multiple entries from various directions create the spatial quality of a hub, as opposed to a terminal destination. The primary axis through the building, in fact, extends into a public bridge that spans the width of the lake, and Ráðhúsið inhales and exhales the public that it serves. Most non-public spaces inhabit upper levels, allowing the ground floor to accept the city, and interior galleries and cafés offer resting points. The building thereby dismantles one of the stalwarts of western civic architecture - the impervious frontal facade. Its meaning derives from how it is used, not how it looks, and it occupies its environment without dominating it. While Ráðhúsið might feel insufficient in other global capitals, it perfectly suits Reykjavik and Iceland.[9] In the main gallery space of Ráðhúsið, an enormous 70 m² topographic model of Iceland displays the true seat of power in the national identity - the land. The model reveals not only the striking geography of the country, but also the manner in which civilisation has adapted to it: roads follow erosion patterns; cities and towns cling to opportune moments along inhospitable coastlines; thermal power plants take advantage of particularly active geological moments; et cetera. Built environments are always a function of their natural context, but the phenomenon occurs in Iceland in an unusually evident, pervasive, and powerful manner. Nature in Iceland is a physical force that exerts limitations, and a cultural authority that regulates social engagement. The topographic model in Ráðhúsið is thereby not unlike the eighteenth-century Nolli map of Rome – an artefact that is both physically and culturally accurate. Its placement in an important public space underscores the extent to which geography defines cultural identity.

Nature is the venue of everyday life in Iceland, not because its citizens indulge in recreational uses of nature, but rather because the built environment is embedded within both the limitations and the potentials of its natural context. Herein lies the essential difference between Iceland and its European peers, who associate culture with urban development, and view nature as an escape from civilisation. In Iceland, the cultural significance of geography and infrastructure exceeds that of urban design and architecture. Over the past two decades, the development of the Reykjavík Capital Area has lost sight of its place in the world, and the Vatnsmýri design competition provided an opportunity either to correct or to reinforce past mistakes.

Scalar Distortions

Following the spirit of the competition guidelines, most of the teams that participated in
the Vatnsmýri competition (including Jonathan
F. Bell and I) treated Reykjavík as a typical
European capital. Proposals tended to privilege
self-referential urban forms, such as grids and
boulevards, and to address landscape through
conventional parks that were adjacent to, and
isolated from, the urban fabric. With few exceptions, the synthesis of fabric and landscape as
extolled by landscape urbanism (which was
emerging as a new paradigm at the time of
the competition) is absent.[1] Considering the
importance of nature to the identity of Iceland,
Reykjavík would have been an ideal context
in which to promote ecology-based planning
principles. Furthermore, the domestic airport
that occupies the core of the redevelopment
area is built on top of a once rich ecosystem
(vatnsmýri in Icelandic means "swamp"). Most
entries, however, honour the runways as though
they were archeological ruins, and ignore the
potential of natural forces to order the development of the site. Geometry trumps ecology.
Sustainable strategies were identified as a
primary concern in the competition guidelines,
but most design teams seemed to consider
sustainability as something that is applied
onto a normative urban fabric, as opposed to
something that generates a site-specific fabric.

My awareness of the symbolic power of
landscape in Iceland led to our adoption of
Þingvellir as a primary design premise for
our project, which was titled *City of Seams*.

Þingvellir is the first significant work of
architecture in Iceland. Stretching along the
Reykjanes Ridge on the American-Eurasian
continental rift, it is a geological rift (or seam)
that accommodated the founding of the world's
first parliament in AD 930, and it served as
the seat of parliament continuously until the
late eighteenth century. The transformation
of the raw site into a work of architecture
was an act of occupation, not construction.
While some modest and relatively temporary
structures housed the practical affairs of the
annual assembly, the primary parliamentary
actions occurred in geology, not architecture.
The first Icelanders recognised the site as
a special moment in the landscape, where
communities from across the island could meet
and devise the rules of their society. At Lögberg
(Law Rock), lawmakers debated issues and
pronounced rulings above a vast plain, in front
of a giant shear in the land. Þingvellir thereby
embodied both the eternal power of the earth
and the ephemeral strength of a political
structure. Architecture and urbanism today are
rarely that dramatic or effective.

Þingvellir suggested to us a notion of "seam
urbanism" that could mediate the inevitable
discontinuities caused by infrastructure and
the rich juxtapositions inherent in city fabrics.
We envisioned seams as spatial opportunities
comparable to geological rifts, and as
alternatives to two paradigms of planning: the
nineteenth-century, Haussmannian practice of
masking urban fissures behind homogenous

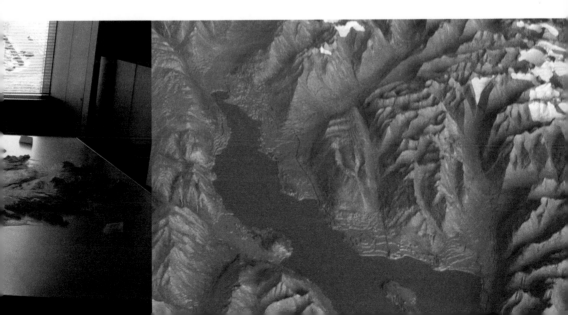

street façades; and the twentieth-century, modern practice of scarring the fabric with indiscriminate formal collisions. *City of Seams* rejected both the harmony of boulevard urbanism and the brutality of urban renewal. Seams allow planners to embed infrastructure into densely populated environments and to resolve abrupt adjacencies in ways that create unconventional and thereby vital public spaces. Seams provide material richness, formal adventure, and social unpredictability.

In our proposal for Vatnsmýri, the existing north-south runway on the site is transformed into an urban condition that aspires to the geological/architectural condition at Þingvellir. This primary seam accommodates a transportation hub that provides a distinct gateway into the city, both for national and international travellers arriving from the airport on a new Maglev connection, and for local and regional travellers arriving by car or public transportation. As sprawl erases the physical integrity of the boundaries of the city, it is becoming increasingly difficult to discern precisely where the capital begins, and we sought to create a spatial, as opposed to a graphic, indicator of "city." Inspired by (but not indebted to) nineteenth-century train stations, the hub ensures that visitors, as well as Icelanders, immediately sense the physical integrity, as well as the international significance, of the capital city. At the same time, it does not announce itself as a focal point or a clearly definable monument, but rather as a layered threshold. The hub abandons the frontal, façade-driven paradigm of urban architecture and accommodates both the heterogeneity of the surrounding fabric and the complexity of programmes that inhabit, and lie adjacent to, it. The hub is a linear organisation of spaces, and operates a vibrant, multi-functional public space, permeable from multiple directions and orientations. Pedestrian walkways, tram tracks, cycle paths, and single-lane roads pass through it, overlap each other, and diffuse the otherwise formal dominance of the seam on the site. The aim was to blur distinctions between architecture, urbanism, infrastructure, and landscape.

Regrettably, the form of the hub (as with some examples of landscape urbanism) suffers from an overly literal application of geological imagery, and the secondary and tertiary seams that emanate from the primary seam, and order the redevelopment area, adopt figural geometries that better suit expectations of certain programme requirements, such as those of a business district and a university campus

expansion. The deep context of the swamp, which could have regulated the formal logic of the entire area, is suppressed in favour of the surface context of the runway, and conventional tropes of urbanisation that disrespect the logic and scale of Reykjavík. The scale of the redevelopment plan, in fact, was its fatal flaw. Typical of international competitions, most of the entrants probably never visited the site, and therefore may not have understood the extent to which the scale of the redevelopment was incompatible with Iceland. Our adoption of Þingvellir as a guiding principle of our proposal was an attempt not only to engage the national identity of Iceland, but also to mediate the scale of the project, as I had great difficulties imaging the realisation of the aspirations of the competition in the city that I had just visited. In the end, however, we failed to appreciate the extent to which the fabric of a more modest redevelopment could have been devised through a specific revitalisation of the existing swamp. The heroic scale of Þingvellir overshadowed the modest scale of Vatnsmýri.

What is Architecture?

In the wake of the 2008 economic collapse in Iceland, the Vatnsmýri redevelopment project became unfeasible, and methodologies of spatial engagement that challenge normative practices of space making began to flourish in the capital region. Many of these methods, which other essays in this book discuss, existed before the crisis, but they received more attention in the sober economic climate that followed it. The ironies are dense: whereas the international proposals for the Vatnsmýri redevelopment would have heightened the detrimental effects of the boom that it was supposed to alleviate, local strategies could have provided both functionality and cultural meaning within the unique context of Reykjavík. Grassroots strategies of development demonstrate that architecture sometimes arises not through massive construction, but through small-scale intervention and/or occupation. Despite the recent resurgence of destructive pre-crisis development mentalities, alternative strategies have established a foothold that hopefully may inform the next round of large-scale development in Iceland, and perhaps elsewhere.[1] An example of the global relevance of the case of Iceland is the redevelopment of the World Trade Center site in New York City. On September 25, 2001, a group of architects, planners, and theorists gathered at the Great

Hall at the Copper Union for the Advancement of Science and Art to discuss potential responses by the design professions to the terrorist attacks that had occurred two weeks earlier. Arguments ranged from replacing the buildings that had been destroyed in defiance, to commemorating the loss through an absence of building.[1] In all cases, designers struggled to understand how design could contribute to the recovery, never doubting that architecture and planning would be critical contributors to the cause. The saga that followed, which is too long to chronicle here in any detail, resulted in a depressingly conventional development that fails to fulfill either the functional or the symbolic needs of the city. The rebirth of the site, like the vast majority of entries in the Vatnsmýri competition, is a twentieth-century solution to a twenty-first-century problem.

Nearly every aspect of the World Trade Center redevelopment has been controversial, with the notable exception of Santiago Calatrava's transportation hub. Both the public and design professionals immediately heralded the design of the station, perhaps because people were looking for something to support amid all the other architectural and political controversies on the site. Since the demolition of Pennsylvania Station in 1963, and the near destruction of Grand Central Station shortly thereafter, New Yorkers have yearned for heroic transportation architecture, and Calatrava's project provides it in a seemingly appropriate context.

The station soars above its site and creates a vast public space that captures the sunlight that enters the site on September 11 in a symbolic manner. As the project nears completion (in 2015), however, criticisms concerning its budget and its aesthetic impact have dampened the initial enthusiasm for it.[1] The station may be a compelling and well-executed work of architecture, but it is somewhat overwrought for its function, which is to serve as one of two terminals for the smallest of the region's four commuter rail lines, as well as a transfer station for a subway line. While a critical hub in the overall transportation network of the region, the architectural and budgetary excesses of the project would be better suited to the redevelopment of Pennsylvania Station. Furthermore, the "bigness" and object-like qualities of the project resonate with models of planning that may no longer be relevant to contemporary society.

Meanwhile the temporary station that has functioned on the site, since the reopening of rail service in late 2003, is a triumph of "small" design. Robert I. Davidson, the chief architect of the Port Authority of New York and New Jersey, which is the governmental agency that manages both the commuter line and the World Trade Center site, designed the station. It is a complex network of spaces that evolves in conjunction with the multiple construction projects on the rest of the site (including the new station). The restrictions, complications, and contingencies on the site are profound, as both physical and political forces pose non-negotiable limitations. As a result, entrances to the station, and circulation routes through it, have opened and closed throughout the process. In each configuration, like Ráðhúsið, the station invites the city to permeate it and avoids the conventional tropes of "important" architecture.

Like many of the works of infrastructure and planning depicted on the topographic model of Iceland, the station embeds itself into its environment and adapts to its environmental context. Its raw concrete and steel materiality responds to function and building codes, not aesthetics. The project is nonetheless a well-planned, well-proportioned, and well-detailed built environment, albeit one that foregoes

concepts and conventions in favour of what matters to its users.

Despite its matter-of-factness (or perhaps because of it), the temporary station engages the cultural significance of the site in a manner that the Calatrava station never will. As commuters and visitors to the site pass through its corridors, openings into the vast construction site provide views of both the destruction and the recovery. Its specific meaning is ever-changing, as its spatial logic shifts over time in response to the construction processes on the site. Unfortunately, as time passes, the power of the temporary station declines. When it initially opened, trains entering the site emerged from a dark tunnel and circulated along the perimeter of a vast sunlit void. Even daily commuters would stop their conversations or look up from their newspapers in order to contemplate the meaning of the site. As they ascended to the street level through various escalators, stairs, and open-air corridors, commuters absorbed the scale of the original site and, by implication, a primal sense of what had been lost. Architecture and planning are rarely as powerful or affective as this. Without excessive rhetoric, Davidson created a site of extreme social and emotional significance.

The first street-level entrance into the station, which has been destroyed, occupied the eastern edge of the World Trade Center site and faced the neighbourhoods of Lower Manhattan. A simple tensile canopy marked the threshold between the city and the site of the attacks, which had been entirely closed to the public for over two years when the station opened. Unlike the new station, the temporary canopy was not a remarkable work of engineering or architecture, but it rose above the chaos of the site as a powerful symbol of the rebuilding process. When workers removed it in 2007 in order to accommodate a shift in the circulation routes through the station, it shamefully received no official acknowledgement for what it had meant to the city. Although the local press covered the daily activities that occurred on the site in excruciating detail, the canopy disappeared without notice or recognition. More than the other entrances into the station, the original canopy was iconic, not because it sought to articulate a higher meaning, but actually because it did not do so. It was a simple construction that understood its time and its place. The destruction of the canopy and the eventual disappearance of the temporary station is apt. All architecture expires, and the best examples understand their precariousness and allow for new generations of construction to provide new levels of meaning. In a sense, the process mirrors that of nature, which is why the notion of the built environment as a living ecosystem holds so much promise for future development, both in Iceland and abroad.

1 W.H. Auden and Louise MacNiece, *Letters from Iceland* (New York: Random House, 1969), pp. 26 -27.
2 Vatnsmýri, Reykjavík: *A Call for Ideas* (2007 competition brief), p. 2.
3 Alan Greenspan coined the term "irrational exuberance" in 1996, during the first bubble economy of the internet revolution, to refer to the danger of falsely escalated economic expectations.
4 Reference to Kenneth Frampton, "Towards a Critical Regionalism: Six Points for an Architecture of Resistance," in *The Anti-Aesthetic: Essays on Postmodern Culture*, edited by Hal Foster (Port Townsend: Bay Press, 1983).
5 Interpretation based on 1836 map of the capital and 1876 perspective of the area, both graphics posted at: http://howlandiceland2011.wordpress.com/historic-reykjavik-maps/
6 Interpretation based on 1876 map of the capital by Sweyn and Benedikt Sveinsson posted at: http://howlandiceland2011.wordpress.com/historic-reykjavik-maps/; the original statue in the square, Iceland's first public sculpture, has since been replaced, see: http://cia.icelandicart-center.is/news/august05/city.htm.
7 Arna Mathiesen of SCIBE noted at the Reykjavík symposium that, since the economic collapse, protesters have used this space in between the two buildings to launch eggs at parliament members during the ceremonies.
8 The potential consolidation of the city government into a work of architecture was discussed throughout the twentieth century, but no action was taken until the late 1980s, which signals an interest in, but also a lack of true need for, an architectural expression of city government.
9 SCIBE symposium attendees noted that initial reaction to the building and its siting on the lake was controversial, but that residents eventually adjusted to it.
10 A Graham Foundation conference in April 1997 on Landscape Urbanism is considered to be the origin of the discourse. The most significant publication on it is *The Landscape Urbanism Reader*, Charles Waldheim, ed., (New York: Princeton Architectural Press, 2006).
11 Unfortunately, the city has recently revived the winning entry of the Vatnsmýri competition, which is a regression; some SCIBE participants worry that the original proposal's housing will become hotels.
12 See Julie Iovine, *Designers Look Beyond Debris*, in The New York Times, September 27, 2001.
13 The budget of the project has more than doubled to over $4 billion; its precise location is not over the tracks, as is conventional, and its underground mall is expected to generate more traffic than its function as a station.

Into the Firmament

Valur Antonsson, on the work
of Ásmundur Ásmundsson

Into the Firmament, video stills.

Consider a society that has been immersed
in an ideology, one catering to the wishes of a
ruling class; now consider that society in the
present day, in a time when nothing gets done
or built – be it goods or services – without
the security of capital exchange. What would
be the defining trait of that society? We can
trace the history of capitalist accumulation
back along a winding road, on which every
turn with hindsight seems inevitable, and
yet, we have to admit, which of us was not
taken aback at each and every step along that
road? A world unhinged by such a force is a
world in need of answers. The quest for its
characteristic emblem, its brand – the allure of
The Grail so to speak – has perhaps become
synonymous with the soothsayer's job – to see
past the lure, deep into the very heart of the
beast; divining a fate that is attached by some
diaphanous means to a firmament above – the
abode of our makers.

A soothsayer would have privileged access
to the world and its beings, and would send us
back an answer, often the question itself in an
inverted form. It would always be depicted as
an image, more often than not in the form of a
beast, a terrifying nameless Thing, a truth-maker
that thwarts our will, and directs our fate.

The artist Ásmundur Ásmundsson has
spent the last decade or so examining such
images; not the ancient versions, but ones in
our ready-made world, often clichés. He pokes
fun, twists things, re-enacts them, and always
with a critical eye to reveal their ambiguous
character, and their potential for acting as
emblems for the forces that dominate our daily
life. With one such work, *Into the Firmament*
(2005), Ásmundur delves into a truly potent
concept, and brings to life the ideology of
supply and demand.

The spectacle of the champagne tower,
whereby glasses are built up into the shape
of a pyramid. The uppermost glass is filled to
the brim, and then more and more champagne
added so that the melliferous liquid cascades
over the glasses and down the sides, as though
an obsequious crowd were waiting down below
in quiet anticipation for their glasses to be filled.
Spoon-fed by the firmament, their insatiable
hunger can only be fulfilled by this spilling
over, and trickling downwards, down to those
unfortunate enough to be at a lower level.

It is an ideology that would provide an
escape from the guilt that such a fantasy
engenders, as well as providing the image
through which the guilt becomes a virtue.
Greed is good. The more the better, and the
more will flow. Liquidity is the very force of
life itself; we are life-givers. The moral of the
story is encapsulated in that image, and yet
it escapes us as we become transfixed on its
soluble nature. In a similar manner to the way
capitalism itself operates – the real products of
life are made invisible while our fascination is
gripped by these ambiguous images; they may
not signify the products they represent, but they
offer the potential for being exchanged over and
over again. That is what makes them so alluring.

'You've got a year before the crisis hits.'

Robert Aliber, a University of Chicago specialist on financial crises speaking in public in Reykjavík, 2007.
Story has it that this became his opinion after driving around the capital, counting the excessive number of building cranes, and seeing the level of borrowing implicit in the number of construction sites; the frenzy of property speculation could not be supported by the economy.

The fragile, effervescent and ephemeral nature of the Icelandic banking boom - symptomatic of any boom, the ever-changing name and nationality of Mr Jay Gatsby the Great – it is literally transubstantiated in the work by Ásmundsson, *Into the Firmament*.

'Liquidity?' you say.
An abundance of it.
A shortage of it.

Well, it's not just a figure of speech anymore. Instead of crystal glasses, sturdy barrels of oil coalesce into a pyramid which overflows with hardened concrete. It contains an allusion to the colloquial sense of the Icelandic word for 'concrete' ('steypa'), which is 'bullshit'. But no form of words would have as powerful an effect as this image, turned inside out, now in full view when it had been hidden; visible, being seen, the meaning of liquidity. A soothsayer's job is to look into the future; an artist, however, is divining something else, something too painful to recognise in the moment, too embarrassing to accept with hindsight – something that is all too present.

Into the Firmament, detail.

'This is a rotten society,
this is altogether loathsome.
There are no principles,
there are no ideals, there is nothing!
There are only opportunists
and power-hungry individuals
...perhaps 30 years ago
I started to notice in the conversations I had
- if you work in the media you meet lots of
different people each day -
a certain change.
realised that the conversation was about interests
...there were no ideals, no principles...
it all went completely out of control
in the first decade of this century.
At that point this society became disgusting.
It was disgusting
because it was as though anything was for sale.
As though one could buy anything.
Buy people. Buy views.
As though nothing was sacred.
If it was possible to get money out of it,
then it was the obvious thing to do...'

Styrmir Gunnarsson, previous editor of *Morgunblaðið*
(a daily right-wing newspaper that for decades was the most widely read in Iceland)
explaining his comment in the Special Investigation Report on the financial meltdown, Sept. 26, 2012

Into the Firmament, concrete, oil barrels, Keflavik, Iceland 2005.

2.

Agents of Change after the crash

NEYSLUMYNSTUR 1990-2009

A decorative platter, a collector's item, traditionally illustrating events of pride, shows in this case the consumption patterns in Iceland 1990-2009 (source: Statistics Iceland) ; an ironic reminder of the excessive materialistic attitudes and show-off lifestyle that went along with economic growth. The platter was a token of a new kind of creativity.

by hugdetta.com

Traces (Spor)

**Arna Mathiesen on a work
by The Art Nurses (Listhjúkkur)**

'Traces' was performed at the foothills of Eyjafjallajökull in October 2010. The volcano had erupted in April that year and caused considerable disruption to air traffic across the globe for six days. Icelanders once more felt the eyes of the world watching their country because of a strange and uncontrollable crisis. It wasn't because it was a freak show, or an omen of what was to follow. It was a reminder that an epicentre in a tiny place, supposedly at the periphery, could produce global consequences. The economy and the planet is shared, no matter what.

On the one hand: The overview – looking down from the top, onto a building site frozen in time, an empty vessel.

The big machinery lying silent, cash evaporated and the Polish workforce gone from the scene. The skeleton of a building site was all that remained. The scene of a crime? Or a scene in the distant future, to inspire great masters of music? Or a prison, a debt prison?

On the other hand: Trying to grasp for breath, on the other side of the explosion.

Out of control, a catastrophe of unimaginable global proportions.

Crawling out from the ashes. Despite confusion all around, reduced visibility and the risk of choking, The Art Nurses get down to Doing

something, and welcome in anyone who wants to join them. They use small tools that are close by. They apply the logic of the handmade, needlecraft – stitch by stitch, with the precision only the hand can create. It's the alternative to Doing nothing – they choose the option of carrying on with further work, developing whatever is there already. Is it because it's half done, or because a change of direction is needed, in the way it's made, in the way it was meant to be? Are they using their own hands to embroider new visions for a new future?

Each little stitch is meticulously threading a new path, following designs of the past… is it an option to add a personal touch… to embellish with texture and colour, if you so wished? Is it mending, is it embroidery, or is it art? Is mending in fact an art? Nursing, painstakingly stitching together a wounded body.

The Art Nurses… the Florence Nightingales of an ongoing crisis.

The overall view from above depicts the whole story, seen at a glance. The story from the ground, where visibility is limited, is where the unexpected could happen, leaving traces that might be valuable, even beautiful, but that may or may not disappear.

Top Down / Bottom Up

Emmanuel Gianotti and Arna Mathiesen

During the boom Reykjavik experienced fast urban growth. Infrastructural networks were expanded, with commercial development lined up, like beads on a string. New suburban neighbourhoods were built on the outskirts of the capital area and these developments went hand in hand with radical downscaling of the social housing sector.

After the crash the large-scale urban transformations came to a virtual halt, halfway through completion. A whole building sector collapsed, resulting in massive job losses, especially in construction, and incomes were reduced. This situation ushered in new challenges. People found more time for private activities, and smaller initiatives with scarcer resources were applied to fulfil changing needs.

Only groups that have had exceptionally fruitful years since the financial crash, lawyers among them, are still having their houses built in the same style, albeit a rather more sober version. Much of the commercial space is still empty, and new neighbourhoods that were under construction before the crash have not been prominent on the public agenda since then. On the contrary, the focus has been on the old city centre where there have been some interesting, but small initiatives, promoted by the municipal administration. Larger plans for increasing density in the city centre have just been approved in a new master plan.

Even though attention seems to have turned away from the developments on the outskirts, the constructions from the boom are still firmly in place. Some of them are close to functioning as run-of-the-mill neighbourhoods, others are in a half-finished state and some are not even constructed, with just a handful of streets and a few buildings that stand alone, apparently in the middle of nowhere.

Keen to know more about the phenomenon, we investigated what was happening on site. Were these places entirely devoid of creativity, innovation and/or resilience? How did the inhabitants react to the crisis and the abrupt ending of the construction process? How did the institutions deal with the circumstances? What sort of opportunities did those neighbourhoods have to offer?

1. Inhabitants' reactions

During our visits to the outlying neighbour-hoods three to four years after the crash, the first impression was that almost nothing had happened since the meltdown of 2008. The scene appeared frozen. However this transpired to be not entirely true.

Some inhabitants changed their houses to adapt them to new requirements; separated couples split up houses into two units instead of one, as they could not afford to move. Job activities (small firms) were moved to the home, the intention being to save money by not having to rent a work space. Young people postponed moving away from their parents' house. Construction strategies were shifted, from buying all the services from building companies, to DIY – doing it yourself. Some had good fortune with a house, as artisans in construction or as house buyers purchasing at the right time, when loan products were in their favour. Those who could afford it, saw opportunities in further developing their houses, and even buying up surrounding properties so that they could be adapted to secure the views of a mountain. Another option has been to put up different types of flats that are more suitable for the current market, thus making money at the same time. This has also had the effect of creating more diversity in the building mass, breaking up the monotonously planned settlements.

The activity of building companies has acquired a rather more grassroots-like character. While the big building companies went bankrupt (and proceeded to start up with a new organisation later on), some very small and flexible carpentry firms have displayed resilience during the boom. Some companies have even blossomed after the crash, and their services been more in demand for minimising building damage resulting from fast building procedures by colleagues, against whom they previously found it a struggle to compete.

Little is known about how widespread such occurrences were, but the impression we got while working in architecture student workshops was that in some streets most of these categories were represented, albeit in a rather ad hoc manner, and obviously depending on the individuals concerned, rather than being an organised process.

We were aware, too, of examples of people operating on the fringe long before the boom took off. Although these people seemed untouched by the collapse, they also adapted their practices to the new conditions, both for their own advantage and the benefit of others. Some of them will be presented in more detail at the end of this part of the book: the carpenter starting up a coffee place, the chemical engineer investigating the soil, and so forth.

The way in which the new neighbourhoods were designed did also act as a trigger for original activities by people from other parts of the city. When people from the countryside move to the capital, they often chose to move to the outskirts; many find raising children 'on the asphalt', as the saying goes about the urban environment, something to be avoided (in retrospect an interesting saying, considering how extensively the new developments are covered with asphalt nowadays). On the other hand, the outskirts have a bad reputation (chiefly among many living in other parts of town) for being peripheral and monotonous, offering a limited range of housing for a predetermined lifestyle. After the crash this has acted as inspiration for people who would rather live in the centre, but cannot afford it, to find a place of residence instead in industrial areas, in buildings that were not designed for residential use.

Although many of these activities were indeed individual and un-coordinated, there are certain signs of people getting more organised. A feeling of solidarity increased, and began with small things, like sharing tools or working together in networks or groups; a kind of timeshare under the public radar. There is a tradition for DIY in Iceland, although in the boom this shrunk to next to nothing, one of the reasons being that people worked such long hours.

On a different scale, something along the lines of mass movements in the context of the city, has emerged. It is difficult to estimate to what degree these are influenced by popular and recent trends that are springing up internationally anyway, but the benefits perfectly compliment some of the new needs in evidence since the crash. These practices don't particularly have anything to do with fringe developments, but some of them clearly have different spatial aspects from one place to another. Growing food has exploded in popularity, even amongst the younger generation which certainly wasn't common in the boom years. The use of a bicycle as an alternative means of transport has also taken off. Practices that were fairly usual just a few decades ago, such as making traditional foods from raw materials for the winter and handicrafts like knitting, have become more valued again. It may not alter the financial situation a great deal but perhaps it makes people feel better regardless.

There is evidence of increased awareness when it comes to making better use of local resources. Local farmers have organised themselves, and shops selling local produce have popped up in the city (see: http://beintfrabyli. is). The second hand market for furniture and clothing has flourished.

Social media and other web-based networks have aided house owners in their efforts to let out space to tourists, and to sell other products that help improve the household economy. Squatting is a further activity that visibly emerged in Iceland during the boom.

As part of a public demonstration, the graphic designer Gunnar Júlíusson painted the road across the surface of a copy of *Gálgahraun*, one of Kjarval's paintings of the lava, and the activist Ómar Ragnarsson commented:

'This main road will cut through the area in which the maestro Kjarval found many of his motifs, forsake its stillness and destroy some very beautiful lava formations, Grænhóll, Ófeigskirkja and Álfakirkja. It will also disrupt three well-known ancient paths over the lava which emanate the scent of the distant past.'

With the lack of rental space and so many buildings standing empty on the outskirts, house occupation would seem a perfect way to shine a light on the important resource that could cater for a dire need currently present. Public squats have, however, been mainly established in old buildings in the centre – ones that were under threat of being torn down because speculators have wanted to build replacements that could reach higher prices than the 'worthless' old buildings. As such, this is activism that can be viewed as a response to the financial opulence of the boom years. Uncertainty regarding the ownership of some of the building stock has brought about a form of squatting that is different to the kind normally associated with anarchists in dreadlocks (their favoured hairstyle). In some cases no rent has been collected for months, because the ownership was unclear; the bank had collapsed, or on occasion people simply stopped paying their mortgages, claiming the loan products were illegal.

In the context of infrastructures (as opposed to individual buildings), actions are more organised. The group Hraunavinir (Lava Friends), for example, protested in October 2013 against new road constructions, which were planned across a lava field, allegedly for improving access to a residential area on the periphery. This lava landscape was important subject matter for the painter Johannes Kjarval (1885–1972), the Picasso of Iceland so to speak. The group is closely linked to a network of environmental activists that were also busy operating before the crash, questioning the need for the energy infrastructures in the Icelandic interior to occupy large parts of the country, threatening the eco-systems. Four environmental organisations brought the case to court before construction works started.

Another example of coordinated citizen protest is the resistance to developments in the most dense part of the city centre, enforced in the name of increased densities. Protests like these were common before the crash as well, but current building trends may well trigger more of them. From the point of view of the citizens that have some interests and insights into the making of the city (architects among them), this can come across as muddled, if not corrupt, politics. It is difficult to establish the facts when meetings and decisions are made behind closed doors, and professionals inside the system have signed an oath of silence.

Finally, the biggest single factor bringing people together in an organised way is probably mortgage debt. Actions have been taken (lobbying, public protests, judgments in court etc.) against the banks and the state, to try to solve the financial problems households are facing. People gathered together, protesting on the main square week after week and month after month, new political parties emerged, and the Homes Association (Hagsmunasamtök heimilanna) was formally established.[1] Money difficulties are severe in the outlying neighbourhoods, and meetings have been held in local schools there to discuss how the problems can be tackled.

2. Institutions' reactions

So what is the public policy since the crash? The expansion of the city and the spatial and environmental problems of the outskirts are not subjects arising regularly in public debate.

At a presentation for a new design policy in the making for Iceland, in a conference in 2011, two kinds of innovative pilot projects were displayed: luxurious spas under private owner-ship (resorts not dissimilar to Blue Lagoon), and exclusive (and so-called innovative) luxury food products; very expensive sweets made on site with local products found in great supply. These two types of design are thoroughly grounded in local qualities (Icelandic nature and Icelandic foodstuffs) and they aim to produce something both useful and comforting. However, they are exclusive products that are ultimately made not for local people, but for others to enjoy - wealthy tourists, or those who can afford, and are willing, to pay good money for them. The design policy is supposed to be about generating more currency and more jobs, and achieving cost effectiveness through design, as well as promoting Icelandic design abroad. Despite the crash, and even though one sentence in the document was devoted to stipulating that the built environment should be designed, the new design policy makes no mention of the potential of larger-scale urban design, or a re-evaluation of the outskirts, for improving quality of life for the citizens.

City centre events, described earlier, involve participants with no financial influence: students, artists and activists that come up with a playful idea, make it happen and then move on. The stunts are temporary, usually lasting just for a summer, and leaving no permanent traces. And yet they are little shoots for the gentrification processes that are underway in the city centre, with hundreds of hotel rooms within the older building mass, and in new buildings too. These processes are steered by the players with access to capital - investors, developers, contractors, speculators and finan-ciers - with the helping hand of the municipal administration, which has legitimised plans for substantial new developments centrally in town, plans which hardly differ from those before the crash. With these massive developments approaching, the politicians (many of whom live in the city centre) emphasise the acclaimed superiority of the centre. Their claims include making the city centre more available to a larger number of inhabitants, and making it possible for everyone to cycle to and from work. The architecture firm that won the

competition for the large plans has published announcements in the daily press criticising the master plan, and stressing the architects are not being consulted and their proposal is being misconstrued.

One of the development areas cuts off the sensitively dimensioned structure of the old city from the waterfront (a development not unlike Skuggi from the boom, as described in 'Spatial Inequality in Reykjavík', part 1). The other plan affects a central wetlands area, where a local airstrip has been located since World War II. Heated political debates about the airport overshadow most other topics of conversation on urban issues, and divide the nation into two opposing sides. To increase the pressure on removal of the airport (the domestic airport of the region), building has started around, and as close to it as possible. This patchwork is well on its way to resembling a typical suburban sprawl. It is difficult to believe that housing units, built on grounds as technically challenging as a harbour front and wetlands, can become as affordable as the politicians suggest, especially taking into account the fact that they cover the most expensive land in the country. It is highly likely that speculators see a win, win opportunity in combining this master plan with the wishes to build more hotels for the tourist industry, thriving because of the low value of the Icelandic currency. The city's main argument for the plan is that it will allow 'everybody' to cycle to work, but the solution will in fact not benefit the people that will still be living far away from the centre. In the meantime there is barely a mention of the new industrial area within the master plan, located in the green scarf wooden area on the outskirts, and little concern as to where the local airport can be moved to in the future. When the politicians' attention is drawn to this expansion of the city, as displayed on the master plan, they say yes, and then proceed to assert how revolutionary the plan is for curtailing the expansion of the city.

Meanwhile, the other municipalities in the area continue with the same plans as before the crash for the new residential areas on the outskirts, with slightly less expensive building lots, and a more lenient attitude towards the rule of only one unit being allowed in areas previ-ously reserved for large single-family houses.

The fragmentation of the capital area into many municipalities with their own agendas has repeatedly been shown to be one of the main causes of the expansion ('Going for Growth', part 1). However the system has not been overhauled since the crash.

Small participation projects have been put into practice. Better Reykjavik[2] is an online forum where the public can post their ideas and opinions relating to the policy, priorities and the service that the city provides. This tool is useful for the city to receive suggestions for smaller interventions, and people may get a feeling they are being listened to, as in some cases they can place their vote for different ideas. The forum was launched in an innovative video[3] by the stand-up comedian Jón Gnarr who became the Mayor of Reykjavik City in 2010. His public relations skills have made him the most popular mayor for decades, and very accomplished at repelling any critical voices.

As for the public protests, bulldozers arrived to penetrate the lava before the appeal had been taken up in court, and several lava friends were carried away from the site and jailed for a day. Some of them were prosecuted. The whole scenario has uncovered the truth that the Minister of Finance's family has a piece of land which will apparently multiply in value with the new road, as it opens it up as an attractive proposition for yet another urban development. This very politician was on the committee, as discussion of the road went through the municipal stages, neither did he step out while the decisions were taken. The news didn't cause any resignation.

A popular strategy for pushing through controversial expansions has recently been defined by critics as The Turbine Trick (túrbínu-trixið 2013).[4] This is, for example, well-known in relation to exploitation of energy resources, for running metal smelters. According to standard democratic practices, complicated processes have to be followed through the political system before the exploitation of energy can start. On the other hand, smaller projects (roads, buildings etc.), that have the same goal in mind, do not have to go through these processes in order for approval to get underway. Later in the process, the investment involved with the smaller operation is used as an argument for why the big project needs to be granted approval too. The final decisions are often made in parliament, deals concluded between the leaders of political parties (some even give the impression of having an environmental profile) as the plans are believed to slow down or reverse the urban shrinkages of the same politi-

cian's constituency. The growth strategies have not always been successful, despite involving substantial damage to the environment. For instance, it is highly controversial as to whether the construction of Kárahnjúkar dam (57km^2) in 2007 prevented depopulation in east Iceland. Yet that was used as the strongest argument for building this energy plant, the largest in the country. Since it was started in 2008, it has had drastic effects on the surrounding ecosystems, gradually emerging all the way from the high-lands and down to the ocean.

Changed activities often challenge rigid building regulations and planning documents. Initiatives by smaller groups are criticised by big industries and the public sector for being hard to keep track of, and potentially even dangerous. There is scepticism about anything that might stimulate activity on the black market. Simultaneously, there is political will to transform the building codes, allegedly to encourage the building of smaller, and therefore less expensive, housing units. This can lead to increased profit per m^2 for the developers, and put in jeopardy universal design which has recently reshaped the rules to try to make the built environment more, if not financially accessible, at least physically accessible to all, whether they are wheelchair users or not.

Taking into account the municipal debts after the crash, it is fair to assume that priorities for municipalities are usually determined by their desperate need to straighten out the balance sheet at the end of the year.

The municipalities are selling off land with hot and cold water resources, and public build-ings, and then renting them back on a long-term lease. By doing this, it seems as though they are hiding the bad financial situation by manip-ulating the documented figures in the current budget, regardless of any long-term negative costs to the public.

The radical processes, outlined above in these two most recent examples of top-down approaches, can be said to depend on big fixes, large operations. These fixes are sensitive to the big players with financial clout, but not to the general public who are in need of different solutions, and will end up paying the price for current activities further down the line.
Two parties, both of which had been in power for 12 years when the meltdown occurred, won a majority in the parliamentary elections of April 2013. The winning recipe was a promise to cut

ICELANDIC PROTESTS.

Debt is steering many of the actions both from the top and bottom.

Different Perspectives : Problems and Opportunities

the debt burden for all households.

Economic growth is an outspoken, fundamental premise for new policies for Iceland; it was explicitly launched in May 2013 by a committee on which all the main stakeholders in the Icelandic economy are represented, with the aim of maximising the future prosperity of the nation.[5] Of the 44 university degrees possessed by the representatives on the committee, thirteen are in the field of business administration, and eight are law degrees. No architects, urban planners belonged to the group, although it was claimed to be interdisciplinary.

In the sixties, in opposition to the general opinion of social scientists about the urbanisation of the so-called underdeveloped countries, William Mangin and John Turner stated that the slums were not only a problem, but also a solution to that problem.[6] They were looking at the positive characteristics of squatter settlements; opportunities for individuals, and social progress. In the need for a roof over their heads, and having access to only limited resources, people used their creativity to improve the neighbourhoods in which they were living, building housing by themselves, getting organised to make their actions more effective, and trying to get support from public and private institutions.

This position was criticised because it was seen as legitimising policies that promoted minor improvements, but failed to tackle the deep roots of the poverty. Nevertheless, some recent programmes such as the Favela-Bairro project in Brazil and The Integral Urban Project in Medellín, aimed at increasing the spatial quality of the slums, have proved to be much more effective than the clearing of such settlements, with the consequent construction of new ones on the periphery.

Comparing the built environment in the Reykjavik Capital Area, left over after the financial crisis, to slums might sound absurd. The Icelandic situation undoubtedly looks like a problem stemming from abundance, even though it resulted in serious financial difficulties for many. The need for housing was over-estimated, inflated by the ample financial resources in Iceland during the boom. Even so, the experiences in the slums offer some interesting thoughts. The first is the capacity to make new assets from scarce resources which sounds like a sensible idea for Iceland and, more generally, for a world threatened by the depletion of resources. The second is the prospect that most of the settlements, unless they are exposed to hydro-geological or any other sort of risk, can be improved, recycled or even transformed into something partially different. This strategy of recycling is often much more effective and less costly than erasing and rebuilding a new neighbourhood somewhere else. A third point is that a house cannot provide all the services needed by one family, because some of them are provided by the neighbourhood or by the city. Resources can therefore be saved by building collective strategies, not purely individual ones. Finally, it is worth keeping in mind that the ability to organise, and to drum up external support, is essential. Many of the programmes that successfully regenerated the slums involved the community being able to organise, and rally some kind of support from other sections: national institutions, municipalities, NGOs, students, political parties, and so on.

On this basis, it could be very useful to apply the same viewpoint adopted by Mangin and Turner to the case of Reykjavik: change the perspective and start looking at these neighbourhoods not simply as a problem, but also as an incredible opportunity to rethink the city and its relationship with the territories around the capital area.

At this point in time the new suburbs just don't seem necessary, and perhaps more than that, a big mistake that should be removed as soon as possible. However, these neighbourhoods are there and they are lived in by many people. After all:

1. Even if they were possibly the outcome of a collective, incorrect evaluation about the actual needs and the real possibilities, they are also the expression of a certain way of life, which cannot be overlooked. We cannot assume that everyone is willing to live in the centre of town.

2. A large number of people reside in those places, often without the necessary services, sometimes living in half-finished houses and in such unfavourable economic circumstances that they couldn't move even if they wanted to.

3. A huge public investment was made in order to construct an extensive infrastructural system (streets, pipes, heating systems etc.). If this is not put to use, it will be a tremendous waste.

4. The neighbourhoods in question cover approximately one fourth of the capital area, which as a whole is housing two thirds of the country's population. It is highly unlikely that the population of the metropolitan area will shrink over a longer timescale.

In conclusion, instead of starting new projects which will demand an incredible amount of resources, recycling or retrofitting the neighbourhoods on the outskirts seems like a reasonable way forward, and would be an important step for the whole town.

In order to proceed, a first step would surely be to get an overview, and understand which processes are in place bottom-up. Mapping the activities arising from the initiatives of the inhabitants can suggest certain possibilities in the way of development. They show alternative ways to re-use the built environment with scarce resources, ways which are often more sensitive to the local environment and also create opportunities to build a sense of community, often sorely lacking in the areas. Moreover, the scattered initiatives satisfy specific and urgent needs that should be the point of departure in a renovation project.

Although there are some individual examples of innovative use of space, no collective claims or any kind of social movements seem to be emerging, aside from those that are directed particularly at people in the direst financial straits - The Home Association for example. Singular initiatives in scarcely populated and spread-out parts of town can be so weak and dispersed, that even if they are interesting, innovative and respond to an immediate need, they may not have the power to conglomerate into something more structured that has an effect on a broad scale. It seems that support from an external source is needed, in order to start a real process of renovation for the outlying neighbourhoods. This might in turn inspire a bigger group of residents to use the built environment (such as housing) as a resource for their own advantage, in ways that would help them overcome their problems.

It would be desirable if the support were to come from institutions. However, neither the municipalities nor the national government seem to be very concerned with the outskirts, as discussed earlier. On the contrary, the projects proposed by the official urban planners hardly differ from the urban development of the boom period; they seem to be a direct continuation of it. In fact, they can even be interpreted as an accelerated stage in the competition between the municipalities. In this scenario the central (and largest) city of Reykjavík plays out the queen of spades; the centre of town against the ongoing expansion of the other municipalities. These efforts (on which the municipal planners are employed to use their expertise and energy) may attract more taxpayers to the municipality with the best housing product (location being part of the equation), but they can also seem quite absurd, bearing in mind the surplus of housing built during the boom.

In this context, what could be done by architects and planners? After investigating and mapping the interesting activities initiated by the inhabitants, as a second step there are several options, which could complement one another:

a. Publicising the initiatives that are in place, and bringing to light the problems and potentials of those areas are actions that can create a public debate, the aim being to generate an awareness which is almost totally absent at the moment. Making the neighbourhoods on the outskirts an object of public concern is the path to getting support from private foundations or institutions, as well as helping strengthen and expand the creativity that is surging from the bottom-up.

b. Creating some kind of relationship between the initiatives of the inhabitants, which at present are too dispersed. Links and networks can save time for resourceful individuals, and empower them to get better at what they are doing and resist forces that pull in another direction. When individuals coming from different backgrounds make the effort to cooperate on shared solutions for a common goal, it creates a broad base for communication and produces a variety of perspectives. Potential conflict (a familiar challenge from discourses and initiatives after the crash) can be dealt with by tried and tested methods from cultures with extensive experience in collective designing and collective space. The Danes have experience of designing shared solutions when it comes to housing. Thus they have developed valuable tools in terms of design issues and conflict resolution. The Co-design concept applied in Lathi, Finland, and the Transition Town movement which started in the UK, can also be useful role models. Retrofitting the city with spatial solutions that enable the shared space to be in focus can in turn increase social cohesion.

c. Providing new perspectives, helping with the visualisation of new options and alternatives, showing their spatial implications. Architects and planners can provide a more general vision in which the smaller problems and initiatives of everyone could be contextualised.

The projects we developed with students during two workshops, presented at the end of the book, followed the last route. On one hand, each group developed a different strategy that dealt with the specific conditions of each neighbourhood, trying to gain benefit from the local opportunities they found. On the other hand, they did also attempt to position the neighbourhoods within a more general vision for the city, and so indicate a direction of development for the whole metropolitan area. A broad overview of this kind can help in generating public debate about the future of the city, and prompt some institutional support. The result could be a transformation of single initiatives by inhabitants into a real process of renovation for the neighbourhoods on the outskirts, reaping benefits for the whole city.

1 http://www.heimilin.is/varnarthing/english/about.html
2 https://betrireykjavik.is/
3 http://bit.ly/1dQeUk3
4 http://www.youtube.com/watch?v=F0I1LNIPUKc
5 http://samradsvettvangur.is/
6 William Mangin, 1967, 'Latin American Squatter Settlements: A Problem and A Solution'. Latin American Research Review, 2 (3): 65-98; John Turner, 1968, 'Uncontrolled Settlements: Problems and Policies'. International Social Development Review, 1: 107-128.

Hole in the Hill

Hannes Lárusson

Vernacular architecture in Iceland, the turf house heritage, is a hidden mystery. Hardly any information on this tradition, more than 1000 years old, is accessible in a foreign language. The Icelandic turf house is a dug in, and perhaps also metaphorically speaking a dug out, hole in a hillside. It is a dwelling shaped as though a piece of grass carpet has been lifted up like the back of a camel in which to make space for the inhabitants to crawl. Local intellectuals and politicians have been under the impression that the mud hole, as they officially call such a house, is something of which to be ashamed – for its diseased dirt and its ugliness. However, there is now a new renaissance on the horizon. Thanks to Peter Jackson and his New Zealand crew, the educated Icelanders have been recently finding an acceptable and neat entrance back into the local turf house by sliding in through the Hobbit hole – probably via an unconscious association with the cosiness of the English pub, as experienced on excursions abroad.

I have recently overheard conversations among scholars claiming that Bilbo Baggins was an Icelander.

I recall a meeting with a specialist, and an advisor in entrepreneurship and design, working for an official committee. After sketching out the Icelandic turf house tradition, explaining that through the centuries all our ancestors lived in houses made of organic materials – turf, stone and soil – I was met with eyes of authoritative scepticism and a sarcastic smile. "You have to sell me this idea!" The conversation came to an end with me correcting my account, and substituting an Icelandic architectural legacy that actually consisted of the Chinese wall circumscribing the island, with the pyramids and the Great Sphinx in the centre, and the Colosseum and the Eiffel Tower proudly at the heart of Reykjavik.

It has always been a bitter pill for many Icelanders to swallow, the truth that practically everyone lived in turf houses, including the priests, the landowners, the district marshals and officials, the common people and the workers, along with their cows, horses, sheep, dogs, hens, roosters, cats and mice. For twenty-eight generations out of thirty, the inhabitants and the livestock of the island were crawling in and out of mud holes. Of course the upper class and the well-to-do lived in bigger holes, a sort of luxury burrow, and owned more of them.

The Icelandic turf farmstead is a cluster of interconnected houses, often with additional structures for keeping animals, storing and processing food, or sheltering equipment and sea vessels. A typical farmstead consists of a central cluster of 10-15 houses with 3-10 satellite structures. The average turf farm of the latter part of the nineteenth century would have contained at least 15 houses; they would all have made extensive use of turf, unshaped stones of various kinds and compacted soil, as well as (contrary to popular belief) a considerable amount of timber. In the early 1930s official figures estimate that 3,665 turf farmsteads were still functioning in Iceland, and that twenty years before that (approximately one hundred years ago) the number was about 5,360. A simple calculation gives us roughly 80,000 turf houses; if those within villages, others that were among more modernised farmsteads, as well as the freestanding ones along the shore or inland were included, the figure would be closer to 100,000 – densely spread all over the country. In less than two decades, an official cleansing programme – dreamt up by politicians and rationalised by academics – managed to wipe these structures off the face of the earth. Aside from the structures themselves, the positive memories of what had been on the whole good, modest and happy dwellings were targeted, the purpose being to convince everyone that the houses were dark, damp, cold, smelly and foul; not a single happy creature could have been found in these horrible mud holes, except maybe

Pastor Guðmundur in front of a turf house early twentieth century; a truly green and resilient architecture.

some unfussy mice families, and the bacteria responsible for tuberculosis and leprosy.

If a generous estimate were made today it might amount to 60-80 turf structures still above ground, and less than ten farm clusters still standing, none of them complete with their satellite houses. More than 99.9% were destroyed. As recently as 2011, one of the very last remaining clusters, in the south of the country, was bulldozed away under official supervision, reducing the remnants to a few photographs, a simple plan drawing and a brief description. For most Icelanders these documents are of greater importance than the object itself, despite the fact that the object is of medieval, or possibly even Iron Age, origin. If Bilbo Baggins and the Hobbits were ever Icelanders, it seems that Saruman and his apprentices have also found their homeland.

A while ago I had a visit from a group of children aged ten. As they entered the exhibition space, they caught sight of a nice model on a table, of a traditional turf farmstead, about 1:50 in scale. Two energetic boys immediately walked up to it and started to touch the model and trace out the outlines and details of it with their fingers. I was slightly worried about the fragility of the model and said rather sarcastically: "Probably the best way to look at a model is with your fingers". This statement caught the attention of the lively group, and they lined up, one by one, to carefully trace the contours of the model with their fingers, and then they resumed their running around and noisemaking. When it comes to vernacular architecture, exploring with your body is the only way to enter the house.

Cleansing of a buddha statue in Bamiyan in Afganistan, destroyed with dynamite in March 2001 by the Taliban.

A turf farmstead, before and after the 2011 bulldozer cleansing.

Run for your Life

Tinna Grétarsdóttir and Bryndís Björnsdóttir

As an agent of change, artist Bryndís Björnsdóttir's alter ego **i(m)material girl** is off and running at Ásbrú Enterprise Park, an abandoned NATO base (United States Naval Air Station) situated on the outskirts of Reykjavík. The aim of her marathon is to incite a conversation about the measure of one's worth, limitations, and possibilities within a neoliberalist system.

In 2009, in the wake of Iceland's economic meltdown, large-scale protests were held against Iceland's neoliberal regime, successfully overturning its right-wing government; now, the neoliberal architects are back. Only vague memories of the so-called economic meltdown, and whispers of the public outcry that followed, remain. That popular and public outcry has dwindled to just small groups that pay for access to their streets, in organised events like the Mickey Mouse Arion Bank marathon. At best, it corresponds to what Paolo Virno calls "publicness without a public sphere".[1] People, it seems, have lost their verve to contest the alienation and exploitation of neoliberal capitalism.

Iceland has become something of a laboratory for neoliberals to experiment with new forms of entrepreneurialism. Ásbrú Enterprise Park, the former NATO base, has become one of its most promising experiments. It is currently being transformed into "an economically, culturally and ecologically sustainable environment that emphasises creativity and innovation."[2] It is described as a sketchpad for innovative agents; but, much like its previous occupants, these agents of innovation must stay alert, awake, and on the move. If they stand still in the context of today's "mandatory entrepreneurialism",[3] they too will be relieved of duty. Nonetheless, the park has created an excellent opportunity for agents of change, like i(m)material girl, to think through concepts such as transition and becoming. Specifically, it affords them an opportunity to examine the effect of this process on the park's principle protagonist, the creative worker as entrepreneur.

The history of the Ásbrú Enterprise Park site dates back to the 1940s (World War II), when Iceland agreed to the short-term establishment of a U.S. military base on the Reykjanes Peninsula. With the advent of the Cold War, however, the U.S military used the site for over 60 years. The base, fenced off from the Icelandic public, incited both protest and prosperity. The U.S. occupation of Icelandic soil enraged many Icelanders. Large-scale demonstrations were held, the most famous of which took place in 1949 when police used tear gas against the protesters. While the American military presence, and the international airport it maintained, met with significant opposition, it also led to an influx of wealth, foreign goods, and local employment opportunities. It boosted Iceland's national economy and ushered in a golden age of consumer choice and international contact.

In an attempt to prolong this golden age, a new brand of creative entrepreneurism, affective performativity, and communicative brilliance is being sent to the Icelandic economic front of international networking, nation branding, tourism, etc. There seems to be no shortage of happy conscripts willing to contribute "to the lofty national project, right in step with marketing specialists, PR people, cultural managers, tourist agents, cultural economists, cultural advisers...and other specialists in creative thinking."[4] With the traditional industries such as aluminium smelting becoming increasingly unpopular, Iceland's neoliberal experimentalists are now attempting to tap into a cheap, renewable resource to fulfil the market demands of a neoliberal consumer culture. But what will become of art and artist when they have "been diluted in society like a soluble tablet in a glass of water"?[5]

1 i(m)material girl running the Life Vein with a torch in hand, 2011.

The neoliberal ideal assumes that there is "only one liveable reality".[6] Its reality is one in which "excessive imagination is out of the question".[7] According to the neoliberal ideal, reality can, and must be, accounted for in exclusively quantifiable terms. Every gesture is conceived and conveyed as a calculable unit to be managed. If something can be measured, it is real and manageable; if not, it is "set aside as impractical and utopian."[8] The call of this neoliberal reality "obliterates the breathing space for an awareness of what is possible."[9]

Artists are particularly sensitive to the tragic reductionism of this world view; however, self-preservation demands that they nonetheless account for themselves in these impoverished terms. To this end, they ally themselves with technocrats to acquire a set of magic productivity values meant to represent their feasibility, productive capacity, and realised output. This colonisation of artistic production by the neoliberal demand for quantitative performance measures has given rise to what are now called the creative industries. Advocating numbers (investment, revenues, consumption, etc.) is the only legitimate language when it comes to validating art.

The Association of Icelandic Visual Artists even seems to subscribe to this practice, enthusiastically advocating its members to adopt the MU agreement. Although it represents an interesting step towards the remuneration of artists' work, the MU agreement, signed by the Swedish Arts Council and the Swedish Artists Association in 2009, stipulates that the amount artists are to be

paid is contingent on the size of the audience they can draw.[10]

However, the terms of the neoliberal discourse, as manifested by continual neoliberal reforms, have become a form of "creative destruction."[11] These reforms, and the terms that now frame Icelandic political debate, have reinvigorated debilitating social institutions and undermined those that could have produced a genuinely new set of social, political, and critical values.

I(m)material girl's running route in Ásbrú Enterprise Park is the newly named Life Vein – a street that links together Ásbrú's public, domestic, and labour areas. Running the Life Vein, i(m)material girl holds an unlit torch in hand. Her act is an act of discontinuity. It is a performance piece intended as a staunch criticism of the penetration of neoliberal enterprise culture into the world of art and artists. In a newspaper article published on the day of her performance, i(m)material girl called for other creatives to join her. Unfortunately, despite her invitation, she ran alone. No one came.

This, however, should not be taken as a lack of support. More likely, her peers were simply working. As an indebted yet energetic multitasker, i(m)material girl represents the ever-growing number of immaterial labourers in the neoliberal era. The restructuring of the economic and socio-political world since the 1970s has often been described as post-industrial, post-modernist, post-Fordist—concepts that are associated with the platitude flexibility (e.g. flexible labour, flexible working hours, flexible movement, flexible communication).[12] Though it has an attractive veneer, it is also associated with increasingly precarious living and working conditions. Though such conditions have always been true for the artist, they have become normalised by the neoliberal, post-Fordist regime.[13] As an artist pointedly aware of her current political status, i(m)material girl understands the importance of staying innovative, flexible, and fit. Her blue jumpsuit marks her as a highly skilled creative labourer, with room to move and sweat. The immaterial labourer must always be on the move. She must, for instance, run even when her feet and her mind are out of sync.

This new mobile and isolated workforce is barred from the traditional means of improving its status, unless one counts perpetual schooling and its associated price tag. Working alone and without rest, strikes and worker solidarity are out of reach to the immaterial labourer. While moving from one temporary project to another, i(m)material girl must be willing to work for very little and sometimes for nothing at all. She must also be willing to work on her off-hours to realise her own creative projects and perpetual deadlines. No clocking out. Her life becomes work itself if she is ever to make manifest her fantasies of self-realisation and autonomy. Work makes her who she is. It penetrates her body, and her body's basic functions (e.g. communication, emotion, sociability).[14]

Moreover, asserting her gender, **i girl** reminds us that this unpaid economic sector has typically been designated as women's work. While all sexes can be found on the creative factory floor, it is perhaps best characterised as being feminised, or as "a mockery of a limited work day; leading to an existence that always borders on being obscene, out of place, and reducible to sex."[15]

Neoliberal enterprise culture tells the self-responsible, self-employed, and self-marketed creative workers that they are in control, yet only at the price of insecurity and vulnerable working conditions. It encourages anticipated conformity, eliminating the artist's radical imaginative powers, and forces the question, "[W]hat are we becoming in and through work…?"[16]

If i(m)material girl's mute critique went unheard, it nonetheless reflected the main criticism made against the arts today, namely that "art [has] lost its own voice," that it has given up "any utopian plan to really intervene in the world."[17] Moreover, her performance was an act of self-creation. It was an attempt to unmask the governing relations that constitutes the autonomous creative entrepreneur. As an embodied state of what is expected of the artist today, i(m)material girl's run finished down a dead end street. Yet, running along the "Life Vein," i(m)material girl gave the current state of affairs a good run for its money. As Bifo states, "irony is an opening of a game of infinite possibilities".[18] Right now, it's necessary to imagine possibilities of alternative mechanisms of self-realisation, especially those that don't lead to possessive privatisation of the self. Transitions and in-betweens such as Ásbrú Enterprise Park always carry with them a state of ambiguity. So does the affective labour of the overworked body in a vulnerable state. Nonetheless, in such conditions, unforeseen encounters can take place; experiences that are "not reducible to logic, reason or morality", and that might inspire acts of transgression.[19] Get a life and reclaim your body, as well as control of who you might want to become. It's time for another run.

2 i(m)material girl catching her breath after her run, 2011.

1 Paolo Virno in Susan Kelly, "Asking, We Walk", in *Performance, Politics and Activism*, Peter Lichtenfels and John Rouse (eds), New York: Palgrave Macmillan, 2013, p. 117.
2 See Ásbrú website at http://www.asbru.is/english/
3 Mark Fischer, "Indirect Action. Some Misgivings About Horizontalism", in *Institutional Attitudes: Instituting Art in a Flat World*, Pascal Gielen (ed), Amsterdam, Valiz, 2013, p. 110.
4 Ásmundur Ásmundsson, Hannes Lárusson and Tinna Grétarsdóttir, *Koddu* (exhibition catalogue), Reykjavík: The Living Art Museum, 2011, p. 25.
5 Gielen, Pascal, *The Murmuring of the Artistic Multitude: Global Art, Memory and Post-Fordism.* Valiz, Amsterdam. 2010, p. 2.
6 Pascal Gielen (ed) "Institutional Imagination. Instituting Contemporary Art Minus the 'Contemporary'", in *Institutional Attitudes: Instituting Art in a Flat World.* Amsterdam: Valiz, 2013, p. 26.
7 Ibid, p. 25.
8 Ibid, p. 25.
9 Ibid, p. 25.
10 See Frida Yngström presentation at The Association of Icelandic Visual Artists' website at http://sim.is/hagnytt/

11 David Harvey, "Neoliberalism as Creative Destruction." *The Annals of the American Academy of Political and Social Science* 610 (March 2007): 21-44.
12 Martha Macdonald, "Post-Fordism and the Flexibility Debate", *Studies in Political Economy* 36, (Fall 1991) 177-201; Michael Hardt and Antonio Negri, *Empire*, London, Harvard University Press, 2001; Michael Hardt and Antonio Negri *Multitude: War and Democracy in the Age of Empire,* New York, Penguin Books, 2005; Pascal Gielen, *The Murmuring of the Artistic Multitude: Global Art, Memory and Post-Fordism.* Valiz, Amsterdam, 2010
13 Isabell Lorey, "Governmentality and Self-Precarization: On the Normalization of Cultural Producers", in *Art and Contemporary Critical Practice. Reinventing Institutional Critique,* Gerald Raunig and Gene Ray (eds), May Fly Books, 2009; Isabell Lorey "Virtuosos of Freedom: On the Implosion of Political Virtuosity and Productive Labour", in *Critique of Creativity: Precarity, Subjectivity and Resistance in the 'Creative Industries'* Gerald Raunig, Gene Ray and Ulf Wuggenig (eds), London, May Fly Books, 2011; Pascal Gielen, *The Murmuring of the Artistic Multitude: Global Art, Memory and Post-Fordism.*

Valiz, Amsterdam. 2010
14 See Nina Power, "Don't Smile, Organize", in *Work, Work, Work. A Reader on Art and Labour,* Cecilia Widenheim, Lisa Rosendahl, Michere Masucci, Annika Enqvist and Jonata Habib Engquist (eds), Berlin: Sternberg Press, 2012.
15 Donna Haraway, "A Cyborg Manifesto Science, Technology and Socialist-Feminism in the Late Twentieth Century", in *Simians, Cyborgs and Women: The Reinvention of Nature,* New York, Routledge, 1991, p. 166.
16 Kathi Weeks, "Life Within and Against Work: Affective Labor, Feminist Critique, and Post-Fordist Politics." *ephemera* 7.1 (2007): 233-249. http://www.ephemerajournal.org/sites/default/files/7-1weeks.pdf
17 Pascal Gielen (ed) "Institutional Imagination. Instituting Contemporary Art Minus the 'Contemporary'", in *Institutional Attitudes. Instituting Art in a Flat World.* Amsterdam: Valiz, 2013, p. 31.
18 Franco "Bifo" Berardi, *The Uprising: On Poetry and Finance.* Los Angeles. Semiotext(e), 2012, p. 169.
19 Claire Bishop, *Artificial Hells: Participatory Art and the Politics of Spectatorship.* Verso, London & New York, 2012, p. 18.

Dyndilyndi

Margrét H. Blöndal

www.dyndilyndi.is

Dyndilyndi, is a project that started in The Reykjavik School of Visual Art, when it collaborated with over 400 students from several fourth grade classes from primary schools in the city. The students came with their teachers and worked in several groups, each under the guidance of one artist. The materials were simple: paper, scissors and glue; the assignment: a dwelling for an animal. Each student considered which animal to select before knowing the assignment. The range was diverse: jellyfish, lynx, Labrador Retriever, owl, baby Arctic Tern, river trout, mother salmon, butterfly, seahorse, ground beetle, blue whale, hamster, monkey and so on. We discussed the needs of each animal, whether it longed for security, darkness, freedom, flow, space … and the students cut, bent, positioned, then glued. The scale was very small even for the largest animals. The students worked hard, and the more they worked the more the animals, despite their invisibility, started to take on the needs of their creators. We suspended some branches from the ceiling and put on display some pedestals, and when the dwelling was ready the creator found a suitable location for it. Once all the dwellings were in situ some of the inhabitants wanted to communicate with their neighbours, so all of sudden a ladder sprung up to the highest branches, a path developed between the fiercest creatures and the cutest, and a swing was made for the creatures that longed to see their friends. In the end a whole community had arisen, and the students invited their family and friends to come and have a look.

A few months later the school was invited to participate in Reykjavik Children's Culture Festival. The principal, Ingibjörg Jóhannsdóttir, asked me to see if I could come up with a way of developing this project further. I contacted sixteen adults, all active in their fields: acting and theatre direction, architecture, writing, web design, music, visual art, radio broadcasting, choreography, product design, fashion design and soundscape. I guided them through the community, explaining aspects from single individuals to the surroundings, the pathways, the stories behind each creation and so forth. The artists had nine months in which to develop their ideas and throughover that time the ideas multiplied and were transformed into various forms of appearances, with participants from all generations. On April 17, 2010, there was an opening in The National Gallery of Iceland in Reykjavik and the programme continued until May 2.

Dyndilyndi – verði gjafa gagnstreymi is a project about giving and receiving; about how one seed can fertilise various fields. The content of the assignments touches us all since it tackles life itself without the representation of a visible figure. The dwellings became tiny, fragile and forsaken, constructed with sincerity and care by their creators. It was like a microcosm of the world, with its mixture of sympathy and fear, and the characters were a combination of mild, inventive, shy, cruel, playful and cunning.

The adult artists did not create works especially aimed at children but were true to their own working methods. At the exhibition itself we invited more children to participate in a workshop and so the stream of ideas continued to flow.

Sara María Skúladóttir made various collarbones.

The *lyricist* and musician Megas during his performance of seven new songs with a young female choir and a harp.

Ornithologists performing the work by Kristín Ómarsdóttir.

The age of the audience ranged from those in their first year to those over ninety.

Young students participating in a workshop in The National Art Gallery during the course of the exhibition.

Soundscape by Elísabet Indra Ragnarsdóttir and Rikke Houd, based on interviews with the student participants of the workshops.

A refresher course for teachers.

The actress Edda Björg Eyjólfsdóttir performing The Earthworm by Haraldur Jónsson, under the direction of Harpa Arnardóttir.

Rehearsal for Magga Stina's piece at The National Art Gallery.

Some of the instruments were made by the students themselves in collaboration with the instructors from The Reykjavik School of Visual Arts.

Students on a tour around the exhibition. Cushions by Sara María Skúladóttir, a work by Hugin Þór Arason hangs from the ceiling.

Students moving around the work by the choreographer Margrét Bjarnadóttir.

Workers from several occupations took part in performing Kristín Ómarsdóttir's 34 plays; bakers are performing here.

A hot dog salesman performing a piece by Kristin Ómarsdóttir, with his young son Þórður accompanying him.

A new entrance for The National Gallery of Iceland, created by Theresa Himmer and Kristján Eggertsson. The entrance had three doors, for flying, walking or crawling creatures.

The Sociopolitical Role of the Architect

Hildigunnur Sverrisdóttir

Every single subject in the social – and consequently political – context of our country is challenged by the very fact of being tiny, as a being, as a person, as an ego, as a society in vast surroundings.

We are 300,000 Individuals

However, our web of infrastructures never seems to reflect this fact. True, we are probably more inclined to have a risk-seeking, problem-solving attitude, but even when viewed through the most rose-tinted glasses, an element of absurdity can be detected when it comes to the Icelandic context. And the sad thing is that this element causes a ridiculous amount of resources to be consumed; desiring it, giving it all it takes, then losing it, because we shun critical and abstract thinking, and we refuse to take our egos out of the equation.

The vibrant issue of the moment, the building of a new National University Hospital, is a perfect example of a problem that is screaming out for a solution, underpinning the centrality of the role of the academic and the professional in a societal context. The people that society traditionally calls upon to gather specialised abstract know-how, are trained within strategic fields of responsibility (partially at society's expense) in order to be accountable, for the greater good of society.

Taking Responsibility for a Standpoint

In the 1960s, the London-based architectural and planning practice Llewelyn-Davies, Weeks, Forestier-Walker and Bor was commissioned to work on a new hospital in Reykjavík; not a holistic solution to meet all the needs, but rather to establish a health science centre. The old hospital was outdated, and its preclinical research units scattered around town in different kinds of industrial and commercial housing.

Many were sceptical about establishing a university hospital in the Icelandic context. They felt that people should be educated in more dynamic melting pots abroad – and the local health system should mainly serve, not educate or undertake fundamental research. Some professors at the very same institution were even quoted as saying that the University of Iceland was a second-rate university, that it should be closed down and the students sent overseas.

Some of them, curiously enough, became central to the planning of the hospital, working alongside economic governmental representatives and the Llewelyn-Davies, Weeks, Forestier-Walker and Bor team. When questioned about the schizophrenic aspect of their situation, they admitted it - but seemed resigned to laying their scepticism to rest so as not to jeopardise their academic status.

This example bluntly states my first point of concern - the priority repeatedly given to individual interest, along with an inability and lack of will to maintain the abstract, specialised point of view; to see the wider picture, and translate it from there to other subsystems of society – a fragile and small society that cannot really afford to make mistakes on such a scale as this.

If academic freedom and peer review is worth anything, it is worth exactly that; to show a sufficient degree of respect and aspiration for society to state the obvious, to mirror, criticise, take responsibility for its evolution.

In turn, by doing so, society might eventually learn to understand and, from there, even welcome the specialised vision, understanding that it would be strange and unnatural to demand the world to look the same from the standpoint of a doctor as it does from that of an architect.

The Will to Power - the Power of Will?

After decades of planning, with dedicated support from the government, the firm's design was finalised in 1978: it was to be 16 buildings with linking corridors, located on the same site as is currently being considered. The construction could at long last begin. But, to cut the

story short, after much ado, only a single one of the 16 units was actually built. And in fact that took ten years. The full will of the authorities, and very little opposition, produced one out of sixteen buildings, in a time span that outdated the original plan.

Redoing (and thus repaying for) things in Decision Phobia

The next extremely important point comes in the aftermath. In my lifetime, I have witnessed a threefold design of that very hospital. After hearing about the firms design from relatives,

I later worked at an office that collaborated with a foreign design firm, and won an international competition for the commission to plan the hospital premises. As an employee, I followed that process from the sidelines. Only a few years later all this was thrown out, and for the third time I am witnessing this cycle repeating itself. Who pays? Obviously the architects that take part, since the planning is repeatedly subject to competitions where many offices end up working on their proposals without getting paid – but sadly, enormous sums are also taken from public funds – funds that could be distributed other ways, buying equipment, financing research or supporting the health sector.

Good planning is crucial - don't be mistaken - but: How often can a miniscule society pay for the clothes of the same emperor? And why are there so few children out there stating the obvious?

An even sadder fact is that architects seldom praise, with any certitude, the spatial placement of the relatively massive hospital complex within the fragile tissue of the metro village – with the exception of the very team that sits on the commission at a given time.

Why do architects not find themselves forced to point out that a national motorway running through the most fragile part of the urban tissue is not necessarily a good idea? That an intervention of this size will maintain the

obvious urban rupture already created by the current hospital and the main road? Why, from an urban point of view would this be interesting or good?

Whose Utopia - for Whom do these Bells Toll?

The current planning committee of the new hospital describes a wonderful dream. One can't help but *believe*, due to the convincing power of the semiotics used in the press material - or maybe out of mere denial - that there is an underlying understanding and agreement on how to prioritise and plan. But then again – *who* exactly are the people responsible for this consensus? What are their premises? Obviously, we all dream of top quality services – but what is the basis for the decision-making? Is it a utopian vision or simply our attitude towards life; that we equate human rights with getting nothing but the best? At what cost – and do we even have the money to begin with?

The Burdening Fact of Democracy

And so, the central problem has to do with the abstract and complex woven fabric of infra-structures that have to be taken into consider-ation - in many different professional languages, calculated, reinterpreted, and translated. We need to come to a consensus – which is not the same as forcefully demanding us to blindly agree, crossing our fingers and praying for the best. One could wish for a development in our democracy that would form an agonistic field, in order to get the big picture out there, in every conceivable and relevant language, to negotiate, understand the benefits of sharing doubts and opinions in order to strengthen the base of the decision- making, trying to analyse and understand over how many levels, both democratic, urban, global even, this problem stretches. Interestingly enough, the discourse does not seem to succeed in transcending extremely limited realms of professional and political discourse. It seems to be caged in parallel discussions, lacking the ability to reach an appropriate collective discussion field of the various stakeholders, incorporating the maximum number of relevant arguments at any given time.

Apparently, the idea of this transcendence of the discourse threatens its "stability". One would think that a balance of such fragility - and a situation denying itself an objective trial before its concrete execution - should immediately raise doubts. Is there balance, if its stability is threatened by the obvious being pointed out?

We are too few, wearing too many hats. It is, of course, absurd to expect that a majority of people in this society has a carefully constructed opinion on socio-philosophical matters. Representative democracies were surely developed in order for people to send their representatives into the political field, to take action according to the respective interests. But here in Iceland, as seems to be a somewhat central problem within western society, the individuals appear somewhat lost in the woods of hazy and tangled visions and unclear promises - as well as premises. It lies increasingly in the hands of each subject to more or less individually carry out their political participation, as the political party dialogue becomes estranged from social interests. The problem - as well as the gift - is that we have different abilities. To believe that we can, each of us, individually operate on so many different levels of complexity in our everyday life would be to maintain the Übermensch nonsense that dominated pre-crash discourse in Iceland. It is simply impossible for an individual to keep track of the complex bundle of questions on a societal level, building opinions on a multiplicity of issues, based on critical arguments and thought. Ultimately, however, this does not mean that we have the luxury of not caring. This is essentially why we chose democracy. But our channel of discourse, stamina and investment into the continuous collective dialogue, refinement and progression of critical debate, seems to be challenged by powerful sedative agents. We seem to be simply too busy; with work, with life, with trying to stay "happy". Ignorance is also power. Could this be the reason why so many of us seem to wish for a strict, but kind, fatherly figure to come and save us once and for all; our whisper for a benevolent dictatorship?

The Four-Dimensional Reality of a New Paradigm

Back to the sociopolitical role of the architect. Although this by no means makes architects the sole experts in the decision-making field, I sincerely believe that design thinking has an important role to play with our post-grand-narrative society. Designers and architects are a rare breed when it comes to the training of thinking four-dimensionally in space and time. The fact is that we are trained to operate on multiple levels simultaneously, think through and plan abstractly, to prepare for ignition, construction, be ready for change of direction along the way, and be able to produce an instant translation of that change into multiple professional languages. Ours is not the luxury of being able to express ourselves within one realm of knowledge. On the contrary, we are trained to receive information, put that information into a complex web of context - social, material, economical, aesthetical, ontological and always, always, by nature, political.

It is the misfortune of the profession to fail to embrace this responsibility. Because we are always too busy. Because we fail to invest in critical discourse within our field, fail to carry out the real messages about our findings to the outer world, fail to refine, reflect and re-appropriate our status of knowledge according to the findings of other realms. I want to propose two things:

On one hand, that we put all our effort into searching for our equivalent of Hippocrates' oath, whether we are architects, engineers, flight attendants, as citizens - that we ignite our vocation as specialists, partakers in society before we are vendors of service or products.

On the other hand, wouldn't it be hope-provoking if we could make the most of this meltdown situation and define the agonistic field that could start in an abstract, yet tangible and loving manner, to solve the central problems of this wonderfully resource-rich, but scarcely populated, island, to come up with a genuine suggestion on how to be a miniature democracy in the absurdity of vastness.

One could say that the vitality of the field of architecture in a given nation is a good indicator of the overall strength of its economy.
The mass unemployment of Icelandic architects after the economic meltdown lends validity to that assumption.
However, to say that architects are useless for society in a time of crisis would be nonsense, and the case of Iceland again supports that view.
Below is an attempt to map the fields in which architectural expertise could be useful.

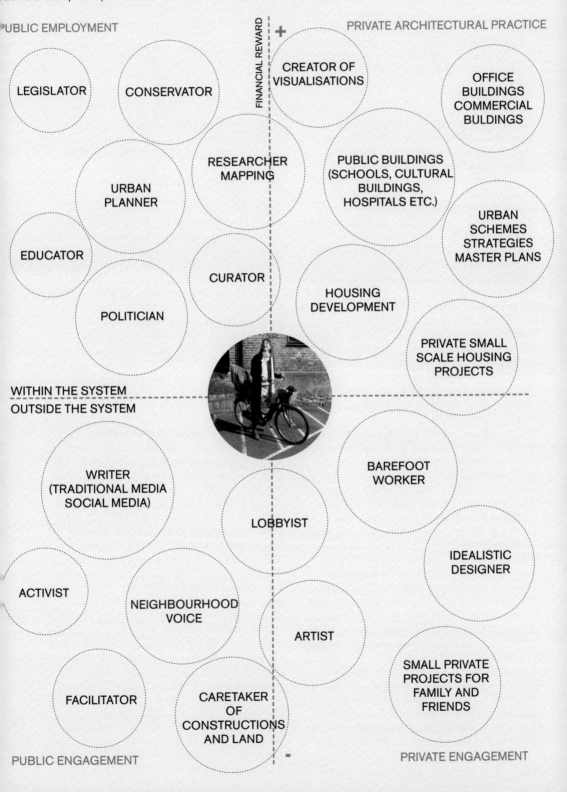

PUBLIC EMPLOYMENT

FINANCIAL REWARD

+

PRIVATE ARCHITECTURAL PRACTICE

LEGISLATOR

CONSERVATOR

CREATOR OF VISUALISATIONS

OFFICE BUILDINGS COMMERCIAL BULDINGS

RESEARCHER MAPPING

PUBLIC BUILDINGS (SCHOOLS, CULTURAL BUILDINGS, HOSPITALS ETC.)

URBAN PLANNER

URBAN SCHEMES STRATEGIES MASTER PLANS

EDUCATOR

CURATOR

HOUSING DEVELOPMENT

POLITICIAN

PRIVATE SMALL SCALE HOUSING PROJECTS

WITHIN THE SYSTEM
OUTSIDE THE SYSTEM

BAREFOOT WORKER

WRITER (TRADITIONAL MEDIA SOCIAL MEDIA)

LOBBYIST

IDEALISTIC DESIGNER

ACTIVIST

NEIGHBOURHOOD VOICE

ARTIST

FACILITATOR

CARETAKER OF CONSTRUCTIONS AND LAND

SMALL PRIVATE PROJECTS FOR FAMILY AND FRIENDS

PUBLIC ENGAGEMENT

−

PRIVATE ENGAGEMENT

Local Agents of Change

Arna Mathiesen

Getting Inspired

Inspiration is needed, for looking at new possibilities and practices in the formation of the built environment, especially for the young before they pursue university studies or buy expensive homes, both of which cause an accumulation of debt. Those who have already become debt slaves also need to be reminded of the alternatives. Getting inspired was one of the main objectives when we made preparations for design workshops that would focus on the site of the crash. This was a particular concern because there would be foreigners working with us – people who have never before seen such a site, and certainly had no experience of living in similar surroundings. It didn't seem at all inspiring, to be faced with the mainstream processes; ones that seem to create environments that may be leading the world to the brink of resource depletion, poison the atmosphere and ground, and in many cases produce an air of apathy too. Inspiration had to be sought elsewhere.

Through my remote links to Iceland (having lived abroad for decades) and by following the developments via social media sites and news feeds, I gained the impression that even if nothing was actually being built after the crash, a lot of activity was taking place. There were meetings and talks going on all over town. Every week a global celebrity of one kind or another appeared on Icelandic television to talk about their cutting edge research, and concluded that the situation in Iceland demonstrated their theories exceptionally well. Blogs were full of debates about what was wrong, as well as discussions about why new things being proposed wouldn't work either.

Asking around, we were given some leads to a number of people (mentioned as though they were eccentric types) that might be able to offer different perspectives. While most of the proposed solutions of the global agents on television came out of the field of economics, the local agents tended to look for answers that were directly connected to the built environment. We called them up to find out whether they would tell us what they were doing; fortunately they were happy to share.

The Entrepreneurial Spirit

It transpired that our good local agents of change were doing their own thing, apparently without being steered by the system that entangled most people, causing problems. Their practices proved to be entirely relevant in the face of the crisis. They were actively using the built environment they reside in, often combined with the nature surrounding them, to improve their quality of life. The principles they applied for their interventions were the keys to their success. They were making changes to their environments and recognising opportunities that would better satisfy their needs, in line with their convictions about what constituted a good life. Moreover, they were doing it without causing trouble for anyone else. In fact, they were making a better environment for their fellow citizens as well, and also providing models that could inspire others. After the crash these agents seemed to thrive like never before.

Making acquaintance with these people acted as a reminder that if you have a good idea it may well be worth trying to realise it. It may involve a considerable amount of work, and failures will be encountered along the way. It may pretty well take over your life, but at the end of the day it can reward you in ways that you couldn't possibly have imagined. If you can find the entrepreneurial spirit in yourself, and use it to take charge of your surroundings, rather than waiting for the government or some large-scale entrepreneurial company to do so, I believe it could make you more resilient if a crisis in the system were to occur. The more you manage to put the wellbeing of yourself and your neighbours at the heart of your activities, the less you get trapped within a system that may not have been designed for your own good.

Win Win Combinations

Our agents' stories elucidate and expand the tale of the crash that is read by looking at the built environment itself. They make it clear that the agency of an individual is a highly valuable resource in the city. Their stories also demonstrate that it should be possible for public policies to better encourage and stimulate the sort of activities the agents have undertaken; such activities could become more mainstream and influential in the city.

In the belief that the wheel doesn't have to keep being reinvented, I invite the reader to keep the principles of permaculture in mind when reading the stories. These principles were originally theorised by two Australian ecologists, Bill Mollison and David Holmgren. Their inspiration came from watching and analysing the natural processes of complex and resilient ecological systems; rainforests that, despite many challenges, have continued to evolve over millions of years. Permaculture principles can be applied during the design process of any environment, from the small-scale private house right up to the garden, street, or urban landscape. They can be used by anyone and everyone, not just professional designers:

Observe and Interact	*By taking the time to engage with nature we can design solutions that suit our particular situation.*
Catch and Store Energy	*By developing systems that collect resources when they are abundant, we can use them in times of need.*
Obtain a Yield	*Ensure that you are getting truly useful rewards as part of the work you are doing.*
Self-regulate; Accept Feedback	*We need to discourage inappropriate activity to ensure that systems can continue to function well.*
Use and Value Renewables	*Make the best use of nature's abundance to reduce our consumptive behaviour and dependence on non-renewable resources.*
Produce No Waste	*By valuing and making use of all the resources that are available to us, nothing goes to waste.*
Design from Pattern to Detail	*By stepping back, we can observe patterns in nature and society. These can form the backbone of our designs, with the details filled in as we go.*
Integrate	*By putting the right things in the right place, relationships develop between them and they support each other.*
Use Small, Slow Solutions	*Small and slow systems are easier to maintain than big ones, making better use of local resources and producing more sustainable outcomes.*
Use and Value Diversity	*Diversity reduces vulnerability to a variety of threats, and takes advantage of the unique nature of the environment in which it resides.*
Use Edges; Value the Marginal	*The interface between things is where the most interesting events take place. These are often the most valuable, diverse and productive elements in the system.*
Creatively Use and Respond to Change	*We can have a positive impact on inevitable change by carefully observing, and then intervening at the right time.[1]*

Please take note of the principle of valuing the edge. Edges and intersections, where two ecosystems meet and enrich each other, are where biological diversity is most abundant, and so the potential for creativity is at its maximum. This was our hunch when we made the decision to have the edge of the capital area as the focus for our study in the student workshops.

At the time of writing, more than a year had passed since meeting the agents. Despite the fact they definitely made a big impression, I may not have remembered every detail of what they told us; here is how I recall it.

[1] http://permacultureprinciples.com/

Obtain a Yield

Use and Value Renewables

Design from Pattern to Detail

Use Small, Slow Solutions

Use Edges; Value the Marginal

Hannes is an artist and Kristín is a biochemist and university lecturer by profession. Hannes is also a writer and has written an article for this book.

http://www.islenskibaerinn.com/summary.html

Hannes lives with his wife, Kristín, in a sustainable house he designed and built himself at the farm where he was born in the fifties. It is at Austur-Meðalholt in Flói parish, about one hour's drive from Reykjavík. Hannes is probably the youngest person alive who has grown up living in a traditional Icelandic farmhouse made with earth, stones, turf and driftwood. For the last 20 years the couple has been building up Íslenski Bærinn - The Icelandic Farm, a cultural and educational institution with the main emphasis on the aesthetics and building techniques of the Icelandic turf house, interpreted and presented in the context of both vernacular and green architecture.

In addition to the original farmhouse, one of the few remaining in the country, there are several other buildings on the site, representing different periods and styles in the same tradition, all built with local and/or recycled materials - everything from a chicken house to an exhibition hall. Hannes has even built an oval beehive, his theory being that it is better for bees to fly within an oval than a square. The bees in the oval hive are indeed producing more honey than those in the square hives; and honey will of course be offered, along with other local produce and refreshments, as soon as the institution opens.

Hannes has a wide selection of tools for cutting turf in the traditional way. Some of them he has saved from ruin, and others he has carefully forged himself. Hannes puts these tools to use during workshops when he lectures about this tradition, as well as providing practical training which results in real building projects. The farm is one of very few where only organic methods have been used. He grew up with a grandfather who as a farmer even refused to use tractors, so everything was done by hand or with the use of horses. The biological diversity on the site is quite striking, as no artificial fertilisers have been applied.

Hannes has collected documentation, with photographs and drawings, about the Icelandic farm for many, many years. He is hoping to open his grand exhibition early in the summer of 2014. The exhibition hall is more or less ready, with a beautiful floor covering made from offcuts from the numerous granite and marble kitchen counters that were installed during the boom - Hannes and Kristín rescued them from being sent to a landfill. Local and international volunteers helped with the painstaking task of laying the floor and it has become quite a piece of art. Iceland is one of the most popular countries for all kinds of volunteer work. It therefore presents local agents of change with an excellent opportunity to get things done, and for young people to travel and learn.

The last portion of finance required for the exhibition is still missing. The new government has said that they want to support Icelandic traditions but what do they mean? Well, it doesn't sound all that promising if one considers the fact that the cultural channel on public radio has recently been more or less closed down; the only cultural radio channel in the country! Hannes has tried to contact them for their support, but…no response so far.

Bergljót has studied veterinary science and is an entrepreneur, manager and guide.

http://islenskihesturinn.is/

Bergljót (Begga) set up a company after the crash: Íslenski Hesturinn - The Icelandic Horse. For Begga it was the chance to live out her three passions: the Icelandic horse, Icelandic nature and social mingling. Offering tourists the opportunity to get to know the lovely Icelandic horse breed is the company's main business, but these horses are a special five-gaited breed and are very comfortable to ride - probably the most comfortable breed on the planet. Traditionally, such an activity has belonged to the countryside, and mainly benefitted tourists. Only a relatively few years ago, however, it was not unusual for people of all classes, including the urban dwellers, to have their own horse as a hobby. Many would still like to do that today, but cannot afford to keep a horse and/or don't have the time to take care of one properly. This therefore created a new opening that Begga has identified, and responded to. She makes it possible for these Icelanders to learn about the horses and to go riding.

Only a few decades ago the horse was an important part of life as it provided an effective means of overland transport. Begga wants the Icelanders and the horses to find each other again. It would be sad to lose the important contact we have had with this animal. The Reykjavík Capital Area is unusual because there are many places where horses can live and there is immediate access to a varied spectrum of nature types. This constitutes a great quality of life ... landscape, horses and people in harmony, all within the city limits. How many capital areas can offer such a prospect?

Not only has this venture changed things for local people who miss not having a horse, but it has also provided a means of intro-ducing tourists to the outskirts of Reykjavík and its exotic surroundings, with unique geological formations and other interesting landscape features.

Begga's language skills are instrumental for her work; she speaks many languages, having lived all over Europe, studying and working before she started a family. The stables that the family run is one in a cluster on the fringe of the city. It happens to be the only place left in Reykjavík with sheep farming, something seen frequently in the capital when I was growing up some 30-40 years ago.

Unfortunately it's not uncommon for horse stables to get shifted out to the periphery, but now the municipal planners have decided to make it even more difficult to ride on the fringe of the city, as they are confining the horses to circles that really limit activities. In such a sprawling city, however, there is plenty of space to cater for all kinds of animals that can enrich the diversity and quality of life in town.

Begga's family spends a lot of time together because they are all helping with the business and they all love horses. At the same time, this activity is supporting the whole family finan-cially. They are doing it step by step; recycling things they had from before, and finding use for items that others are throwing out. It is not how things were done in 2007, throwing out perfectly usable possessions, then taking a loan and buying everything new, the most elegant kind of new.

TripAdvisor may not always be right, but Íslenski Hesturinn has been at the top of their list of interesting things to do in Reykajvík for 2 1/2 years, that is from six months after it started up. Begga's motto is: 'I love what I do and do what I love.'

Obtain a Yield

Use Small, Slow Solutions

Use Edges; Value the Marginal

Creatively Use and Respond to Change

Integrate

Catch and Store Energy

Self-Regulate; Accept Feedback

Use and Value Renewables

Produce No Waste

Creatively Use and Respond to Change

Mörður is an inventor.

http://tofrar.com

Mörður is a man of many ideas and many projects. He loves to learn about smart ways to do things sustainably. Putting the sustainable methods together into more complex systems, to get maximum yield, is Mörður's ultimate goal. Aquaponics, and soil production from waste, are on the agenda, ideally in recycled landscapes and buildings. Finding the win-win combinations is the key to success.

Mörður has taken courses in innovation to achieve his goals. They focused on developing equity through promoting products that thereby contribute to a green economy; a model based on sustainable development and a branch of economics, called ecological economics. Mörður hopes, however, to contribute to the more radical idea of what is known as The Blue Economy, using the waste of one product as an input to create new cash flows and reduce waste. It remains to be seen what will happen, now that the new government has spent all the money allocated for developing a green economy on cutting taxes for the so-called 'quota-kings' - a few individuals who alone have the rights to exploit the fisheries commercially.

Mörður has been living in an enterprise park that has become established in the buildings the American army left behind in 2006. These buildings have great potential, that is if all the blocks of flats were to be filled with people. However, the state is hanging onto whole buildings and the reason is rumoured to be that they don't want to 'disturb' the market. If all those empty apartments that the state and the banks have taken over were placed on the rental market or put up for sale, they fear the prices would drop, and all the people who are so 'lucky' to own something would be left in the position of owning a little bit less. It might result in lower house prices. In the meantime, all the people who cannot afford to buy a home (including those who have lost their homes because of the crisis) become even bigger losers, and buildings gradually fall into dilapidation.

Since a car accident some 10 years ago, Mörður has been unable to do very much in the way of physical work and he tries to figure out new paths for improvements. Were it not for applying this psychological survival strategy, and focusing on positive projects, he would be on the verge of falling into an abyss of despair. As a result of the crash, the health system - the crown jewel of the welfare state - has been hit with austerity measures and so his doctors have stopped doing any more testing to search for a diagnosis. Mörður applies the same strategy for coping with his health limitations as he does for his other projects; he turns the problem into an opportunity.

Mörður has now established a permaculture centre on a farm outside Reykjavík. It is called Töfrastaðir (Magic Place), a slight deviation from the original place name Torfastaðir. Töfrastaðir has already attracted lots of people, even from abroad, who want to participate in, and contribute to, the experiment for developing practices that promote earth care, people care and fair share - the proclaimed aims of permaculture.

At the moment Mörður is preparing a 72-hour permaculture design workshop for next summer. People will travel from overseas to provide expertise and help Mörður build a permaculture network for Iceland.

Gunnar is a carpenter by profession.

http://www.alaborg.is/
http://www.ishamar.is/Forsida/English/

Gunnar runs a bistro/café/art gallery, Álaborg, with his wife Guðlaug, but his main occupation is managing a building company and carpentry workshop that produces components for buildings both old and new.

Gunnar originates from Vestmannaeyjar, an island south of Iceland. The mountain on the little island started erupting in 1973, to everyone's great surprise as no one knew it was a volcano. Ashes covered the village on the island, and lava flooded over parts of it. The inhabitants of the island were evacuated overnight and housed on the mainland until the lava had cooled down and the town had been cleaned up. Gunnar, who was educated as a carpenter, participated in reconstructing the town and put up a factory which prefabricated elements for new buildings. When building activity on the island declined again, he moved to the mainland to seek new opportunities.

Gunnar relocated into the old industrial buildings of Álafoss in Mosfellsbær. Álafoss draws its name from the waterfall, and an industrial settlement was established there in 1896. The water in the river was instrumental for the textile industries there, both for powering the wheels of the factory and for cleaning the raw material - wool from the Icelandic sheep. The river used to be warm because of the hot springs nearby, hence the name Varmá (warm river).

During the boom years, a new development was emerging next to Álafoss, but the design of it was not at all in keeping with the old industrial cluster. A new road to the development was also planned, so massive that it would have dwarfed the historical site completely. Fortunately some activists managed to get the size reduced, but it nevertheless still looks rather like a misfit.

Not long after the financial crash Gunnar sat in his garden and pondered on what to do, now that the building craze had come to an end. A few tourists were walking down the road and wandered into his garden, then kitchen, asking for a glass of beer; they assumed they had found a cosy restaurant. Gunnar gave them beer and an idea was born (or at least confirmed). Gunnar and his wife started up a café on the first floor of their house, just beside the wood workshop. There is a space to 'park' horses and a fountain for them to drink from.

Despite the decline in building activity after the crash, Gunnar is surprisingly busy with his carpentry. In the bubble period he was competing with companies that promised to build faster than he could, as he didn't want to compromise his craftsmanship for speed. But now he is sought after to repair damage caused by fast-track building, problems created for example by concrete not being allowed to dry before building proceeded.

The famous artist Dieter Roth used to live by the same river. Gunnar travelled widely with Dieter, assisting him with shows and exhibitions. In addition, he became involved in a little-known aspect of Dieter's creative activity: the artist owned a lot of properties, houses and apartments all over the world which he developed in many ways, altering them and installing furniture and different objects. A special contract was made between the two. Dieter demonstrated with drawings, complimented with just a few words written on them, what he wanted to get done, including how he wanted the objects to be arranged in the room. Then he was off to his next venture. Gunnar did his best to interpret the drawings, constructing and installing everything on site as a whole, as Dieter had visualised it. For many of these projects no words needed to be exchanged between the artist and the carpenter.

Observe and Interact

Obtain a Yield

Self-Regulate; Accept Feedback

Design from Pattern to Detail

Use Small, Slow Solutions

Observe and Interact

Obtain a Yield

Self-Regulate; Accept Feedback

Integrate

Use and Value Diversity

Vilhjálmur is a chemical engineer by profession. He used to be the CEO of the Research Council of Iceland for 25 years before he retired from the post. He was also on the board of directors of the Icelandic Forestry Association for years, and at the time of the interview he is President of the Horticultural Society of Iceland.

Vilhjálmur and Áslaug have their second home in woods that they and their family created themselves on a moraine, an inhospitable environment for life or growth, left behind by an ice age glacier and volcanic ash fall. This barrenness had been exposed by the catastrophic erosion resulting from centuries of overgrazing by sheep, and other livestock, after the settlement of Iceland. A nearby soil section shows clearly that the original vegetation, which included rich birch forests, gave up the ghost in the distant past as wind and water erosion started about 1100.

The weathered and windy place was not considered very suitable for growing anything when they started the project some 50 years ago. Sheep were running free on the land, and still are in many places. Visiting nowadays, however, is like coming to another country. Quiet woods in Germany spring to mind. It is sheltered between the trees; fruit trees and roses from all corners of the world are flourishing, bees are buzzing and birds are singing.

How was it possible to make all this life out of apparent nothingness? Being the scientist and engineer that Vilhjálmur is, he observed the structure of the soil, collected samples for analysis and came up with a recipe for mixing ingredients to improve its quality and thus speed up the evolution of the site: one part lifeless local soil, one part horse manure and one part porous volcanic sand.

Vilhjálmur has gradually planted many different species and varieties of woody plants and perennials, from both seeds and his own rooted cuttings. When he travels abroad, he collects samples of interesting varieties, brings them back home and tries them out on his land. Over the course of the years many plants have not survived but Vilhjálmur has selected and propagated those that show their ability to cope with the rather hostile environment. An example is a variety of poplar, with an unusual leaf shape that can better withstand the winds. Vegetation and shelter have steadily been built up, with the result that microclimates have been generated, accommodating more and more delicate plants. The topsoil gets thicker and richer with more organic material being created, and local biodiversity increases every year, from soil microorganisms to plants and birdlife.

Vilhjálmur takes the view that the Rio Convention on Biological Diversity, originally tailored for preserving the Amazonian rainforests with their multitude of species developed over millions of years, cannot be applied to places like Iceland that are lacking in biodiversity because of its extensive man-made deserts, and the remoteness of this ocean island. He holds the controversial opinion that there is no good reason for preserving a man-made, lifeless desert land, when we could instead be making a productive and pleasant environment on the same spot. And it is not hard to agree with him that sheltered outdoor spaces are few and far between in Iceland. The controversy crystallises in the debate about the Alaskan lupine, thought to be an invasive species that should be eradicated. Vilhjálmur's experience suggests, however, that the lupine plays an important role in reclaiming the organic content and fertility of Icelandic soil, and that it retreats once that role is played out, all within the lifetime of a generation or two.

Vilhjálmur could not have properly managed even a fraction of his 17 hectares of man-made woodland without the aid of many helping hands. Now in his seventies, he has been troubled with back pain. However, modern technology makes light of such obstacles and now he can go off digging more holes for planting trees with the help of his Italian mini excavator.

Úlfar is a cook by profession.

http://www.amazon.com/%C3%9Alfar-Finnbj%C3%B6rnsson/e/B001JO4VCY

Úlfar has rearranged his house and garden to evolve around local food stuffs. About 30 years ago, when he was still studying, he was the first cook in Iceland to promote the use of Icelandic herbs found in the wild, and develop a special Icelandic cuisine. This was considered a rather strange and eccentric hobby at the time, but has in later years become a fairly popular fashion in the coolest restaurants of the Capital Area.

Úlfar turned what used to be the garage of the house into a fully equipped professional kitchen, opening up onto his garden, which is stuffed full of herbs he has taken from the wild, planted and cultivated. There he sits, surveying his garden, and then experiments with what he discovers in it; prize-winning cookbooks have resulted from his nearby finds.

It is not only herbs that Úlfar chooses to eat and write about. He also keeps rabbits, doves and fish in the garden. The fish are for pleasure only and the rabbits are just too loveable. It was only when he began breeding white doves that cannot be distinguished one from the other, that he was able to slaughter them and concoct interesting dishes.

Around the corner Úlfar has some geese hanging, the catch from last week's hunt. There are also many types of vegetable growing and seedlings are started off in the greenhouse, to which he has redirected the gray water (as well as hot water). Doing so elevates the heat in the greenhouse during the winter, and thus extends the growing season.

Artificial landscapes are spread around the garden, made from materials rescued from nearby surroundings. Stuff that was apparently useless to others became new building blocks for Úlfar. Some of the components came from a development just next door to where he lives, which was underway before the economy crashed. During the course of digging the foundations for the new buildings, they were in the process of scraping away the top layer of soil - about the best agricultural soil in the Reykjavík capital area. There were also lots of stones being dug up. Úlfar went down to where the truckloads were being driven away, the stones to landfills and the soil to golf courses. "Just bring this stuff to my garden, it's easier" he told them, and as he stood on his home-made hill, watching the trucks approaching, he suddenly heard the prime minister of Iceland on the radio; the speech he gave ended with the dramatic words 'God bless Iceland'. The trucks then drove away for the last time, and didn't come back…until recently anyway; one wonders if the building mania will start again now the GDP seems to be on the rise.

Observe and Interact

Catch and Store Energy

Obtain a Yield

Use Edges; Value the Marginal

Creatively Use and Respond to Change

Integrate

Use Small, Slow Solutions

Use and Value Diversity

Use Edges; Value the Marginal

Creatively Use and Respond to Change

Björk is an environmental ethnologist.

http://bukonan.wordpress.com/about/

A few years ago Björk moved, with her partner, Tómas, to the small farm Brennholt in Mosfellsdalur, on the outskirts of Reykjavik. Tómas's parents relocated there from the city, in the early 1960s. They had a greenhouse and grew tomatoes, grapes and vegetables in the outside garden, all organic. Tómas grew up in Brennholt and there he observed, learned and worked with his parents and sister to grow their own food, and live off the land in harmony with the environment. Now Björk and Tómas have taken over and are carrying on the organic gardening tradition, along with keeping bees and chickens.

Björk and Tómas grow heirloom tomatoes, chili peppers, cucumbers, onions, potatoes, lettuce, beets, broccoli, cauliflower, strawberries, celery, and all kinds of herbs. All the lettuce is grown outside, using only sheep manure as fertiliser. No plastic is allowed anywhere near the plants, the gardens are weeded by hand and pesticides have always been out of the question. The organic lettuces are delivered to restaurants in Reykjavík twice a week in the summertime. The chefs can't wait to get their hands on that salad and the customers love it.

Insects are very helpful for the natural environment and Björk never views them as a problem. She believes that nature finds its own balance. The poplar and the birch occasionally suffer because of insects, but each summer is different and the birds are happy if there is an increased insect supply to eat. Björk disapproves of how eager many people are to spray poison all over their trees: 'The pests get stronger but the environment gets weaker. People need to learn that insects are very helpful for nature, and they are not our enemies'.

The beautiful hens (a local breed) love to lay on their eggs and are very caring of their little chicks. They also eat all the household's leftovers. So much food gets wasted nowadays and here is the evidence that it can be used to make chickens happy, and encourage them to stroll around outside all day and lay healthy eggs. Furthermore, Björk has sourced locally grown organic grain for the hens, as she hated feeding them anything which contained genetically modified soy. She is now considering starting a little project with an organic vegetarian restaurant in Reykjavík to generate more organically grown leftovers for her fowl.

'A fairy tale' is how Björk describes her cooking, showing the blog she produces about food making, with many wonderful recipes. She tries to use local ingredients as much as possible, and creates things from scratch. It's fun, tastes great and is cheap if you have the time to do it. Two days a week she works at a Steiner Waldorf school, where she assists in the kitchen doing what she loves most - cooking and baking from scratch.

Björk found inspiration in her own parents' way of life. When she was growing up in the countryside, they produced most of the food they ate from scratch. But she is also impressed by the Indians she lived with in Canada, where she was studying their folklore. The book she wrote in cooperation with the late elder Garry 'Morning Star' Raven has just been published - *The Seven Teachings and more: Anishinaabeg share their traditional teachings with an Icelander.* Anishinaabeg are 'the original people lowered down to Mother Earth by Creator'.

Björk has been considering whether to keep some Icelandic goats, to do her bit to save them from extinction; she has already learned how to make goat cheese in Canada. That idea is on hold for now... she is just too busy at the moment.

Björk claims the best exercise in the world is digging and planting, and after that watering everything, and then harvesting. All these activities are beneficial for people and for nature. 'You and your friends gain so much in many different ways and have fun at the same time, just by growing!' Björk herself eats well and is free of debt. She is surrounded by plants and animals, and is extremely happy.

Ólafur is an architect by profession and has now retired.

Ólafur and Svava live in a greenhouse. After developing a fascination with the idea of living in a house that had a winter garden, Ólafur decided to design a new home. It is basically 480 m² of greenhouse, seven metres high; it contains a 100m² single storey flat-roofed building in the middle of it. The construction was finished in 1996.

In Iceland the rain sometimes comes in horizontally, with ferocious cool winds that make good insulation and protective layers a must, so as not to get cold or wet. In this particular building the greenhouse takes care of all this, so the house inside it has no need of insulation or rain protection. Between the inner house, and the outer walls of the greenhouse, a person is actually outside, but nevertheless protected inside the greenhouse.

The inner house is smaller, and less demanding of resources in terms of materials and energy, than an average family house, because the in-between space takes over many of the usual functions of a traditional house, in terms of both social activity and building physics.

The inner house, which is cruciform in shape, is constructed of pumice. The concrete gives good natural insulation, provides thermal capacity, and capitalises on passive solar gain. Each room is ventilated on two sides, usually by means of sliding timber patio doors with an opening window diagonally opposite. Air change requirements in the inner house are met by natural air movements travelling from the outer to the inner house.

The greenhouse is built from laminated timber, strengthened with steel and aluminium bracing. The enclosure consists entirely of single panes of glass on all but the east gable; that is solid in situ concrete, to provide stiffening. The glazing is 6mm in the roof and 5mm in the walls, calculated to withstand wind and snow loads. There are no sub-frames, glazing is set directly onto the construction, using flat aluminium beads and butyl ribbon seals. About 10% of the roof area and 5% of the walls are made up of automatic window openings. These are driven by an electric motor (a well-known technology in commercial greenhouses) set to maintain a maximum temperature of 20°C. Despite single glazing, condensation is avoided by securing sufficient air volume to dispel moisture. The ridge ventilation system and the local coastal climate also play their part. Rainwater from the roof is collected, stored and used for watering plants.

The building project has proved that enough solar gain exists on latitude 64, even in February, to provide comfortable living conditions in the greenhouse garden. It is a lovely space, with a special climate in which can be grown all kinds of plants that don't grow outdoors in Iceland. A vegetable garden yields produce, and the inhabitants enjoy eating outside the inner house most of the year. There are a large number of fig and apple trees here, and they bear a generous amount of fruit. The grandchildren like to stay, and they choose to sleep in a hammock, or on the roof of the little house.

Even though most of the in-between floor area is taken up with soil for growing things, bugs do not cause a problem as it freezes here a couple of times a year; some plants also need that to enable them to flower.

The whole scenario was an experiment, and there was considerable uncertainty about whether it would be successful. Since Buckminster Fuller's work, there has been much speculation about living in spaces of this kind, but few have gone to such lengths as Ólafur to test whether it might be a good idea. He has managed to prove that it works wonderfully well, and has provided a comfortable home for himself and Svava.

Catch and Store Energy

Use and Value Renewables

Design from Pattern to Detail

Integrate

Use Edges; Value the Marginal

Obtain a Yield

Use and Value Renewables

Use Small, Slow Solutions

Use and Value Diversity

Creatively Use and Respond to Change

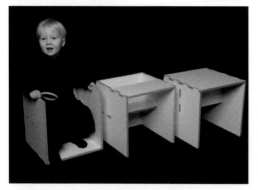

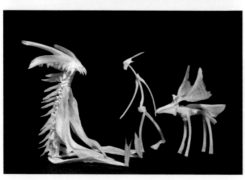

Róshildur and Snæbjörn are industrial designers by profession.

hugdetta.com/, http://grettisborg.is/index.html

Róshildur and Snæbjörn graduated from the local Arts Academy, into a ruined economy. Under these circumstances they realised they couldn't expect to come across any clients who would want to employ them for projects which required their specialist knowledge, industrial design.

For that reason, they decided to make their own projects, influenced by the steady stream of tourists for whom the Icelandic nature and cheap currency are major attractions.

Róshildur and Snæbjörn bought a run-down building in the city centre and as well as a design workshop, they decided to make a bed and breakfast facility out of it. The building was in a much worse state than they antici- pated, so many components had to be rebuilt from scratch. The project (Grettisborg) ended up as a very special type of guesthouse, filled with design objects from different periods. Some are their own design, and all of them are for sale.

Not only do Róshildur and Snæbjörn offer a different kind of accommodation compared to the mainstream hotels in Reykjavík, in terms of the design and arrangement of objects, but their concept is also more personal, with a view to human relations and the services they recommend for their guests. They can tailor a trip for anybody. They are, after all, professional designers.

Bringing this project to fruition was interesting, but not always easy. It did not neatly fit into the commonly used model of opening a guesthouse, for which the rules and regulations are made. Information about how to tackle this dilemma was lacking, and asking the municipal officials didn't resolve it either. They simply didn't know how to match the unusual setup with the existing rules, or vice versa. This made things tricky, as they needed to avoid doing anything "wrong", and being punished before they even knew it.

There seems to be a missed opportunity for municipalities to help citizens apply their creativity in initiating interesting and rewarding jobs, thus making a more pleasant environment for the benefit of the whole town. They should be helping them find a clear path through the jungle of regulations, ones that were put in place not for them, but for different sorts of operators, with different circumstances. In this respect they could surely learn from the city of Lahti in Finland, which devotes a whole department to co-designing the city. With small and medium-sized businesses, the department creates job opportunities that are sensitive to the inhabitants' needs and the surrounding ecosystems.

Another issue is the competition with those in the same field: large hotels being marketed through Hotels.com, and smaller outfits that have a less serious approach and function in the black market, disregarding the rules. How much of the profit is channelled to websites and does not benefit the country at all? That question remains unanswered. Iceland would do well to consider other countries with more experience in this. A short trip to the Canary Islands, for example, leaves one wondering where all the profits from the tourists are going. The place does not exactly ooze prosperity, despite decades of mass tourism. It could make an enormous difference to creative local people who want to put their soul into a venture (rather than focusing on profit only) if the state were to play a more active role by openly discussing, deciding and changing policies to steer the development of tourism; the built environment and the local people would both be beneficiaries.

Back to Róshildur and Snæbjörn, in their studio where they create beautiful things - a model-making kit for children, for instance, made from fish bones, just like the one great grandad used to make.

Þorsteinn lives at Elliðahvammur, a farm where he through decades has tried to find strategies to live off his land, successfully.

The short distance to the capital, where the largest markets in Iceland are to be found, has been helpful for running the business. In the boom period, a new residential area suddenly sprung up around the farm.

Þorsteinn welcomes new neighbours, but 'the developers, with the help of the municipality, wanted to bulldoze over my farm as well' he told us, 'no one, except those that have direct experience of this, can imagine what this kind of violence feels like!' Lawsuits about the matter are still ongoing.

Þorsteinn is a pioneer. He does grow trees commonly found in Iceland, and vegetables like potatoes, carrots, beets, cauliflowers, pumpkins, tomatoes, squash, cucumbers, lettuce and radishes. However, he also grows various kinds of apple and cherry trees, plums, pears, grapes and other species that were considered impossible to grow in Iceland just a few years back. Most of these he cultivates in greenhouses (it's even possible to grow bananas in Icelandic greenhouses), but some have been planted outside.

Greenhouses are a great idea in Iceland. Half of the year there is light in abundance on latitude 64.1333° N.

To improve the temperature and light in the winter, a portion of the huge amount of hydropower, generated by the big rivers, could be utilised. If the greenhouse farmers of Iceland were offered the same electricity at the same price as the aluminium corporations, it would be very good business for them to grow all the fruit and vegetables necessary to feed all Icelanders, and more besides. But they aren't. In fact they have to pay many times more for it. This means that it is hard to compete with cheaply produced vegetables and fruits imported from other countries.

Over the years Þorsteinn has turned his hand to many, many things. He has bees now, and makes interesting products from wax and honey. In addition, he offers tourist accommodation in a small hut which has a turf roof. The main industry though is egg production. It is a pleasure for the new neighbours to be able to pop by the farm, and get some honey and eggs straight from the farmer, despite the fact they live in the city.

Many of the people on the edge of the capital area, who have animals and experiment with alternative agricultural practices, know each other even though they may be quite a long drive apart. They pay each other visits, to socialise, to learn something new, to exchange goods (an example would be eggs for horse manure, which is a good fertiliser), or maybe just to rest their horse and have a cup of coffee while they are out enjoying a ride. This community is an ecosystem in its own right, together with its animals and plants.

Observe and Interact

Obtain a Yield

Use and Value Renewables

Design from Pattern to Detail

Creatively Use and Respond to Change

Auður is a gardener and carpenter by profession.

http://rit.is/

For Auður the economic crash represented an opportunity. She could finally focus all her resources on what she enjoyed most - gardening. She teaches, and writes about gardening for the magazine she runs with her husband, photographer Páll Jökull.

Auður suspected what would happen when the crash hit (yes, people could feel it coming) and it did - there was an explosion in the interest in gardening. People flocked in large numbers to courses about growing their own food. Since the crisis hit, her company has run courses for about 1500 people, and there are others providing this service too. According to Auður, the interest is not really declining, although for some it may be just a passing fad. She says this level of interest would have been unthinkable before the crash. It is not about getting something to eat to stave off poverty, she says, it is about valuing small things, and getting contact with the ground.

Collecting the fruits at the end of the day is a bonus, and some people seem hardly to believe their eyes when the crop starts to ripen. Programmes for becoming a professional gardener have never been so popular, and Auður is adding to her own gardening educa- tion too. She is building up her knowledge about greenhouse gardening through course- work, to round out her previous education as a gardener and carpenter.

Before the crash, it was mostly elderly people who grew food, and they weren't so much in need of education because they had a long training to fall back on. I remember it well from my childhood: more people used to have a vegetable garden back then, for potatoes and rhubarb if nothing else. That certainly applied to old people like my grandpa, for whom the notion of having potatoes to last the winter was important.

Times have changed. Today, many of the young have never grown anything in their entire life. And when they attempt it, they love the contact with the soil. It counteracts stress. Having something edible popping up through the earth provides an added bonus for the whole experience.

In the immediate aftermath of the crash, it was rather difficult for Auður to run her publishing company as people weren't paying their bills. But she knew there were better times ahead, so she looked for temporary solutions. Flexible as she is, she moved the company to her home. People soon started paying their bills again, and the number of subscriptions increased.

Auður's investigations into the potential for growing edibles is moving forward in many directions, rural and urban ones. These developments are well received by the readers of the magazine who love the inspiration she gives them.

Auður has also made an impression on the children in her neighbourhood. In the harvesting season they come round to the garden for a chat, and to taste different types of vegetables. They are amazed that so much edible stuff is coming up out of the ground!

Morten is a Norwegian cycling activist who moved to Iceland many years ago. Morten's personal circumstances have altered so that it would now be easier for him to live elsewhere in the world, but it is by no means straightforward for him to leave Iceland since the crash.

On day one of the collapse, Morten's apartment diminished in price by 50%, as calculated in foreign currencies, because the Icelandic currency was devalued so drastically. At the same time his mortgage expanded by 30%. The result is that Morten would have very little money to purchase a flat if he moved back to Norway. That in itself would not be too bad, as the rental market is more developed there.

Living in Iceland in these turbulent times is an exciting affair, so Morten is staying put, and enjoying it a fair amount. Catastrophes throw up new opportunities for those who are interested in changing the way we operate in the world...for better or for worse. Iceland is lucky to have Morten, and some of the other creative souls from abroad, as they have frames of reference that differ from those of average Icelanders, who are not so proactive in pushing for better solutions.

Morten is genuinely interested in sustainability. The basic tenets filtered into his consciousness back in his childhood during the hippy era. Morten's master's thesis in 1989 covered the greenhouse effect, and before coming to Iceland he worked at the Centre for Environment and Development at the University of Trondheim. Sustainable development was an important theme throughout certain facets of engineering education and research.

Morten is acutely aware that it is not always particularly easy to apply sustainable principles within mainstream practice, if they require radical measures ie. big changes. That's the case whether or not the changes might reduce costs, and improve the image and sales value of the project or firm. Some of his friends, who work in large engineering firms, owe their livelihoods to large-scale infrastructural projects such as power stations, highways or aluminium plants. They feel they have to be careful about raising critical questions, as do others who are university teachers or public servants, in case it resulted in the loss of their jobs. Rather than being excessively critical in public about many of the doubtful (in the context of sustainability) activities that engineering firms or public bodies become entangled in, it is safer for those friends to focus on less controversial, but nevertheless important, issues that could improve public health, resilience and reduce the ecological footprint...like bicycling.

Morten was leader of the Icelandic Cyclists' Federation (LHM) for four years. Inspired by one of the main messages from the big international Velo-city cycling conference in Dublin in 2005, which he attended, Morten has strived to increase cooperation with various partners sharing some common goals. This aim has since been developed by the board members, as well as by the offshoot Bikeability Iceland. The Cycling to Work campaign, initiated and run by the cycling committee of the National Olympic and Sports Association of Iceland, is one example. It seems to be the most popular campaign of its kind in the world, having a participation rate of 3% of the total population. Another type of collaboration is the constructive dialogue with the municipalities in the capital area regarding solutions for improved access for cycling. And thirdly, the cycling conferences in Reykjavik are significant, with Bikeability Iceland being especially active. The conferences pull in various partners according to theme, ranging from the Public Health Institute of Iceland and the Surgeon General, to city departments, government, ministers, teachers, road safety officials and members of the tourism sector.

Morten stays fit, cycling from one event to another; the grassroots are bubbling with new initiatives.

Produce No Waste

Self-Regulate; Accept Feedback

Obtain a Yield

Use Small, Slow Solutions

Creatively Use and Respond to Change

70 MANNS, 3 FERÐAMÁTAR.

Samtök um bíllausan lífsstíl.
www.billaus.is

Catch and Store Energy

Obtain a Yield

Use and Value Renewables

Produce No Waste

Creatively Use and Respond to Change

Linus Orri is a musician.

Linus Orri (aged 21 when he talked to us in a design workshop) had hardly found the need to purchase any food for many years. He came to tell us about his experiences in intentional communities, that are residential in nature with social cohesion and teamwork at their heart. He brought with him lots of fruit that he put down in the middle of the table that he wanted us to sit around, rather than him standing up and telling his stories from the podium. The fruit was from a dumpster.

Dumpster diving it is called, salvaging perfectly good food that would otherwise be wasted. For three and a half years he was part of a collective called Food Not Bombs and they would gather once a week to dumpster dive for loads of food. A big lunch was then prepared, set up on a stand in one of the central squares and served to whomever passed by. The purpose was to reclaim public space for a community action, and to highlight how much waste the consumer society produces. More than a third of all produce gets thrown away at some point in the process.

Since the crash, dumpster diving has moved on from being mainly the occupation of the young, people on the scrounge or Vietnamese immigrants, who seemed to have become part of the ecosystem a few years back. Now what one would call 'ordinary' people in 'ordinary' clothes, of all ages, can be seen checking for food and other valuables in the dumpsters.

Linus has also been a driving force for a bicycle workshop that provided a space for people to repair their bicycles for free, by giving them access to tools and know-how; the hope was to pass on skills and make people independent, rather than relying on professionals to fix their equipment.

Linus has lived in many kinds of intentional communities: some big, some small, some secret and some public and extrovert, organising many cultural events, temporary to varying degrees. The point of joining an intentional community is the conscious desire to live there, to take care of the place and to contribute with what you have, to make life better and easier for yourself and those who might live there with you.

Linus Orri is an anarchist. He believes that it is best to organise without hierarchies or power structures, so that everyone gets to make their own choices and people are acting in solidarity with one another.

One type of intentional community is a squat, people taking over and inhabiting a building that nobody else seems to care about. Such buildings have often been left by their owners with open windows, so rot sets in. The owners obviously want them to dilapidate and fall apart so that they can build something new, which can be sold for considerably more money. When money is all you see when you look at a building, you are only going to treat that building in a certain way.

Linus suspects that some house owners might see squatters as a part of their scheme to get rid of unwanted buildings. Once the squatters have taken possession of a property, the owner sends round the police to evict them but makes sure the police destroy the building to a large extent while doing so, and then they have a proper excuse to tear the structure down.

The New City

Magnús Jensson

The city:

A cooperative project on creating the future city

About the project:

It will cover all aspects of designing and constructing a new city, the next generation urban society.

Target group:

Prescient, progressive people who are interested in social reform, a greener environment and sustainability.

The project is a cooperative assignment. What distinguishes it from everyday regular discussions is that a) the new city will be built from scratch, with no effort spent on tackling accumulated, immovable problems and b) the citizens of the new city will choose the prescient progressive path towards its goal, with no effort spent on convincing the conservative elements. The city's objective is to set an example to new cities around the globe, from the very moment of its completion.

The backstory:

The inaugural meeting of the organisation (although there had in fact been a number of precursory ones) was held in December 2012. It took the form of a series of micro lectures, with short intervening discussions, in which, among other things, issues of sustainability, city planning and e-democracy were dealt with.

The activities of the organisation:

An e-consultation website is currently being prepared. Board meetings (Alþingi), accessible to the general public, are being held every Sunday. There will also be regular seminars, work meetings and workshops.

The organisation expects new members to bring pilot projects and experience to the group discussions. The organisation applies for subsidies, and contributes to a successful interdisciplinary collaboration.

The aims:

That a new generation of cities should emerge on a global scale; that this should occur through preparation and work on the concept of the new city, both academically and manually, by means of an interdisciplinary collaboration.

Products:

(In chronological order) lectures, websites, articles, workshops, television programmes, publications, city.

There is a lack of examples and models for testing the sustainability concept, especially large or comprehensive ones, but it remains the case that sustainability must always be based on collective thought.

The presumption is that, in due course, the concept of the city will become clearer, a lot of people will develop an interest in joining as citizens, and that will be the cue for location scouting and actual physical labour.

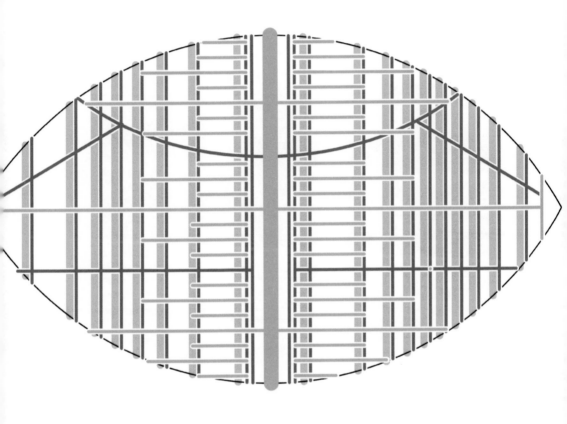

3.

Urban Systems current status

Geology

Kristín Vala Ragnarsdóttir

Iceland is located on the Mid-Atlantic Ridge. It stretches from the North Atlantic to the South Atlantic, and is the location of a gradual divergence between the North American plate and the Eurasian plate in the north, and the South American and African plate in the south (Figure 1). This ridge is formed by volcanic activity, as magma wells up from the Earth's mantle. Iceland is held up high over the oceanic floor because of a so-called hot spot that further funnels magma to the surface, but from deeper down in the mantle. As a result, the island is volcanic and has a young geologic age; it ranges from roughly 15 million years in the north-western and eastern fjords of the island to a recent age within the rifting zone that goes through Iceland from the south west to the north east; it comes on land at the tip of the Reykjanes peninsula and continues north eastwards, only a handful of kilometres from the Reykjavik outskirts, through to the Þingvellir rift valley. In central Iceland the rift zone has shifted towards the east and continues north eastwards from the Kverkfjöll area, through Krafla to the Skjálfandi fjord in the north.

The oldest rocks in Iceland are formed of Tertiary basaltic lava flows that can be viewed in the fjords like a layered cake that typically gives a cross section of tenths to hundredths of lava fields, one lava flow on top of another. About 2.8 million years ago an ice age developed on Earth, and until 10,000 years ago when the ice age ended, volcanic rocks formed either under glaciers creating hyaloclastite rocks, or as interglacial (warm periods during the ice age) lava fields. Hyaloclastites are made of volcanic ash and breccia that have been glued together through alteration processes involving chemical reactions between volcanic glass and minerals with water. Hyalocastites form the mountains that we can see in the Reykjavik area (Úlfarsfell, Bláfjöll) and along the Reykjanes Peninsula (Keilir). Sometimes the eruption material build-ups went above the glacier, and lava flows formed on top of the hyaloclastites (Esja). Surrounding these hyaloclastite mountains are interglacial basaltic lava flows (generally referred to as grágrýti or grey basalt lavas) and post-glacial lava flows. The majority of the Reykjavik area is built on grey basaltic lavas; the outskirts of Reykjavík (Mosfellsbær for example) is on hyaloclastites and parts of Garðabær, Álftanes and Hafnarfjörður are located on postglacial lava flows, which are 8,000 years old (Figure 2). Iceland has virtually no forests, due to long-term grazing, excessive logging for construction, the use of firewood for cooking and iron exploitation in the wetlands. Wherever you are in Reykjavik you can see the mountains in the north (Arkafjall, Skarðsheiði, Esja), in the east (Hengill, Bláfjöll) and in the south (Keilir). Icelanders consider it important to their quality of life to be able to see these mountains.

It is interesting to contemplate what the chances of volcanic eruptions in the Reykjavik City Area could be. As Figure 2 shows, there are postglacial lava fields in the vicinity of Reykjavik (pink in colour) and some of the houses are built on them. Since the Reykjanes Peninsula rift zone is still very active, it is conceivable that an eruption could start where it could directly affect the built environment by lava flowing north from Heiðmörk down a valley to Reykjavík (Elliðaárdalur), as well as further south to the built environment in Garðabær, Álftanes and Hafnarfjörður (Figure 3). The new developments in the Reykjavík area are shown in green, the potential lava flows in grey. There is no apparent planning undertaken when new building spaces are decided, to be sure there is no danger from potential new lava flows. While lavas would devastate both the built environment and potentially also the drinking water reservoirs for Reykjavík and the other townships, if any ash is distributed (there is only a small amount of ash, known as plenian, from the type of eruption that can be expected), it could actually improve the soil in the area, if no more than a couple of centimetres is deposited on the land (see soil discussion below). However, the health of the people in the area could be adversely affected by the ash, as well as dust

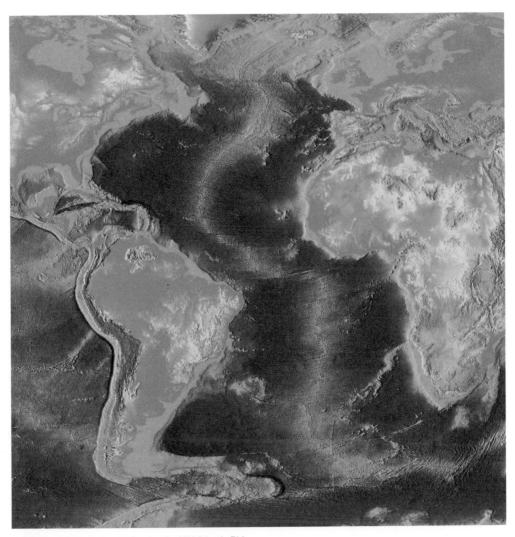

1 Map of the Atlantic Ocean showing the Mid-Atlantic Ridge.

storms in the aftermath, and volcanic gasses.

Soil develops on top of rock formations as a result of physical and biogeochemical reactions that occur with time in the presence of water. The rock gradually breaks up to form loose material composed of alteration minerals that form soil, by the accumulation of organic matter from mosses, fungi and plants that live and die on the soil surface. Soil is thus a mixture of weathered rock minerals and organic matter. The soils of the Reykjavik area are formed in aeolian and tephra deposits that overlie the basaltic bedrock. These deposits weather rapidly to form so-called Andosols.[1]

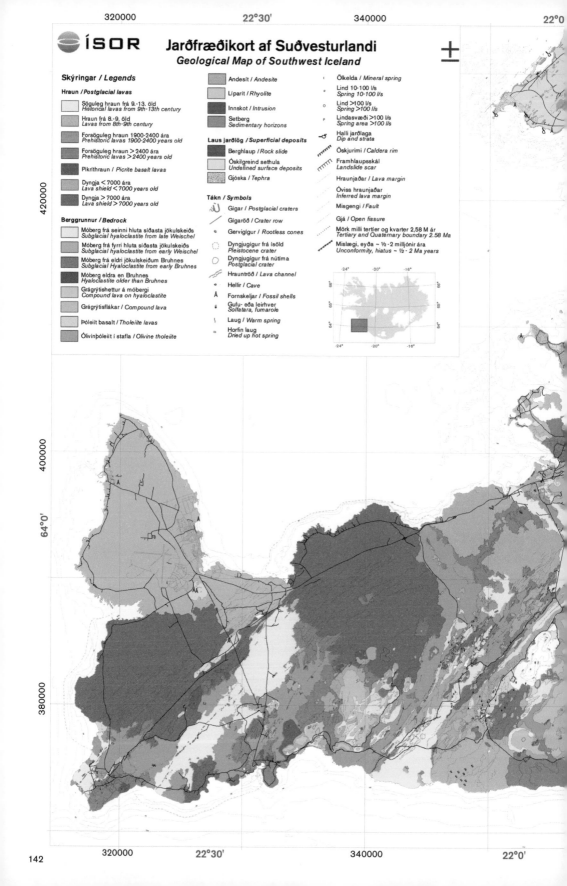

ÍSOR   Jarðfræðikort af Suðvesturlandi
Geological Map of Southwest Iceland

Skýringar / Legends

Hraun / Postglacial lavas

Söguleg hraun frá 9.-13. öld
Historical lavas from 9th-13th century

Hraun frá 8.-9. öld
Lavas from 8th-9th century

Forsöguleg hraun 1900-2400 ára
Prehistoric lavas 1900-2400 years old

Forsöguleg hraun > 2400 ára
Prehistoric lavas >2400 years old

Píkríthraun / *Picrite basalt lavas*

Dyngja < 7000 ára
Lava shield <7000 years old

Dyngja > 7000 ára
Lava shield >7000 years old

Berggrunnur / Bedrock

Móberg frá seinni hluta síðasta jökulskeiðs
Subglacial hyaloclastite from late Weischel

Móberg frá fyrri hluta síðasta jökulskeiðs
Subglacial hyaloclastite from early Weischel

Móberg frá eldri jökulskeiðum Bruhnes
Subglacial Hyaloclastite from early Bruhnes

Móberg eldra en Bruhnes
Hyaloclastite older than Bruhnes

Grágrýtishettur á móbergi
Compound lava on hyaloclastite

Grágrýtisflákar / *Compound lava*

Þóleiít basalt / *Tholeiite lavas*

Ólivinþóleiít í stafla / *Olivine tholeiite*

Andesít / Andesite

Líparít / Rhyolite

Innskot / Intrusion

Setberg / Sedimentary horizons

Laus jarðlög / Superficial deposits

Berghlaup / Rock slide

Óskilgreind sethula
Undefined surface deposits

Gjóska / Tephra

Tákn / Symbols

Gígar / Postglacial craters

Gígaröð / Crater row

Gervigígar / Rootless cones

Dyngjugígur frá ísöld
Pleistocene crater

Dyngjugígur frá nútíma
Postglacial crater

Hrauntröð / Lava channel

Hellir / Cave

Fornskeljar / Fossil shells

Gufu- eða leirhver
Solfatara, fumarole

Laug / Warm spring

Horfin laug
Dried up hot spring

Ölkelda / Mineral spring

Lind 10-100 l/s
Spring 10-100 l/s

Lind >100 l/s
Spring >100 l/s

Lindasvæði >100 l/s
Spring area >100 l/s

Halli jarðlaga
Dip and strata

Öskjurimi / Caldera rim

Framhlaupsskál
Landslide scar

Hraunjaðar / Lava margin

Óviss hraunjaðar
Inferred lava margin

Misgengi / Fault

Gjá / Open fissure

Mörk milli tertíer og kvarter 2,58 M ár
Tertiary and Quaternary boundary 2.58 Ma

Mislægi, eyða ~ ½ - 2 milljónir ára
Unconformity, hiatus ~ ½ - 2 Ma years

420000

400000

64°0'

380000

0   4   8   12   16 Km

Andosols are generally fertile soils that can store large amounts of water, but they are very susceptible to frost. These soils are classified as Brown Andosols.[2] Wetlands have formed in the depressions with soils that are higher in organic content and can be up to several metres thick, but they are mostly classified as Histic Andosols or Gleyic Andosols. In between, there are areas of poor vegetation covered with silty materials on the surface; these soils are also defined as Andosols (Vitrisols according to the Icelandic scheme), and they are dominated by poorly weathered volcanic glass and basaltic rock fragments.

The dominance of Brown Andosols in the Reykjavik area is due to the fact that the overall chemical composition of basaltic hyaloclastites, interglacial and present lavas are all the same, even though the depth of the soil on recent lavas is shallower than soil formed on ice-age volcanic rocks, as soil formation is slow in the cold Atlantic climate.

The grey basaltic lava was used as a building material in the 19th century, the Alþingi (parliament) building in the centre of Reykjavik being a good example. In the middle of the 20th century laws were passed to ensure that all houses of more than one storey had to be built from iron-reinforced concrete and more recently buildings have been raised with a reinforcing steel frame (for example a 17-storey tower in Borgartún).

Many of the Reykjavik area shorelines have been created using infill from the rocks found in mines outside the Reykjavik area. These fillings are part of a major operation that has occurred over the past 50 years and on these harbours, roads, industrial and residential areas have been developed, with no apparent thought for climate change and an imminent rise in the sea level, that could be as high as two metres this century.[3] The soil that will develop on these fillings is also Brown Andosol because of the basaltic material used for the filling. It is important to note that soil that has been scraped off the bedrock in one area of Reykjavik has been transported to place on top of the rock fillings, as well as onto golf courses, that are scattered around the Reykjavik area. This particular movement of material is one aspect of a monumental movement of material by man that is now annually more than ten times that of all natural forces,[4] causing a major alteration of our planet.

1 Soil map of Iceland. http://k-sql.lbhi.is/desert/kort/ice_soilmap_apr02.pdf
2 Arnalds O. (2008) *Soils of Iceland.* Jökull 58, 409-421.
3 Leverman A., Clark P., Merzeion B., Milne G., Pollard D., Radic V. and Robinson A. (2013) *The multimillennial sea-level commitment of global warming.* Proceedings of the National Academy of Sciences. DOI:10.1073/pnas.1219414110.
4 Wilkinson B.H. (2005) *Humans as geologic agents: A deep-time perspective.* Geology 33, 161-164.

2 Previous page: Geoligical map of Southwest Iceland

3 Below: Map showing where lavas could flow in future
eruptions: lava flows in grey, fissures in orange
and new building developments in green.

Water

Ursula Zuehlke

The hydrological cycle, driven by the sun, describes the natural movement of water: water evaporates or transpires through vegetation, forms clouds, falls on the earth's surface, remains there in depressions or piled up as snow, melts, infiltrates into the ground and flows freely above or below surface, forms streams into lakes or the oceans, and evaporates again from all stages.

In urban areas, the hydrological cycle is modified by changes in the vegetation cover, impervious surfaces (mostly roofs, roads and car parks), faster runoff in drainage facilities, reduced infiltration and evapotranspiration, modifications in the flow of streams and withdrawal of water from reservoirs,[1] yet the water supply system is fundamental to any city.

In the Reykjavík Capital Area, water enters as precipitation, as groundwater or surface water streams, and sometimes from the sea. Geothermal water, fresh drinking water and process water is supplied from wells, and some embedded water is imported via food and products.

The pathways through this system reveal what happens; water in the capital's rivers supports salmon, produces energy, allows for recreation, nourishes green areas and gardens, or it just passes through the city. Along its path, the water may get contaminated to a larger or lesser extent. Freshwater and hot water for space heating pass the distribution system, flow through homes, factories and swimming pools, and are then dealt with in the sewage system. Alternatively, it remains for some time in wetlands, poodles or lakes; when there is overflow, it may leak into basements of buildings. Ultimately, water leaves this system when it enters the ocean, most of it through rivers and the waste water system. A certain amount enters the atmosphere, and some of it is carried away, embedded in products.

Hydrology

Rain in Reykjavik, along with the wind and the hilly topography, are commonly used as excuses to bike less and drive more, even though precipitation in Reykjavik is only 800 mm in an average year. 7% of that falls as snow,[2] but the snow often does not remain for prolonged periods. Precipitation increases considerably with land elevation, consequently the mountains surrounding Reykjavík receive much more. Precipitation in the skiing area Bláfjöll, 30 km outside of town, is 3000 mm.

In residential architecture, flat or only slightly sloping roofs suggest that rain would not be an issue in Reykjavík. However owners frequently discover leakages.[3] Due to the strong winds, umbrellas easily get damaged and are actually a rare sight.

The capital area is situated on the coast, by the sub-arctic Atlantic Ocean (see map overleaf). The ocean is simultaneously a rich source of food and a sink of city waste water, albeit treated. The rising sea level is perceived as a threat only in the distant future.

The coastal location of Reykjavik benefits industrial areas and makes sea transportation possible. There is a wide-reaching 'blue ribbon' of cycling and walking paths along the shore, and many inhabitants simply enjoy the sea view from their homes and elsewhere. The Gulf Stream brings to Iceland temperatures that are warmer than expected for its location just south of the Arctic Circle.

Throughout history, water has been a factor in city planning: the wetlands at Vatnsmýri (Water Marsh), which are close to the earliest settlements, provided peat as fuel, and water for an early clothing industry.[4] [5]

For many decades, while the population of the city was growing rapidly, wetlands were avoided for establishing new neighbourhoods,[6] and that is one reason why the built area is so dispersed. The trend has continued to some

extent to the present day, but for different reasons, such as the higher locations offering better views. However, the lower areas are being drained and developed, and they accommodate, in particular, transportation axes and the city airport.

The geology of the bedrock determines whether water enters an area as groundwater or surface water. Where the lava is young, it is porous and virtually all the water seeps into the ground, flows as groundwater streams and resurfaces again in certain locations, for example at Straumsvík in Hafnarfjörður. These types of conditions prevail in the southern part of the capital area, and account for the absence of rivers there. Older bedrock is less permeable, and for this reason more water runs off on the surface, forming rivers in the northern part of the capital area, including most of the city development.

There are rivers and lakes with their surrounding green areas, and four rivers within the Reykjavik area are home to salmon. In one of them, Elliðaár river, a small hydroelectric power station, established in 1921, produces electricity (3.2 MW) from October to April.[7] However, the western arm increasingly suffers from polluted runoff in the lower parts.[8] Varmá (warm river), used to carry natural warm water fed by hot springs close by, most of which have disappeared today.[9] Úlfarsá river is in a slightly better condition: new neighbourhoods allow an ample buffer zone but again, transportation infrastructure encroaches the river and threatens the water quality and the natural flow.[10]

The rivers at the margin of the capital area still flow in their natural beds, but the creeks on the Reykjavík peninsula were buried in pipes below ground during the first half of the 20th century. Of those, Lækurinn connects the pond in the city centre with the shore, and its reopening is under discussion today.[11] Another creek, Laugarlækur (Washing Creek), also carried warm water in the past and it was used for washing clothes, as well as for bathing.

The lakes in the capital area are typically 1-2 km² in size, or smaller. They are increasingly encroached upon by the expanding city, examples being Elliðavatn, Urriðavatn in Garðabæ or Ástjörn in Hafnarfjörður. But they remain popular as peaceful recreational areas, and angling is a favourite pastime in Elliðavatn. The pond in the city centre has fared the worst. Historically, it has served as a waste dump, and subsequently duck feeding became popular there, which also entails some pollution by affecting the composition of the flora and fauna. Air pollution, and unclean runoff from the city centre and the airport, are among the factors that disturb water quality and biological resources.[12] [13]

Iceland implemented the EU water framework directive in 2011, and this aims to achieve good qualitative and quantitative status for all water bodies, including the shore. Judging by the samples taken along the shore, coastal water quality is rather good, and the heated beach in Nauthólsvik was awarded the blue flag ecolabel for beaches and marinas. Bacterial counts are lower in summer than in winter, and they occasionally exceed the allowed limit, often because of waste water outlet overflow. Short-term monitoring with the use of mussels has shown that heavy metal load at the waste water outlet is within limits.[14] [15]

Industry also contributes to freshwater and sea pollution. The aluminium smelter at the southern fringe of the capital area is a polluter because of the spent pot linings that are disposed of close to the shore, as well as outfall from air emissions, carried directly to the sea, and through runoff water. The main pollutants in air emissions are fluoride, dust and sulphur dioxide, and also polyaromatic hydrocarbons, albeit in low quantities.[16]

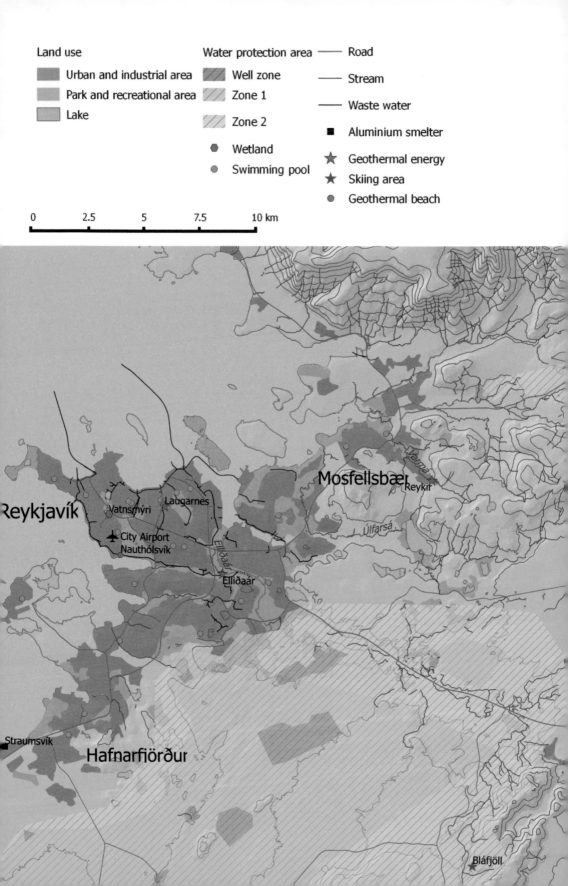

Land use	Water protection area	
Urban and industrial area	Well zone	— Road
Park and recreational area	Zone 1	— Stream
Lake	Zone 2	— Waste water
	Wetland	■ Aluminium smelter
	Swimming pool	★ Geothermal energy
		★ Skiing area
		● Geothermal beach

0   2.5   5   7.5   10 km

Reykjavík

Vatnsmýri

Laugarnes

City Airport
Nauthólsvík

Elliðaár

Elliðaár

Mosfellsbær

Reykir

Varmá

Úlfarsá

Straumsvík

Hafnarfjörður

Bláfjöll

Rainwater Management

Since the beginning of the 20th century, the drainage system in the old town has been laid out as a combined sewer. In the areas built up after the 1960s, the sanitary and surface water systems have been kept separate. The sanitary sewer is connected to the mechanical treatment plants, while surface water is discharged into the sea or the nearest river.

To improve water quality in rivers, a number of retention ponds have been constructed, where heavy metals are supposed to settle

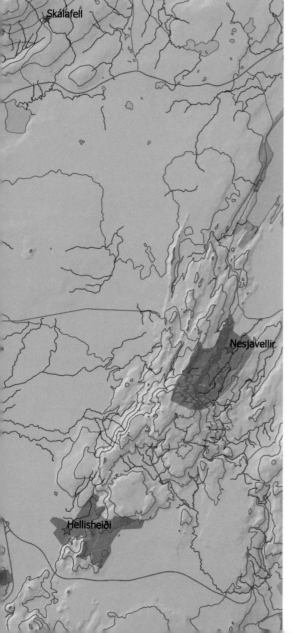

at the bottom, and oils and fats float to the surface where they are expected to evaporate. Furthermore, these ponds are thought to act as a buffer against an inflow, in the event of a major oil or paint spill accident occurring. As for soluble pollutants like road salts, retention ponds cannot do much to help.[17]

Heavy metal pollution of receivers is estimated to increase, as larger areas of their watershed are covered by impervious surfaces.[18] The cause is mostly motorised traffic, but of course rainwater does already contain a certain degree of heavy metals.[19] Sewage connected to the stormwater system, whether intentionally or through error, further increases river and coastal pollution. Similarly, pollutants resulting from maintenance activities, including detergents, oils and paints, can find their way into stormwater drains.

Urriðaholt, a new suburb being planned for Garðarbær is the showcase for sustainable urban drainage solutions, close to a sensitive lake. Swales, or low vegetated depressions, are being proposed along the streets, to allow infiltration of all surface water. Consequently, zinc, copper, lead in paint and building materials are all forbidden.[20] In Kauptún, the nearby commercial area, one of the buildings has been fitted with a green roof, and alternative surface water solutions were explored during the making of the car park area. However, in the course of this process, no thought has been given to the actual construction, size or lack of demand management of the car park itself, despite the fact that it is one of the biggest in the country, and extends into the wetlands.

Floods

In 1799, the rise of the sea level due to high tides, combined with low pressure and wind, brought about the infamous Básenda flood.[21] In the current proposal for the Reykjavík master plan potential flooding areas have been identified, but included among them are areas open for development. The sea level is expected to rise by 0.58-0.99 m up until the end of the century.[22] Planners and politicians, however, perceive the rise only as a threat in the distant future. In view of the various flood events in Europe during the summer of 2013, the question of whether this could happen in Reykjavík should be addressed. Two major floods occurred in Elliðaár in 1968, and then in February 1982, as a result of rain and snow melt;[23] and the dam at Elliðaár burst in 1968.[24] The buffer zone around Elliðaár is large enough to prevent high waters inflicting damage on residential areas. However, varying water flow velocity can cause damage to the riverbed and erosion on the river banks.

Smaller urban watersheds with a high degree of imperviousness can be prone to flooding during heavy rainfall. The maximum rainfall per hour in Reykjavík has been measured as 18.2mm[25] and water regularly flows into basements.[26] New solutions need to be developed in the future, to counteract these trends.

Freshwater provision and consumption

At the beginning of the 20th century, about 34 wells were located in Reykjavík and wealthier families employed people to deliver water to their doorstep. At that time, average household consumption was 18 litres per person per day.[27] The drinking water for Reykjavik comes from groundwater streams in Heiðmörk; it is low in ions and can be delivered without needing further treatment.

Surrounding the wells in Heiðmörk is a water protection area which increasingly gets put under pressure. During the boom, new housing areas were built within its limits; and Heiðmörk is the city's main recreation area, with the attendant increase in transportation and tourism. There has been a recent oil spill in the Bláfjöll skiing region, which also belongs to the protected area, and there are issues with summer house septic tanks.[28] A high voltage transmission line is being planned through the area, and this is to feed an aluminium plant in Helguvík; risks will inevitably accompany this construction.

Average estimated household water consumption in Reykjavík today is 150 litres per person per day. Residential consumption is charged by square metres of floor area. Water consumption is metered only for commercial and public users. The total consumption is 26 million m³ (825 litres/s) for a population of 120,000.[29] More than half of the water is used by commercial and public users. There is some water-intensive industry in the capital area, such as fish and meat processing, as well as manufacture that requires water for cooling. The aluminium smelter, south of Hafnarfjörður, produces 200,000 tons of aluminium per year and requires more than 400 litres/s[30] – enough for 67,000 people, a third of the capital region's population.

Water consumption in Iceland is quite high when compared to the World Health Organisation's minimum requirement of 20 litres per person as a minimum for basic hygiene and basic food hygiene.[31] Throughout the rest of the world, agriculture accounts for 70% of freshwater consumption, but not so in Iceland. For instance, to produce one ton of grain, 1000 tons of water is needed,[32] so a water consumption footprint of sorts ('embedded' water) is imported when grain is imported. Likewise, fish production (cleaning, cooling) is water-intensive, and fish exports follow 'embedded' water. Due to the relative abundance of water in Iceland, export of water has been tried or considered; as bottled water, since 1990,[33] [34] and in bulk on tanker ships (100,000 m³).[35] Setting aside the question of whether export of water is beneficial or not, this shows that Icelanders look at their water resources within an international context, in the same way as they advertise their beautiful waterfalls for the tourist market.

Geothermal water

Geothermal water used to come from boreholes within the city area in Laugarnes, Elliðaárdalur and Reykir in Mosfellsbær, and is now complemented from the geothermal areas at Nesjavellir and Hellisheiði. The geothermally-heated water cools by 0.4-2 °C on its 27 km journey to Reykjavík.[36]

Hot water consumption ranges from 1000 l/s during the summer to 3500 l/s during the winter.

With geothermal water production, hydrogen sulfide (H_2S) is released. The intense rotten egg smell from the hot water does not go unnoticed by foreign visitors. It is unsuitable for drinking but is said to be excellent for bathing.[37] There are 20 open air swimming pools in the capital area, used extensively by the locals all year round, and a warm water lagoon at Nauthólsvík. The entrance fees are affordable (although on the increase), unlike the more famous Blue Lagoon catering for wealthy tourists.

Hot water service provision, in new unfinished neighbourhoods with only a few complete houses, has proved wasteful and very costly.[38]

Waste water management

Recently, the capital area has built a new sewage system, with the two treatment plants inaugurated in 1998 and 2002 respectively. Sewage is sent to the plants and, after a mechanical cleaning stage, waste water is pumped 5 km out into the fjord. The sludge is brought to a landfill site. Whenever there is a capacity problem due to intense precipitation, the surplus sewage is discharged through outlets. According to regulation, this may happen 5% of the time. Further biological treatment is considered to be too expensive, because the sewage is very diluted.[39]

Once the water reaches the ocean, its journey through the city is complete.

Reykjavík is a lucky place when it comes to water. It is available, both hot and cold, in high quality and in abundance, and the sea is a nonsensitive receiver for waste water. Furthermore, precipitation and the risk of flooding is relatively low. It must not be forgotten, however, that water is a precious resource, and in the future, even greater emphasis should be placed on managing it sustainably, both in Iceland and everywhere else.

1 Thorolfsson, Sveinn T., *Stormwater Management in Cold Climate*. Trondheim: NTNU, March 14 2012. http://bit.ly/18ffq5g

2 Jónsson, Trausti, *Snjór í Reykjavík og á Akureyri*. Reykjavík: Veðurstofa Islands, March 15 2012. http://bit.ly/1dJgztB

3 Jónsson, Kristján, 'Að búa í margra bala húsi – eða húsi sem lekur ekki neitt'. Reykjavík: *Morgunblaðið*, 30 September 2007. http://bit.ly/1dJgEh1

4 Náttúruskóli Norræna hússins. *Sýning um fuglana, gróðurinn og mannlífið í Vatnsmýrinni, um náttúruna í borginni og mikilvægi endurheimtar votlendisins*. Reykjavík: Umhverfisraduneyti.is, 2012. http://bit.ly/1cTy0mc

5 Isaksen, Oddgeir, 'Minjar undir malbiki Fornleifaskráning í þéttbýli'. Reykjavík: *Skemman*, January 2011. http://bit.ly/1eBCnmE

6 Kristjánsdóttir, Sigríður, *Þróun byggðar út frá náttúrufarslegum forsendum*. 2005. http://bit.ly/17H3r11

7 Virkjanir-Elliðaárvirkjun. Reykjavík: Orkuveita Reykjavíkur, 2013. http://www.or.is/um-or/virkjanir

8 *Aðgerðir gegn mengun í Elliðaám*. Reykjavík: Morgunblaðið, 19 October 1995. http://www.mbl.is/greinasafn/grein/228192/

9 *Flokkun vatna á Kjósarsvæði Varmá*. Rannsókna- og fræðasetur Háskóla Íslands í Hveragerði, 2003. http://www.eftirlit.is/files/21/20080315142623671.pdf

10 Thors, Stefán and Sigurðardóttir, Hólmfríður. *Mislæg gatnamót Hringvegar og Víkurvegar og Reynisvatnsvegur að Reynisvatni, Reykjavík*. Úrskurður Skipulagsstofnunar um mat á umhverfisáhrifumun, 2000. http://goo.gl/8mAqlu

11 Helgason, Egill, 'Brúin yfir Lækinn'. Eyjan, October 12 2012. http://eyjan.pressan.is/silfuregils/2012/10/12/bruin-yfir-laekinn/

12 Malmquist, Hilmar J., Ingimarsson, Finnur, Ingvason, Haraldur Rafn and Stefánsson, Stefán Már, *Mengunarflokkun á Reykjavíkurtjörn*.

Reykjavík: Reykjavíkurborg, 2008. http://bit.ly/11hJAEQ

13 Nielsen, Ólafur Karl et al., *Tjörnin saga og lífríki*. Reykjavík: Reykjavíkurborg, 1992.

14 *Vöktun strandsjávar*. Reykjavík: Reykjavíkurborg, Umhverfis- og skipulagssvið, http://bit.ly/1eQaAzj

15 Ólafsdóttir, Kristín Lóa and Steinarsdóttir, Svava S., *Vöktun á vatnsgæðum strandsjávar í Reykjavík 2003-2010*. 2010. http://bit.ly/

16 Hönnun. *Stækkun ISAL í Straumsvík, mat á umhverfisáhrifum*, 2002. http://goo.gl/T8C0GS

17 Vollertsen, Guðbjörg Esther, 'Removal of Heavy Metals in a Wet Detention Pond in Reykjavík'. Reykjavík: Skemman, 2010.

18 Háskólasetrið í Hveragerði. *Mengunarflokkun Hólmsár, Suðurár og Elliðaáa*. Reykjavík: Reykjavíkurborg, 2004. http://bit.ly/18FYNox

19 Gunnarsdóttir, María J., 'Neysluvatnsgæði og vatnsvernd'. *Skemman*, January 2 2005. http://skemman.is/item/view/1946/13275

20 *Umhverfisáherslur í Urriðaholti*. Garðabær, January 10 2007. http://goo.gl/hG7kg6

21 Hjartarson, Árni, 1. *Básendar - Básendaflóð* Reykjavík: Isor, 2010. http://www.isor.is/1-basendar-basendaflod

22 *Aðalskipulag Reykjavíkur 2010-2030, Tillaga, Umhverfisskýrsla*. Reykjavík: Reykjavíkurborg, 2013. http://bit.ly/14O42jv

23 Hróðmarsson, Hilmar Björn, Reynisson, Njáll Fannar and Gíslason, Ólafur Freyr, *Flóð íslenskra vatnsfalla – flóðagreining rennslisraða*. Reykjavík: Veðurstofa Islands, 2009. http://bit.ly/18FYv12

24 *Tjónið af Flóðunum sífellt að aukast*. Alþýðublað, 29 February 1968. http://timarit.is/view_page_init.jsp?issId=202216&lang=fo

25 Jónsson, Trausti. *Mesta úrkoma á Íslandi*. Reykjavík: Veðurstofa Islands, 28 September 2007. http://www.vedur.is/vedur/frodleikur/greinar/nr/1049

26 *Vatn flæðir inn í kjallara í Reykjavík*. Reykjavík: Morgunblaðið, 17 August

1991. http://www.mbl.is/greinasafn/grein/72421/

27 *Vatn – Undirstaða lífs á jörðinni*. Orkuveita Reykjavíkur, https://or.is/media/PDF/vatn.pdf

28 Kravec, Alda, 'Oil Spill In Bláfjöll Ski Area Puts Drinking Water At Risk'. *The Reykjavík Grapevine*, September 5 2013. http://bit.ly/1cJHwZs

29 *European Green Capital Application 2012-2013*. Reykjavík: Reykjavíkurborg, 2011. http://reykjavik.is/sites/default/files/graen_skref/reykjavik_application_round_2ny2.pdf

30 Hönnun, *Stækkun ISAL í Straumsvík, mat á umhverfisáhrifum*, 2002. http://www.mannvit.is/media/files/loka_skyrsla.pdf

31 World Health Organization. *What is the minimum quantity of water needed?* 2013. http://bit.ly/1hqRl41

32 Brown, Lester R., Chapter 2. 'Population Pressure: Land and Water: Farmers Losing Water to Cities'. in *Plan B 4.0: Mobilizing to Save Civilization* 2009 Earth Policy Institute. http://www.earthpolicy.org/books/pb4/PB4ch2_ss4

33 'Stígandi útflutningur á vatni'. Reykjavík: *Morgunblaðið*, October 6 1990. http://www.mbl.is/greinasafn/grein/57284/

34 'Jón Gunnar selur vatn í austri'. Reykjavík: *Viðskiptablaðið*, December 8 2011. http://www.vb.is/frettir/68188/

35 Blöndal, Ásbjörn, *Útflutningur á vatni - Aðgengi að vatni og eftirspurn*. Reykjavík: Samorka, 2009. http://goo.gl/5LQhWS

36 *Nesjavallaæð – frá Nesjavallavirkjun til Reykjavíkur*. Reykjavík: Verkís, 2012. http://bit.ly/1ipFWCW

37 *Visitor's Guide, Icelandic water*, http://goo.gl/f5gx61

38 *Vatnssóun í nýjum hverfum*. Reykjavík: RÚV, April 16 2009. http://www.ruv.is/node/77941

39 Guðmundsson, Þórður Ingi, *Úrgangur til orku - Leiðir til að nýta skólp til eldsneytisframleiðslu*. Reykjavík: Skemman, 2012. http://bit.ly/138Tk5s

Planning

Sigríður Kristjánsdóttir

Historical overview

Iceland's unique location, between two continents, has resulted in the impact of different cultures on the development of the society through time, as well as the effects of the physical environment in which it has grown. Traces of planning ideology from Europe and the United States can be deciphered from the planning documents.[1]

A brief discussion of the main factors currently influencing the planning approach in Iceland follows.

The settlement in Reykjavík expanded directly from being a small village, with detached turf or wooden houses, into a modern town planned according to the principles of ruling ideology.

The first book on planning[2] in Icelandic was published in 1916 by Guðmundur Hannesson, a professor of medicine, who was concerned with the living conditions in the town and the risk that was clearly apparent as the centre had caught fire in 1915. Hannesson proposed legislation for town planning in 1917. The first planning law was enacted in 1921, based on his work. The State Planning Committee was established in 1921 to oversee planning in Iceland, but Reykjavík had considerable say in its own planning. In 1924 a joint municipal working committee (state and city) was charged with making a comprehensive plan for the capital city. The comprehensive plan, proposed in 1927, was never confirmed by the planning authorities. However, it did affect the development of the city in the following decades.

The municipality of Reykjavík bought land outside the built-up area well ahead of development. Almost all development in Reykjavík since 1930 has been on land in municipal ownership and the explosive growth of Reykjavík led to decades of day-to-day ad hoc planning solutions. In 1934 Reykjavík got its first architect to design city buildings and draw up local plans.[3]

Danish planning experts introduced the transportation ideology in Iceland in the 1960s. Planning laws were revised in 1964 and the first master plan, based on the new ideology, was published in 1966.

The next comprehensive master plan was accepted in 1987. A long-term planning office had been established in 1972. By the 1980s the days of long descriptive planning documents were over, and the comprehensive plans were revised every four years following elections. After the municipal elections in 1994, the main objective in the city comprehensive plan became the 1992 Rio de Janeiro Local Agenda 21, the blueprint for a sustainable environment.

Until 1997 it was only urban areas that were covered by planning regulations. After 1997 the countrywide planning legislation covered the whole country, for the first time introducing planning of the interior.

Planning during the economic boom

According to the Planning Act No. 73/1997, with later amendments, which was in use during the economic boom, the country as a whole needs to be planned.

The aims of this Act are:

• *to ensure that the development of settlement and land use in the country as a whole will be in accordance with development plans which are based on the economic, social and cultural needs of the population, and also their health and safety;*

• *to encourage the rational and efficient utilisation of land and natural resources, to ensure the preservation of natural and cultural values and to prevent environmental damage and over-exploitation, based on the principles of sustainable development;*

• *to ensure security under the law in the handling of planning and building issues so that the rights of individuals and legal persons will not be neglected even though the common interest is the guiding principle;*

• *to ensure the professional preparation of development, and active monitoring, to ensure that the requirements regarding safety, durability, appearance and suitability of buildings and other structures are fulfilled.[4]*

The planning system

The Minister for the Environment has supreme control of planning. Development plans fall into three categories: regional plans, municipal plans and local plans. Development plans are presented in a statement, and on a land use map.

• *Regional plan: A development plan covering more than one municipality. The role of a regional plan is to coordinate policies regarding land use, transportation and service systems, environmental matters and the development of settlement in the region, during a period of not less than 12 years.*

• *Municipal plan: A development plan for a specific municipality expressing the local authority's policy regarding land use, transportation and service systems, environmental matters and the development of settlement in the municipality, during a period of not less than 12 years.*

• *Local plan: A development plan for specific areas within a municipality, based on the municipal plan and containing further provisions for its implementation. Local planning provisions apply equally to urban and rural areas.*

In theory, the lower levels of government should operate within the framework of the objects set out in the policy of the higher level. In turn, the policy of the higher level should provide general guidelines within which plans proposed at lower level can be realised. The local authorities examine applications for permission, grant building permits and development permits, and carry out building inspection with the assistance of elected committees and specialised employees.

Other influences

The Strategic Environmental Assessment Act (SEA) was adopted in Iceland in 2006, stressing sustainability issues. Since then, environmental assessment of planning proposals has been mandatory, and planning proposals may be improved following the evaluations.

The legislation related to land use was changed in 2004.[5] The purpose of the law is to regulate the rights and duties of landowners, and facilitate controlled land use given the features of the land, pluralistic purpose of agriculture and the benefits of municipalities and their inhabitants, as well as ensuring that the most suitable land will remain in agricultural use. One of its purposes is to ease the access to land by the public, and to facilitate the change of ownership.

The legislation applies to all exploitable land in Iceland which has not been taken from agricultural use by the master plan or any other. The ministry has never objected to land being removed from agricultural use by planning authorities.

The government-owned Housing Financing Fund (HFF) was established in 1999, strengthening the government's main pillar of housing policy, i.e. giving every homebuyer access to a mortgage at the lowest possible interest rate. The HFF's bond issuance was changed in 2004, lowering its financing cost, and passing lower rates to mortgage borrowers. The HFF's lending terms were also changed, easing the access to credit, as the loan to value ratio was raised to 90% of the purchase price. In 2004 the HFF was for the first time subject to aggressive competition from banks. Housing investment increased significantly, and the demand for new land for housing developments grew.

After the economic crash in 2008

The planning and building act was split in 2010, resulting in separate legislation to deal with planning, and with building and building regulation. The responsibility for planning, and for building regulations, falls under different agencies.

The aims of this Act are:

• to ensure that the development of settlement and land use in the country as a whole will be in accordance with development plans which are based on the economic, social and cultural needs of the population, and also their health and safety;

• to encourage the rational and efficient utilisation of land and natural resources, to ensure the preservation of natural and cultural values and to prevent environmental damage and over-exploitation, based on the principles of sustainable development;

• to ensure security under the law in the handling of planning issues so that the rights of individuals and legal persons will not be neglected, even though the common interest is the guiding principle;

• to ensure public participation in the making of development plans in order to allow the people to influence political decision regarding planning;

• to ensure the professional preparation of development plans regarding appearance and form of buildings and accessibility for all.[6]

The methodology for national planning was also amended. Descriptions of planning proposals are now required, facilitating involvement of the public at early stages in the process.

The Minister for the Environment presents a national planning policy to the parliament for approval within two years after elections. The policy is therefore revised every four years. A regional plan is now mandatory for the capital region but optional in other areas.[7]

The Minister of the Environment decided, in spring 2002, to revise the planning and building act nr. 73/1997, with later amendments.[8] One of the goals set for the new legislation enacted in 2010 was to increase the efficiency and flexibility of the planning process; it affected the publication of planning proposals, changed the development plans and their processing, and gave clarification to their role and the connections between development plans at different planning stages. This was in response to the pressures encountered during the economic and building boom of 2003-2008. The other goal was to initiate a national planning strategy. The government and the municipalities could not reach agreement, and the compromise found kept the main responsibility for planning with the municipalities, while the government was supposed to introduce its vision in the national planning policy, which combines official plans for transportation, urban issues, environmental protection, energy use, and sets out the government's plan for sustainability with a view to land use.

Although the new law was enacted in 2010, shortly after the crash in 2008, it had been brewing since 2002. It included some responses to the pressures felt by planning authorities during the boom, but it did not tackle the root causes of the boom. The law was not articulated in regulations until 2013.[9] It is still too early to judge the effects of the new law and it is difficult to assess if they have had any significant impact.

Discussion of current affairs

There have been dramatic changes to the urban landscape in Iceland between 2000 and 2013. The planning policy in Reykjavik has been oriented around transportation, causing the city

to sprawl. The housing boom between 2003 and 2008 dramatically shifted the benchmarks in Iceland, as well as affecting the planning sector and the physical urban landscape of Reykjavík. The severe downturn has left its mark, where abandoned and half-built suburbs stand as a token of broken dreams.

The extensive swings during the recent business cycle raised public awareness of planning. General interest in planning grew with the raised demand for public participation. In 2009 the first independent academic programme in planning in Iceland was established at the Agricultural University of Iceland.

The population used to be spread fairly evenly along the coast of the country 100 years ago, but nowadays about 64% lives in Reykjavík and the surrounding area, on the outskirts of an active volcanic zone. Regional plans are mandatory in the capital region only. The Association of Municipalities in the Capital Area (SSH) is currently working on a new regional plan.[10] In other regions it had been too detailed in the past, tying the hands of municipal authorities at the lower planning stages.

The City of Reykjavík is the leading force in planning in Iceland, a pioneer in evolving and implementing new ideologies which other municipalities often follow. So-called neighbourhood plans are intended for older districts in which local plans are out of date or missing, and these allow for small-scale developments. New projects on a grander scale require detailed local plans.

In spring 2013 parliament began preparing new legislation on nature preservation which was to be enacted in April 2014. Some overlap between the new legislation and the current planning laws, such as the restrictions on municipalities' planning authority, and lack of public consensus, caused the minister to withdraw the Nature Conservation Act before it was passed.

The Master Plan for hydro and geothermal energy resources in Iceland, a separate law on preservation and energy-utilisation plans commonly referred to as The Frame Plan (rammaáætlun), came into effect in January 2013.[11] This is yet another law dealing with land use planning, partially replacing the regional plan for Iceland's interior (The Highlands). This, too, has caused debate and is under revision.

The current discussion, and postponement and revisions of these new legislations, hint at the importance of wide agreement on these critical issues. Given more time for preparation, the current conflicts and overlaps between the nature and energy preservation acts, and the general planning legislations, will undoubtedly be solved. The national planning policy must lay out the government's vision for development and building in the country as a whole, combining various forms of land use. It must be guided by the welfare of the nation.

Conclusions

At the height of the recent economic boom, the building sector felt hindered by regulations. There was constant pressure to simplify the planning process, increasing its efficiency and speed. The revision of the planning law started well before the crash and it is therefore not an adequate response to the problems which resulted from the overheating and the ensuing collapse.

It remains an open question whether the people of Iceland, or even the relevant specialists, do in fact see the connection between planning, the business cycle and the crisis.

The next revision of the planning laws should consider the incorporation of guidelines which would have countercyclical effects, so as to dampen the boom and bust cycle and hopefully hinder the formation of housing bubbles. It is a topic requiring further research.

1 Kristjánsdóttir, S., *Deciphering the contemporary urban landscape of Reykjavík, Iceland, by applying the concepts and methods of Caniggia and Conzen*. PhD thesis, University of Birmingham, 2007.
2 Hannesson, G., *Um skipulag bæja*. Reykjavík 1916.
3 Kristjánsdóttir, S., *Deciphering the contemporary urban landscape of Reykjavík, Iceland, by applying the*

concepts and methods of Caniggia and Conzen. PhD thesis, University of Birmingham, 2007.
4 See: http://goo.gl/knmuVX
5 *Jarðalög* number 81/2004, http://www.althingi.is/lagas/142/2004081.html
6 http://www.althingi.is/altext/138/s/0742.html Translation by author as official text is not available in English.

7 Planning Act no. 123/2010, http://www.althingi.is/lagas/138b/2010123.html
8 http://www.althingi.is/lagas/138b/1997073.html
9 http://www.skipulagsstofnun.is/media/pdf-skjol/B_nr_90_2013.pdf
10 http://www.ssh.is/
11 http://www.rammaaaetlun.is/english

Economy

Lúðvík Elíasson

Iceland is one of the world's largest islands and also one of the most sparsely populated, with 322,000 inhabitants occupying 103,000 km² (40,000 sq. miles). The country is about the size of Kentucky, somewhat larger than Hungary and a little smaller than Bulgaria. About one fifth of the country has some vegetation. About 63% of the total area is categorised as wasteland, with cold deserts and lava fields included, and glaciers cover another 11%.[1]

Production and Trade

The bulk of consumer and investment goods are imported, whilst the focus for exports has been on natural resources. Traditionally the main exports were farm products but fish and associated products took over as the main source of foreign revenue as early as 1878. The fishing industry accounted for over 80% of the value of exported goods between 1920 and 1970, and 90% or more between 1947 and 1966.

Since 1970, aluminium production has widened the variety of exports. It uses a substantial proportion of the country's electricity output. The value of exported aluminium was on average 37% of goods exported from 2008 to 2012, with fish products averaging 40% during the same period. The majority of raw materials needed for the aluminium have to be imported, and the smelters are foreign-owned. It is, therefore, a relatively small part of the value added in this sector of industry that accrues in Iceland – mostly due to the electricity consumption, and domestic labour. In a sense, aluminium production is a means of exporting electricity generated by the hydroelectric and geothermal power plants, thereby utilising the country's natural resources. The fast-growing tourism sector, and recent marketing drive for Iceland as a film location, adds another dimension to the list of exported resources ie. the natural environment.

Urbanisation and Housing

Urban formation is a recent phenomenon, and the capital region is by far the largest urban area in the country. The rate of urbanisation in the past century was dramatic, and by 2013 73% of the population was living in towns with no fewer than 10,000 inhabitants. The capital region accounted for 205,000 of those inhabitants, or 64% of the population.

Housing policy in Iceland was, for the largest part of the twentieth century, aimed at meeting

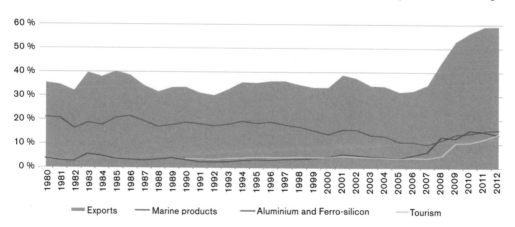

Exports — Marine products — Aluminium and Ferro-silicon — Tourism

1 Exports of goods and services as a % of GDP. Exports of marine products, aluminium and ferro-silicon, plus revenues from tourism, account for three quarters of all exports; each of these categories constitute roughly 15% of GDP.[2]

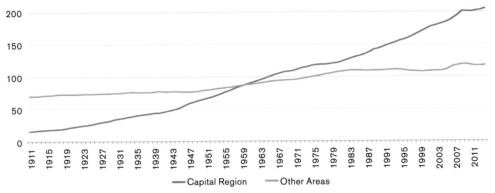

2 Population growth has in the last one hundred years largely been concentrated in the capital region. The graph shows the number of people (in thousands) living in the capital region and in other parts of the country.[3]

the high and increasing demand for housing which stemmed from rapid population growth and, more importantly, rapid urbanisation. The emphasis later shifted towards the financing of housing in general. Housing policy in Iceland has become synonymous with mortgages backed by a government guarantee.

The National Housing Agency, founded in 1957, was the government's main vehicle for its housing policy, and offered both traditional and inflation-linked mortgages. During the early seventies rampant inflation had driven most of the other suppliers of mortgages, banks and pension providers, out of the market as they were not allowed to link their lending to the price level. The Workers' Building Fund had been established in the thirties to finance the building of owner-occupied housing for low income families, but it was taken over by the National Housing Agency in 1970, and subsequently the agency served as the main source for financing social housing.

It was during the eighties and nineties that the National Housing Agency increased its emphasis on financing housing transactions rather than building new houses. Total lending by the agency grew significantly, reaching as much as 6% of GDP in 1991 (fig. 3). In 1999 the body was replaced by the Housing Financing Fund. Any social objectives linked to the housing policy gradually evaporated, and by 2004 the government-owned Fund simply oper-ated as a mortgage bank. Despite leveraging the government guarantee on its funding, it was unable to withstand increased competition in the mortgage market. Since its formation in 1999, losses incurred by the Housing Finance Fund stood at 6% of GDP in 2012 and further losses on its assets, to be realised in the coming years, have been estimated at an additional 2-10% of GDP.[4]

Tradition of "Over-Housing"

During the sixties and seventies long-term borrowing was effectively subsidised by inflation, since the value of repayments kept falling faster than anticipated. A ban on indexation of bank loans in the seventies, along with government-imposed rates of interest, resulted in an increase in demand for lending alongside a falling supply. The government reacted by borrowing more from abroad, and struggled to keep funds flowing through its mortgage programme. As the value of repayments made by borrowers was only a fraction of the value borrowed, this resulted in over-investment in housing. People became too accustomed to being able to buy and furnish houses in a manner they could not have achieved, had they been required to repay the value of the mortgages received.[5] Indexation of debt was legalised in 1979, and it put an end to the use of the mortgage market to redistribute assets from lenders to borrowers. It resurfaced, however, around the turn of the century when ever-increasing amounts of international savings searching for yield, coupled with the advance of newly liberalised Icelandic banks seeking funding in international markets, caused excessive volumes of money to be channelled into the country. The purchasing power of disposable income continued to rise while ample inflow of foreign funding, increased competition in the mortgage market and financial innovation, in addition to universal indexation, all contributed to the lowering of the initial repayment burden of mortgages. The outcome was, once again, homebuyers committing a share of their future income to mortgage payments that was more than they could truly afford.

Recent Housing Boom Bust Cycle

The rise in purchasing power during the past decade, supported by a strong currency and accumulation of foreign debt, resulted in widespread investment in luxury apartments that were beyond the means of most people in normal purchasing conditions. This development did not occur in isolation, but was triggered by external and domestic factors combined. Domestic demand and a rise in asset prices stemmed from certain external factors: the global savings glut,[6] with an increased supply from countries with ageing populations, oil-exporting countries, and others wishing to accumulate large foreign currency reserves; low interest rate policies at the leading central banks; financial innovation, including collateralised debt obligations and credit default swaps,[7] that facilitated increased lending to low income households (known as sub-prime lending); generous rating agencies that awarded top ratings to the funding of such loans.[8]

The domestic factors encompassed both expansionary fiscal policies and loose monetary policy. During the early years of the century, fiscal policies were aimed at raising the purchasing power of disposable income. The government promoted, and participated in, large-scale investment projects in the energy-intensive sector, enacted widespread tax cuts, and led a restructuring of the mortgage market. The formerly government-owned banks were privatised, while changes in financial regulations encouraged them to multiply their lending. Mortgage financing was one of the sectors with the most potential for lending growth, and competition between a number of the

lenders increased the availability of low interest mortgages. Meanwhile, the government-owned Housing Financing Fund tried aggressively to consolidate its share in the mortgage market in the face of this increased competition. Loan limits and loan to value ratios were raised, reaching 90% of the value of the purchased apartment in deals with the Housing Financing Fund, and even temporarily up to 100% on loans with further restrictions with some other mortgage lenders. At the same time, documentation and credit checks were all too often relaxed, particularly by the government organisation. Real interest rates were too low and the currency was too strong. The banks had easy access to liquidity in the national currency, Icelandic krónur, at the Central Bank and could borrow, to an excessive degree, from abroad. Following their privatisation at the start of the century, the banks were operating in accordance with European rules and they opened branches and subsidiaries in other European countries. Attracting foreign funding was easy, at least for a while, but putting the money to use on foreign soil proved not to be. The Icelandic banks eventually reverted to lending within the domestic markets (including mortgages), in foreign currency which had the temporary effect of lowering repayments still further, while driving up asset prices and debt levels along with their accompanying risks.

The country is still recovering from the economy's worst over-expansion in recent times. An inflated exchange rate and purchasing power, coupled with widespread, but short-sighted, optimism, fuelled temporary growth in the

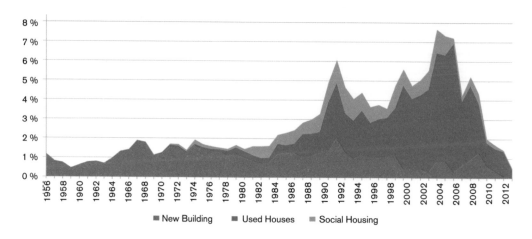

■ New Building ■ Used Houses ■ Social Housing

3 Lending by the National Housing Agency and the Housing Financing Fund, % of GDP.[9]

banking and building sectors. This came to a sudden halt, as the foreign supply of short-term funding for the banks dried up, and the exchange rate plummeted.

During the boom years, demand for luxury apartments was high, and the turnover in the housing market matched it. Many new neighbourhoods were built, particularly in the capital region, and many more planned and later abandoned at various levels of completion. The large, high-class apartments, which were under construction as the tide turned in the financial markets, were no longer in demand.

Looking ahead: Strengths and Weaknesses

Significant success has been achieved in debt-restructuring but nevertheless the economy remains plagued by indebtedness. Capital controls have been in place since late 2008 and these help to keep the currency elevated and support local asset prices. Although this dampened the initial shock, as the economy contracted in 2009, the capital controls are slowly but surely becoming a burden on the economy; investments are guided by their rules and regulations, not just considerations of profitability.

The banking sector shrunk at the time of the crash in 2008, but remains significant. The country's three large international banks, with assets greater than ten times GDP in 2008, are now in the process of being wound up. In their place, three new banks were formed around the existing domestic operations. Refinancing of foreign debt is still largely unresolved, but

market access of financial companies, and large municipal and government-owned firms is increasing. Political risk remains high.

The economy, however, is growing again. Over the past three years real GDP growth has resumed after its two-year drop in 2009 and 2010 when it fell by roughly 10%. Standards of living are still high. The labour force is flexible, and the local currency is still able to absorb some of the imbalances, where required, in order to relax the remaining controls on capital flow. Furthermore, the pension system is still relatively well-funded, and government debt manageable. In addition to this, the country's natural resource management is among the most efficient and sustainable in the world; it ensures continued generation of sufficient foreign revenue to maintain the nation's living standards, despite Iceland's limited manpower resources and its geographic isolation.

A far cry from the dizzy heights of 2005-7, the housing market has nevertheless recovered, and turnover is back at the level seen before the boom years. Real house prices have stabilised at relatively high levels compared to historical averages, but they are currently well below the peak reached in 2007. Debt restructuring is well underway, although there is still considerable risk aversion, and lending has not stopped contracting. Municipalities have been revising their plans, adapting them to the post-boom period, focusing on smaller apartments and denser neighbourhoods than before. Investment in general, and housing investment in particular, is low-key, at a historically small amount.

1 Central Bank of Iceland. *Economy of Iceland*. 2012.
2 Statistics Iceland and the Central Bank of Iceland
3 Statistics Iceland.
4 Special Investigation Commission on the Housing Financing Fund. *Report by the Special Investigation Commission on the Housing Financing Fund*. Alþingi, 2013
5 Jónsson, Bjarni Bragi, *Verðtrygging lánsfjámagns og vaxtastefna á Íslandi*.

Central Bank of Iceland, 1998.
6 Bernanke, Ben S. *The Global Saving Glut and the U.S. Current Account Deficit*. Speech given at the Virginia Association of Economists in Richmond. Virginia, March 10, 2005.
7 Ferguson, Roger W. jr., Hatmann, Philipp, Panetta, Fabio and Portes, Richard, *International Financial Stability*. CEPR, 2007.
8 Special Investigation Commission. *Aðdragandi og orsakir falls íslensku*

bankanna 2008 og tengdir atburðir. Alþingi, 2010.
9 Jónsson, Guðmundur and Magnússon, Magnús S. eds. *Hagskinna – sögulegar hagtölur um Ísland*. Statistics Iceland, 1997 and Special Investigation Commission on the Housing Financing Fund. *Report by the Special Investigation Commission on the Housing Financing Fund*. Alþingi, 2013

Housing

Arna Mathiesen

Between 2000 and 2008, the number of dwellings in Iceland, including those under construction, increased by 26.8 %, whereas the number of inhabitants grew by just 13 %.[1] During the same period, there was also a 33% increase in the number of summerhouses, many of which are inhabitable all year.[2] Around half of the population growth during those years was due to immigration from abroad and a considerable number of those arriving were migrant workers in the construction industry ('The Expansion', part 1).[3]

Following the crash there was a crisis for many homeowners. Negative equity (owing more than the value of a home) among homeowners rose from approximately 6% in 2007 to 37% by the end of 2010.[4] The boom in Iceland puts the future of housing design, urban design, housing production and ownership of housing into a new perspective.

Housing Types in the Boom

The first impression is the striking contrast in housing types in the new neighbourhoods, with accompanying disparities in housing standards, which reflected the increased economic inequality Iceland experienced over the above-mentioned period.[5] On the one hand,

there are quite densely built multi-story apartment blocks, with inadequate outdoor spaces, which tend to be placed on the least attractive sites - the windy northern hillsides, or as a buffer protecting the rest of the residential area from the noisy motorway, polluting industries or prevailing winds. On the other hand, there are detached single-family houses, typically between 300 and 400 m² (3,200 and 4,305 square feet) in size, on the sunny hillsides and/ or by the water. These often have a large part of the private garden surrounded by high fencing to shelter the outdoor space from the winds (a climatic challenge on the barren heaths that has failed to be addressed by the building pattern), thereby greatly limiting interaction between neighbours. While there are certainly exceptions to this dichotomy in splendid penthouse apartments of tower blocks, and unregistered less attractive basement flats in the houses, the aspect of spatial inequalities are better substantiated in an earlier chapter, 'Spatial Inequalities in Reykjavík'.

The block developments had insufficient funds for the design work and it was often undertaken by technologists who had no educational training in architecture or urbanism. For villas and second homes, the standards were set by financial institutions; their innovative

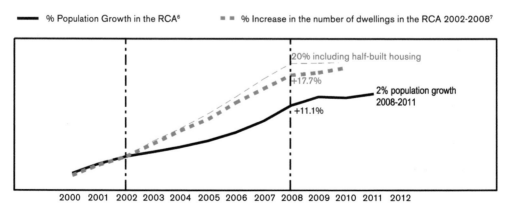

—— % Population Growth in the RCA[6]   ▪ ▪ % Increase in the number of dwellings in the RCA 2002-2008[7]

20% including half-built housing

+17.7%

2% population growth 2008-2011

+11.1%

2000 2001 2002 2003 2004 2005 2006 2007 2008 2009 2010 2011 2012

Availability and Demand

finance packages were designed for buying homes, and viewed the financial elite as role models, reflecting their affluent lifestyles in the built environment. The aspirations can best be illustrated with an example. The top lighting designers were hired to show the buildings (and the future inhabitants?) in the best possible light, quite literally. Even if the specialist found the ideal lighting fixture in a catalogue from an expensive brand, it was still deemed not good enough. Everything had to be specially designed from scratch, so that it would surpass anything available in terms of exclusiveness, even if it meant copying the exact same fixture as the one found in the catalogue.[8] Regardless of how good the edifice looked, illuminating the apparent wealth became questionable after the crash.

The more frequent habitation of areas not primarily designed for residential purposes, such as industrial expanses, is a new trend[9] which can possibly be traced to economic problems. This type of space is not necessarily inexpensive to rent though, and the phenomenon is perhaps also evidence of a demand for alternative housing types from the ones provided in the boom, which were tailored around a traditional family unit of four, living predetermined lifestyles.

Since the meltdown, there are plenty of empty flats and houses. Many of these are in the countryside, but a considerable number are in the greater capital region, as discussed in 'Going for Growth'. This surplus could be treated as a resource, in terms of housing the people. Approximately 3080 apartments in Iceland, owned by loan institutions, lay empty in December 2013, the greatest portion belonging to the state-owned Housing Financing Fund, and half of those defined as inhabitable.[10] At the same time, there was, and still is, a huge shortage of flats available for rent.

The uncertainty regarding the state of the economy following on from the crash converts residential buildings into something beyond a dwelling, and/or a display of the status of its inhabitants. Apartments in the city centre have become popular investment objects for those with excessive capital which, under current circumstances, cannot be taken out of the country as the capital controls severely restrict the export of currency out of Iceland. A new master plan for Reykjavík backs up this trend, as it highlights the qualities of the city centre.

The investments have, moreover, taken on an organised form by the establishment of investment groups of capital owners. These groups have been known to invest in 100 housing units

Typical housing types in the boom settlements.

in the city centre at one fell swoop.[11] As a result, individuals and firms who have capital gained prior to, or after, 2008 can take advantage of the situation, and profit even further at the expense of others who are unable to afford to buy or rent a decent roof over their heads.

Despite the excess of housing units at the time the crash hit, the price of housing has dropped only to the level it was in 2004, and prices are on the rise again.

There is pressure to keep house prices up, because if they drop, homeowners will have paid off a smaller portion of their home, while still owing the same amount of money. When equity (the amount of a home that has been paid off) finally collapses to a position of owning nothing, leaving just debt, the debt is a permanent fixture anyway. This system deviates from the one operating in the US where negative equity owners can walk away without debt, and start from scratch again. A bill to change this, 'Lyklafrumvarpið', was turned down by the Icelandic parliament in 2013. Throughout the period prices are kept high, the housing market remains inaccessible to a large proportion of the population, especially the younger generation, and yet investors profit.

The demand for residential buildings in the centre is at the cost of the new areas on the fringe that shrink before they are completed. So closely linked with the crash, the fringe is not considered a favourable location, and is consequently little in demand.

Ownership

Owning your own home has been considered an important part of welfare, the idea being that an owned home could function as a pension in advanced years. Before the crash, homeownership had been the ruling model for housing in Iceland. From the turn of the century until the financial crash, homeownership was at its peak, when around 90% of the housing stock was owned by the inhabitants.[13] Once the financial meltdown became a reality, however, homeownership turned into a burden for many households, rather than a safety net or even safe haven as it tends to be regarded. The crash has therefore permanently altered the notion of welfare politics through housing.

After the meltdown many people could not afford to pay their mortgages (financial stress), and others were indebted even if they were able to sell their home (negative equity); or in some cases both of these problems arose. The Icelandic króna was devalued by roughly 50%

overnight. For those who had taken mortgages in foreign currencies (as was encouraged in Iceland, but would have been considered a fairly risky business in most countries), the debts doubled. However, the type of loans that about 80% of Icelandic mortgages consist of, could (depending on the composition of the loan) come out even worse as a result of the crash. Such loans are linked to indexes which can change at any time, making future debt unforeseeable. These kinds of mortgages skyrocketed after the crash.[14]

The average equity ratio of the housing mass under private ownership of individuals dropped from 67% in 2005 to 49% in 2010.[15] It effectively meant that Icelandic house owners were, on average, owing more than they had actually paid towards the properties. Everything else was in the hands of loan institutions, for whom the debt of others constitutes assets. These institutions are the state-owned Housing Financing Fund, with 42% of the loans,[16] and banks, almost 50% of which are also state-owned, following a restructuring of the banking system after the meltdown.[17] The banks are also owned by foreign creditors (some of them so-called vulture funds) which can thus be considered de facto owners of a considerable share of the Icelandic housing stock.

Due to the prominent homeownership model, a strong rental market has been lacking, which very much reduces the options for those, ever increasing in number, who cannot afford to buy. Even though it is very difficult for some people to pay their mortgages, they hang on to their property as long as possible because the alternatives to doing that are worse. Housing rent is more expensive and tenants can be thrown out, or the rent raised, at short notice because of the lack of regulation and controls in this market. It is a particularly difficult situation for families with children in local schools.

The economic situation makes it hard for young people to enter the housing market, and rented accommodation is even more expensive to pay for each month; the result is they stay living in their parents' home longer than they would have done before the crash. This alters the sizes of households and the need for space per housing unit (flat/house).

The people, mostly young, who bought their homes during the boom were the hardest hit. They are also the people who are of parenting age and, therefore, often in need of larger and/ or more flexible space. From the beginning of 2009 until the end of 2012, on average at least 1.9 households lost ownership of their homes

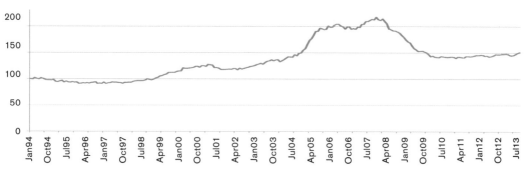

Real apartment prices in greater Reykjavík 1994 to 2013[12]

each day,[18] and many of the inhabitants had to move out. If that figure were to be translated into the American context, it would mean an average of 1900 foreclosures every day of the year.

Policies

The efforts of the state to help the poorer section of the population get a decent roof over their heads started after World War 1.[19] In the beginning, assistance was aimed at helping self-builders complete their houses for their families. This was later reduced to assistance in buying flats, arranged by a state-run mortgage lending institution, founded in the mid 1950s. The State Housing Agency was closed down in 1999 and a new institution opened under the title The Housing Financing Fund, which functions like a bank, and competed with the other banks in offering attractive mortgages during the boom. Social housing had always been under the ownership of the inhabitants, and could not be sold on the open market. However, in 2002 this was changed and people could sell their housing units in the same way as any other property. Now social housing is reduced to much fewer subsidised flats offered to those who qualify for housing benefits, after they have been means-tested.

When the Icelandic banks collapsed, developers stopped building overnight, and many of the building companies went bust. This created multiple troubles for future inhabitants. People had nowhere to turn, having paid part of the purchase price before the building process was finished. They also faced difficulties claiming their rights with regard to building failures caused by the rapid construction speeds during the bubble. With hindsight it is clear that at the end of the day it is the inhabitants who take on all the risks, as the big companies are not held liable when an economic crisis strikes, even though it is fair to assume they profited well in the boom. Many householders are stuck deep in debt, and trapped in residential architecture and an urban environment that is catering badly to the current needs.

New housing policies, launched by the parliament in 2013, stress the importance of establishing a rental market for housing, as an alternative to the house ownership model that holds sway. It is followed up by a new master plan for Reykjavík City, providing new building grounds in a central location. The politicians say that the intention is to give the plots free to non-profit housing cooperatives. It is worth noting that many so-called non-profit housing cooperatives outsource budget management tasks to developers that have a tradition of maximizing their profit margins.

Fast release of the units owned by the state (through The Housing Financing Fund) for badly needed rental homes has been argued against by the Fund, on the basis it would have a negative effect on property values. In the meantime unused units, the result of a period of abundant resources, are left to fall into disrepair, and neither does the state receive any rent from owning them. These policies have recently been revised, and now hundreds of these flats are for sale and for rent, but only for those without any unpaid financial obligations. Pets (which for some might make the obstacles in life a bit more bearable) are not allowed.[20]

In Iceland, the plots in urban areas are usually owned by the municipalities, and people have to buy rights to build on the plots according to the rules in the plans.

Changed Needs and the Design Responses

Adjusting to the needs of the time is inevitable, for individuals and groups whose economic or private conditions have changed because of the crash. A low currency rate, as a result of the economic situation in the country, has triggered mass tourism (e.g. on average 15,000 overnight stays each day in July 2012).[21] If all these people are welcome, they need to be accommodated.

The question remains how, and to what degree, the authorities respond to the changed needs. New housing can be built, and/or the existing building mass can be transformed. Architectural measures are important for both strategies. And both will provide many jobs. A reflection on recent experiences can be a constructive starting point for new design and its implementation.

From the perspective of sustainability, recycling is important. Recall the housing types built in the boom - the large single-family houses and the mass-produced, poorer quality blocks of flats? There is a certain flexibility embedded in the large units. The size makes them easier to redesign and transform into something else, whereas smaller ones often come tailored with minimal solutions that are rather inflexible. All the outdoor space can be remodelled to create a better urban environment. Furthermore, there is an excess of commercial property that has the potential to be converted for other uses, such as housing or mixed-use developments.

This all requires effort, organising and

different attitudes as well as policies. Considering the scale of the task, and based on previous experience, leaving further building projects to financial speculation might entrench the problems. Recent changes (since the crash) in the centre of Reykjavík also indicate that to be the case, as it is more or less being transformed into a field of temporary tourist accommodation quarters, with hundreds of new hotel rooms. This arrangement squeezes out the city's permanent residents, and is founded on the assumption that tourists come to Iceland to experience life in the centre of Reykjavík, as opposed to the interesting geology of the country, which is to be found out of town, and on the fringe of the metropolitan area. Meanwhile the tourist industry warns against a black market, and complains about private households earning income by inviting tourists into their spacious homes.

If the authorities are to take different approaches to planning for the benefit of the housing situation and the general public, the rules determining the function of plots need to be changed, and also the urban context, in relation to job development strategies in the city, needs to be reconsidered. In this respect the public sector could adopt a new role as facilitator; helping the inhabitants to organise, and implement changes, in order to make better use of all the building mass in a way that doesn't accentuate the current problems.

Unfinished buildings of all types might prove easier to alter than finished projects, when it comes to redesigning existing building mass to fit in with new functions. It is worth noting that the different building stages may not necessarily correspond with the economy of the respective inhabitants. When it comes to houses (as opposed to blocks built by developers), it is paradoxical that unfinished buildings are often owned by people who did not come out of the crash too badly, and in fact the ones that are affected most badly financially, took out loans to finish the work, and may not be enjoying their splendid villas very much because of their debt.

Ownership and Design

Ownership is an important premise when it comes to design. The homeownership model put social pressure on the population; not owning your home was stigmatising. Why would one not own one's home when renting was more expensive (rental space being very scarce and hard to find) and one could save, and most

probably make money, by buying a property? Wouldn't it just display a certain foolishness? In the light of the crisis, however, wouldn't it be important to redefine what ownership really is? Is it ownership if you owe more in your home than what it is worth? Is it important to die as a millionaire? Across the scales of the built environment this is architecturally significant since there are totally different design criteria for rental space as opposed to owner-occupied housing. Is homeownership a way to fool people into spending more resources on maintaining something, and consuming unnecessary goods, because they think they own something that they don't really?

Generally speaking, it is fair to assume that if someone lives in a particular environment, they will have greater incentives to improve that same environment, to make it more comfortable, useful or beautiful, than owners who never physically experience that environment - companies, for example, whose aim is to maximise profit (for example vulture funds, or even sovereign states on the far side of the globe).

Housing units, built by companies to be sold on the open market, can exist primarily for the purpose of making profit, although the situation can be dressed up in public debates as helping politicians provide the citizens with housing. From an architectural point of view, this equals design that is known to have sold before, and materials that look neutral and are cheap, but have not been selected for their resilience. With this way of doing things, a large chunk of money disappears into profits for the developer rather than being spent on improving the housing. The more economically beneficial for the developers, the bigger the consequences; poorer quality housing, and more debts, for the inhabitants.

Despite some crucial particularities, housing policy in Iceland has developed in parallel to that in the Nordic countries and others in Europe.[22] Thus the famous Red Vienna[23] housing project (1919–1923) by Adolf Loos, from the heyday of self-build housing, has its matches in Iceland too. Even though there has been a complete transformation of all the systems, there are a few cases where its origins can still be traced. A publicly organised self-build tradition still runs in a couple of municipalities in Norway. This model makes it possible for first-time homebuyers to participate in the building process, and pay the work-related costs of professionals. The model, which expels profit-driven developers from the process of mass-produced housing, has cross-party political resonance and puts the scale of housing developers' profits into an interesting perspective. Take the case of a project of 73 units, designed in the author's architectural practice (2003-2005). On taking over their apartment (this was within the housing ownership model), the owners could sell their unit on the open market, as soon as it was completed, for double the price they paid. The Norwegian example, which has cross political support in its context, provides a reality check when it comes to the true price of building. If Iceland was to take up manifold housing solutions to prevent a monopoly of one system (in which unnecessary profits are hidden) it could draw on the experiences of various such models abroad. Another idea would be to create the kind of conditions that stimulate designers to achieve what they are good at - making the most of scant resources.

Allowing homeownership to be the ruling model creates a culture that has become challenging when faced with reaching agreement on the uses, and maintenance of, the shared space in and around apartment blocks. House owners who live in their own property are probably quite concerned that their house should display their specific tastes, and the way they would like to be represented. In this context, personal tastes and changes in fashion mean more generous, and not always so rational, use of the resources of private space, as time

passes. It was, for instance, quite common before the crash to tear out all the (perfectly well-functioning) floor coverings, kitchen cabinets and even doors, when buying a new apartment, and replace them with alternatives that were new. One might reasonably presume that this particular premise for the architecture drove much of the urban development during the boom, where the ideal was, the more spacious and the more expensive-looking and newer, the better.

An agency that has long-term aims with housing in mind would hardly want to spend considerable sums of money on maintenance, the latest fashions or changing around spaces. For such an owner, a fair price, long-lasting timeless materials and flexible space, allowing and stimulating the inhabitant to flourish and treat the housing well, would probably be the most versatile solution. Owning most of the plots in urban areas (the municipalities), and a large portion of the housing debt portfolio (the state) would be great ingredients for rethinking new housing policies. Until then, it might be wise to make an investment in upgrading all the apartments owned by the state, so that they are inhabitable, and can provide affordable rental flats for all that need them, as a matter of urgency. And who would benefit more, than society as a whole?

1 Statistics Iceland. (Citing: National Economic Institute/Icelandic Property Registry), via Datamarket: See: http://bit.ly/1bAEjxr and http://bit.ly/JrwgZf
2 'Fjöldi sumarhúsa í lok hvers árs eftir landshlutum'. Reykjavík: Þjóðskrá Íslands. http://bit.ly/Kxlv7r (increase from 8.633 to 11.454 summer houses)
3 Statistics Iceland. Population by origin and citizenship. http://bit.ly/19HFMDa
4 Ólafsson, Þorvardur Tjörvi and Vignisdóttir, Karen Áslaug. Households' Position in the Financial Crisis in Iceland in: Working Paper No. 59. Reykjavík: Central Bank of Iceland, 2012, p 1. http://bit.ly/1e9hcac
5 Ólafsson, S. and Kristjánsson, A.S. Income Inequality in a Bubble Economy: The Case of Iceland 1992–2008. Luxembourg Incomes Study Conference, June 28–30 2010. http://bit.ly/1kSZsJ8
6 Statistics Iceland
7 Statistics Iceland (citing the Icelandic Property Registry)
8 Interview in summer 2010 with an Icelandic engineer who moved to Norway in spring 2008 (about half a year before the crash became public knowledge) after his acquaintances in the banks told him what would happen.
9 Information from a telephone consultation in June 2012, with the Fire Department of the Capital Area, which systematically maps this activity, allegedly to uncover potential fire hazards.
10 'Fjölmargar tómar íbúðir'. Reykjavík: RUV, December 10, 2013. http://bit.ly/1eP9Z0t
11 'Leggja milljarða í íbúðarhúsnæði'. Reykjavík: Viðskiftablaðið, November 5, 2012. http://www.vb.is/frettir/77870/
12 map by Elíasson, Lúðvík, Statistics Iceland. Reykjavík: Þjóðskrá Íslands.
13 Ibid.
14 About Financial Indexation. Reykjavík: Hagsmunasamtök heimilanna. http://bit.ly/1mRvJfl
15 Sigurðsson, Sveinn Óskar. Figures from Statistics Iceland presented in: Silfur Egils. Reykjavík: RUV, September 18, 2011.
16 Um Íbúðalánasjóð: Tilurð, hlutverk og starfsemi. Reykjavík: Landsbankinn. http://goo.gl/ZrjiQD
17 Skýrsla um starfsemi Bankasýslu ríkisins 2013. A report on the activity of Icelandic State Financial Investments. Reykjavík: Bankasýsla ríkisins, June 2013, p 27 and 44. http://bit.ly/1gikA9E
18 Greinargerð um fjárhagsstöðu heimilanna. (Figures for more recent developments are lacking).Reykjavík: Velferðarráðuneyti, April 2013, p 20. http://bit.ly/KwFkMw,
19 See: Sveinsson, Jón Rúnar. "Housing in Iceland in the Aftermath of the Global Financial Crisis" in: Forrest, Ray (ed.). Housing Markets and the Global Financial Crisis – The Uneven Impact on Households. London: Edward Elgar, 2011. http://bit.ly/1li4R7C
20 The website of The Icelandic Housing Fund. http://www.ils.is/einstaklingar/ibudir-til-solu-og-leigu/
21 Óladóttir, Oddný Þóra. Ferðaþjónusta á Íslandi Í tölum, apríl 2013. Reykjavík: Icelandic Tourist Board, 2013, p 9. http://bit.ly/1dl8vCQ
22 Sveinsson, Jón Rúnar. Húsnæðisvefurinn. http://husvef.is
23 'Viennese Cooperative Garden City Movement'. Sheffield: Spatial Agency. http://bit.ly/1fQL5TD

Food

Salvör Jónsdóttir

'There are two spiritual dangers in not owning a farm. One is the danger of supposing that breakfast comes from the grocery, and the other that heat comes from the furnace.'

from Aldo Leopold's *A Sand County Almanac, And Sketches Here And There*

Since these words were written in 1949, people's connections to the origins of food have become even more tenuous. Meanwhile, the dangers that lurk in the disconnection with nature, have become more evident. In the effort to reconnect with the natural environment, many seek to spend time in "unspoiled" nature, away from the urban environment. That effort, however, often necessitates that those who wish to reach the unspoiled nature must possess an expensive SUV to get there, and to enjoy the time and space on their own. This will hopefully in turn lead those people to a better understanding of the natural environment's role as the basis for all human existence. Not everyone, of course, may have the means to undertake such an exploration, but everyone does need to eat. As author of this brief overview, I wonder whether a better understanding of the food system, and following on from that humans' dependence on a clean and safe natural environment, might overall increase the appreciation for the need for planning in terms of sustainable land use. An important step in that learning process may be to give people the possibility of producing their own food. According to international agreements, everyone should have the right to eat unspoiled food. This has been acknowledged as a human right, along with other basic needs.

When, in the early 1920s, land use planning in Iceland was recognised as being of public concern, the focus was on housing and the built environment. It later moved to include the undeveloped environment, and sustainable development became the guiding light of planning legislation from 1997 onwards. Although farmland is by far the largest land use category in Iceland,[2] the food system and food planning have been absent from the general discussion about planning until very recently.

Food System, Policy and Politics

The food system has been defined in the planning literature as the "chain of activities connecting food production, processing, distribution, consumption, and waste management, as well as all the associated regulatory institutions and activities".[3] The food system therefore involves policies that may affect what gets produced and how; as well as the ease with which it reaches the consumers.

Policies get shaped by politics in which economics and financial resources often play a role. Apparently there is plenty of food produced in the world, and yet a huge section of the world's population is suffering from hunger,[4] which raises some tough questions about food pricing and distribution. Food has been treated as a commodity by the very large financial institutions[5] and their goal may not be to eliminate hunger. It therefore follows that global food issues will not be resolved unless this is recognised, and acted upon, by means of international agreements. With a growing urban population and a changing climate, the question of how to feed the world becomes even more important to answer. There exists no simple solution to this problem, which may mean that it continues to be ignored by many, or just lip service paid by international institutions and power holders.

This important subject will, however, not be the focus of the discussion here. It should, nevertheless, always be kept in mind since no one in the consumer world of free trade is outside the international food system. Awareness of how that system functions, and the links between the environmental, social and economic aspects of food production and consumption, is crucial for the future development of our man-made environment.

'Everyone has the right to a standard of living adequate for the health and well-being of himself and of his family, including food, clothing, housing and medical care and necessary social services...'

United Nations 1948[1]

Food and Sustainable Development

Sustainable development may be hard to comprehend, since embedded in its definition is a lot of uncertainty, especially when it comes to recognising the needs of future generations.[6] This uncertainty presents a challenge for planning in general too. Not everyone may be interested in sustainable planning of the man-made environment, but everyone needs to eat. Since food production and accessibility touches each of the three pillars of sustainability, there may be an underutilised educational opportunity in linking the food system and sustainable development to the

dining tables of those nations in the world that impact the global environment to the largest degree. In a small country like Iceland, where there seems to be abundant land per capita, space for development and food production may not seem to be a problem. Yet, given Icelanders' modern lifestyle and relative high standard of living, use of both domestic natural resources and imported goods is of concern for those that want to plan for future generations. It should also be noted that only a small fraction of Iceland is arable,[7] whereas a large portion of the land is used for grazing.

1 Small urban garden in Reykjavík, providing herbs for a local restaurant.

Most Icelanders, in fact 64% of the total population, live in the greater Reykjavík area in relatively sprawled settings,[8] calling for high use of private transport and consumption of imported energy. Urban development in the country took place mainly after the introduction of the car, and as a result the city is spread out, with large open spaces, and some opportunities for urban agriculture (UA).

The socio-economic situation, compared to that of other OECD countries, may be relatively acceptable now that the level of income inequality has fallen[9] and the food bill averages 14% of households' expenditure.[10] However, consumption of fresh produce, such as fruit and vegetables, is at the moment extremely dependent on imports, whereas just one third of groceries are imported goods.[11] Healthy alternatives may therefore be costly, especially for low income or bigger families.

Food in Reykjavik

With only 6.3% of its inhabitants living in rural areas,[12] Iceland has developed into an urban society, with the majority of people in the capital area. Interestingly, as the farmers and fishermen have declined in number, so have the grocery providers. Three companies currently control 90% of the grocery market,[13] which creates quite a primitive food system.

Urbanisation happened quickly in Iceland during the late 19th and early 20th centuries, bringing people from the rural parts to the villages and the capital. Early residents of Reykjavík brought with them the tradition of food growing. In 1948 'school gardens' were founded, to improve the eating habits of school-age children and encourage outdoor recreation. Vegetable growing for home consumption was very common in Reykjavik until the late 20th century, and traditional farms could be found within the city boundaries as late as the end of the 1960s.[14]

In the early years of the 21st century, interest in allotment gardens diminished drastically, rising again, among city residents, after the financial crash of 2008. The school gardens were converted to regular allotments in 2011 and are now rented out to families in eight out of ten neighbourhoods within the city. Additionally, the city leases approximately 100 allotments to the Horticultural Society which in turn sub-lets them to its members.[15] It should be mentioned that the geothermal heat in the Reykjavik area makes possible the use of greenhouses, as well as greywater for heating the soil. Many residents already take advantage of this, but in most cases the private greenhouses are built on single home lots.

Farmers markets are not common in Reykjavik, but in the summer of 2013 the city worked with interested sellers to establish an outdoor food market on the Saturdays in July.[16] Furthermore, in recent years several Reykjavik businesses have opened, emphasising their direct chain from farmer to customer, and some farms have begun selling directly to customers via websites and mail order.[17]

Urban Agriculture Policy as Part of the proposed Municipal Plan

The planning committee of Reykjavik decided in the spring of 2012 to make UA a formal activity of the city, by integrating it within the Municipal plan. The motivating factors have come from a number of directions. Firstly, a few requests to keep poultry for egg production have been made to the city, but according to the Municipal plan as it stands this would not be permitted within the ordinance on animal husbandry. Secondly, at public planning meetings in the city's neighbourhoods, people have been vocal in their demands for additional horse-keeping areas, permits for keeping poultry, and for farmers markets.[18] Thirdly, on the citizens' website 'Better Reykjavik', permission for poultry rearing and egg production has been put forth as a suggestion by several people. And finally, among the projects chosen, in an e-based referendum conducted by the city, was an increase in access to allotments. The referendum took place March-April 2012, and citizens voted for the projects they considered most important for their neighbourhoods.[19]

In the proposed plan (published and approved before publication of this book), UA is defined as food production within the city, whether from plant cultivation or animal husbandry, as well as non-industrial processing and distribution of such production.[20]

The proposed policy for UA is based on the following goals:

• *Land and resources should be efficiently used.*
• *Environmental quality and public health should be improved.*
• *Citizens should have access to fresh and healthy foods.*
• *Those interested in producing their own food should have the opportunity to do so, provided that conditions permit.*

The policy itself is then proposed in seven strategic statements:

• *As many as possible of the city's inhabitants will have access to fresh and healthy food.*
• *Conditions will be created to promote vegetable cultivation within the city limits.*
• *As many as possible of the city's inhabitants will be able to grow vegetables for their own consumption.*
• *Allotment gardens will be established in all ten neighbourhoods.*
• *Where conditions allow, citizens may keep poultry for egg production for their own consumption.*
• *Facilities for the farmers markets will be sent up in all ten neighbourhoods to increase citizens' access to fresh foods (the above-mentioned food market that was run in July 2013, initiated this policy).*
• *The city officials will maintain good cooperation with individuals and organisations interested in healthy food production within the city.*

With regard to the implementation of the policy, certain steps are suggested to make way for increased cultivation, animal husbandry and farmers markets in all the neighbourhoods, with the proviso that the local committees and residents must agree. These goals and strategies promote better health and more sustainable land use, they are not put forward to address the spiritual dangers Leopold warned against. It can however be asserted that, as a byproduct of UA, a degree of knowledge and an understanding of the basic elements needed for healthy food production, will be gained by the residents.

Now only the future can tell if Icelanders are willing to accept agriculture as part of urban life in the long run and, more importantly, whether there will be any impact on the nation's attitude towards sustainable urban planning, and respect for a clean and healthy environment.

1 *The Universal Declaration of Human Rights.* Adopted by the General Assembly of the United Nations on December 10, 1948, Article 25(1). http://bit.ly/1e0ELb2
2 Jónsdóttir, Salvör, *Landbúnaðarland í skipulagsáætlunum (e. Farmland in planning proposals).* Research paper funded by the National Planning Agency of Iceland, 2012.
3 Pothukuchi, Kameshwari and Kaufman, Jerome L., 'The Food System: A Stranger to the Planning Field' in: American Planning Association. *Journal of the American Planning Association 66(2).* 2000, p 113–124.
4 See e.g. http://bit.ly/1m2JibA and http://bit.ly/1frkDzH and Kaufman, Frederick. 'Let Them Eat Cash'. *Harper's Magazine,* June 2009, p 51-59.
5 Kaufman,Frederick., 'The Food Bubble'. *Harper's Magazine,* July 2010, p 27-34.
6 See: UN website for *"Our Common future",* Chapter 2: *Towards Sustainable Development.* http://bit.ly/b68FYz
7 Snæbjörnsson, Arnór et al.,

Skýrsla nefndar um landnotkun. Athugun á notkun og varðveislu ræktanlegs lands (e. Report on the use and conservation of arable land). Reykjavík: Sjávarútvegs- og landbúnaðarráðuneytið, 2010.
8 Theodórsdóttir, Ásdís Hlökk and Jónsdóttir, Salvör., *Going for Growth. Planning for Development in the Greater Capital Region of Iceland.* Working paper presented at AESOP 26th Annual Congress, 2012.
9 OECD. 'Crisis Squeezes Income and Puts Pressure on Inequality and Poverty', 2013. http://bit.ly/JUJXjr
10 Statistics Iceland. http://www.statice.is/
11 Samkeppniseftirlitið. *Verðþróun og samkeppni á dagvörumarkaði (e. Price Trends and Competition on the Grocery Market),* 2012.
12 Statistics Iceland. Statistical Series, *Population (2013:1),* 2013.
13 Samkeppniseftirlitið. *Verðþróun og samkeppni á dagvörumarkaði (e. Price Trends and Competition on the Grocery Market),* 2012.
14 *Morgunblaðið,*1948 maí 23, p 2, and Bernharðsson, Eggert Þór., *Saga Reykjavíkur. Borgin 1940-1990. Fyrri*

hluti. (e. Reykjavik´s History 1940-1990), Reykjavík: Iðunn, 1998.
15 Matjurtagarðar. Reykjavik: Reykjavíkurborg (City of Reykjavik), 2012 apríl 4. http://bit.ly/17OwDHV
16 See: Reykjavik´s website: http://bit.ly/1cVCryC
17 See e.g. http://www.akurbisk.is/, http://austurlamb.is/ and http://www.beintfrabyli.is/
18 Reykjavik Planning and Building Department. Proceedings from Public Meeting. Reykjavik: Reykjavíkurborg, April 4, 2012. http://bit.ly/1ajfgLb
19 Kjósum betri hverfi - niðurstöður rafræna kostninga (e: Lets Vote for Better Neighbourhoods - Results from E-referendum). Reykjavik, Reykjavíkurborg, 2012. http://bit.ly/1j514h8
20 *The Municipal Plan Draft.* See city of Reykjavik website (in Icelandic): http://bit.ly/19NLM6P

Definition of UA based on: Mukherji, Nina and Morales, Alfonso. *Zoning for Urban Agriculture,* in: Practice Urban Agriculture. American Planning Association (Zoning Practice), March 2010.

Communication

Hildigunnur Sverrisdóttir
in interview with Arna Mathiesen

A:
Will you contribute to the book Hildigunnur?

H:
I need to consider... I pointed out in a seminar
at the Association of Icelandic Architects that
a certain Nobel Prize winner in economics had
just convinced the World Economic Forum that
economic growth should not solely be defined
by money. The guys at the seminar, notably from
the older generationsclaimed it was their duty
to convince the client about the financial gain of
building ecologically. Interestingly, people gradually began to throw up ideas about how much
one could profit from building ecologically.
But to explain that building ecologically could
be more beneficial for the community in more
complex and variable ways than simply financial? No, that was surely way too complicated
and much more in the realm of the politicians.
I am curious about this.

A:
I saw Saskia Sassen in the paper today,[1] stating
that our built environment has created a more
brutal world. Doesn't the Icelandic crash prove
her point?

H:
That's right up my street - I am preoccupied
with the question of boundaries and autopoiesis of social systems and the balance between
the individual and society as Chantal Mouffe
describes it.[2]
    A big problem in the Icelandic context,
is using obsolete top-down approaches to
describe a 2D reality which might have been
relevant in the times leading up to modernism,
but in a postmodern context things have
resolved into a much more spatio-temporal or
four-dimensional phenomenon, stretching over
many languages. We see capital starting to
behave like water and air, not caring for borders
at all. We see capital starting to behave like
water and air, not caring for borders at all. The
same is happening with structures of society as
such, not describing society in any human way.

It would be great if we could talk about the
Occupy movement and the importance of the
incentives imbedded in physical proximity and
the need to redefine the physical being in the
world. Hmm...

A:
How is it practically possible to tackle the
alienation you describe? Isn't it a challenge to
talk from an ivory tower, in a manner everybody
would understand? Perhaps that's why Sassen
avoids big conferences with other academics,
and prefers to go to smaller meetings with a
good mixture of people?

H:
Many conferences are about ticking boxes
required for scoring points for "research", rather
than the yearning for sharing findings and
getting feedback and dialogue.
    It is useful detecting the historical accumu-
lation of communication before one defines a
system i.e. that even if one works top down,
one defines the bottom up as well.[3] Where
does one find, and how does one detect,
the self-definition of a social system? What
is it that draws subjects into a continuous
dialogue, what do they have in common, i.e. in
which 'language' is the communication within
the system? How do they define their limits
and where is the sensitivity of their limits,
considering irritants and communication to
and from other systems? If it is not possible
to communicate in the same language
between different systems? How do you
convey your message?
    It is as if we think that because we all speak
Icelandic, we have a possibility for mutual
understanding in any given case. Then we
meow and bark at each other and have no
idea why we don't understand each other. But
if we embrace the fact that, even within the
frame of a native tongue, we speak different
"languages" built on our respective experience
and cultural background, that they who bark
don't have the suppositions for understanding

the meowing I produce, it will be easier for me to open the membrane (around me) and try opening up to an understanding of the barking, in the hope there will finally be a good mutual understanding (through the historical accumulation of communication).

Practically It takes time, sending out messages, investing in a dialogue...

Lack of participation comes from not having the mentor/apprentice-relationship that is necessary for people to become stronger on their own premises. Many of us want to partic-ipate in important and relevant dialogue, but within the Association the discourse has sadly at times been held hostage by a somewhat querulant group, misinterpreting, in my opinion, the term 'democracy' (that is: I have my rights to take space, but I am not responsible in the face of society). In the public domain you are alone, you get wind in your sails if things go well, but nobody talks to you if things go wrong. A herd mentality rules, and we are fighting for building up a young school, defining the academic ability within our profession, developing teaching skills within it, at the same time as trying to sustain our studies - and hopefully with a master's programme soon.

The tradition for democracy and a dialogue in our young democracy (sad contradiction) - or lack thereof - is working against us. In fact I sometimes get the feeling that many people here would prefer a benevolent dictatorship, or so the discourse suggests. We must not forget that there are only about 300,000 of us, and one would be unconsciously celebrating the megalomaniac Übermensch nonsense of our country's former discourse, if one would claim that the collective subjects of such a small society would individually have the capacity to focus on their daily tasks, and simultaneously be capable of developing and maintaining a nuanced and strong critical, philosophical, and political set of opinions.

Challenging the marketing and battle language we have adapted to is essential. It steers the tone of the discourse. There is a certain difference between selling something to somebody, winning someone over or concurring in a debate, and encouraging people to reflect on and question their opinions through an honest debate. We might mean the same, but there is an essential difference when it comes to the responsibility for the subject at hand and the results.

There is lots of alternative stuff the public sector has supported, but the central question is, where is the incentive? Why this but not that? Who gets paid? Why should all this happen at the cost of the public? Questioning, not to paralyse, but to encourage the public sector to take responsibility for what gets built on its behalf, how it is developed, where it begins and ends, who develops, questions and puts it in context? What does the public get out of it? Tina Saaby, when getting the post as the Copenhagen City Architect, went immediately to work on defining these processes. That was the basis for her new post.
...

A:
Did you get a mail from me yesterday Hildigunnur? HALLO!!

H:
The essence is: Stop the nonsense, do what we mean and mean what we do!
Until then, do less.

A:
Great! What about the title: "meowing and barking"?

I am seriously trying to put this book together and find people in Iceland difficult to get hold of. I don't have a clue why this is and I put in too many hours doing stuff I would have done differently if everybody had shown their cards right at the start. If people don't respond I tend to think I've stepped on somebody's toes, or that people are on vacation, are sick, can't respond, don't want to, or are offended? This to too much work, I am passionate, but there are limits. I am about to give up on the book!

H:

I hear what you are saying and I understand. It can be frustrating in our profession when we have to be continuously reaching over into new realms and trajectories.

My personal experience (which has been ongoing as Director of Studies at the Academy)... I get on average 50 mails a day, all containing proposals and errands that crave an instant response to some degree. One truly tries one's best, but has to take one's ambitious ego aside and try not to promise anything one cannot fulfil. I beg you to interpret the silence like this. It says that I have not had space to take a stand, determine if I have time, orientate myself within the context enough to give a clear answer – clear answers, on the other hand, mean that there is potential and we can continue the journey.

What if we were to drop everything with an academic context? One can question how sane it is for a population of 300,000 people in a metro-village to run a symphony, two radio stations, TV - you know the deal.

We can essentially only do just a fraction of what one would consider 'normal', if we have any ambition for aiming at the wonderful context found in larger societies.

Then we can only spit in our palms, grope around doing our best sharing knowledge and happiness so that everybody doesn't have to rediscover the wheel (we cannot afford it, nor do we have the time) or we will choke in each other's smoke as we burn ourselves up... Of course you know this from architecture. Architects have the shortest life expectancy amongst academics... if you don't count war reporters.

A:

Before we restructure and become hairdressers Hildigunnur (hairdressers have the longest life expectancy): It is essential to be clear and say: "yes" or "no". If not, this book will end up like the new constitution. Unfortunately it seems it is not going to happen, despite the crash and the aftermath. Things run out of time and all that remains is the memory of an argument, a lost opportunity. Icelanders blame it on the small size of the population, but it can't be just that. For being effective it can be an asset to be few, like when there were just two of us in my office, everything was so effective, running more or less on telepathy.

It is better to avoid the unclear and hairy, no hard feelings, and it's kind of you to give some thought to hairy patterns of communication...

In fact that kind of pattern is considered unprofessional over here, and one would be dismissed from any serious post pretty quickly. Ad hoc might in fact be the privilege of small societies, since there is only approximately one of each type of specialist...so, nowhere else to turn. Some say system changes should be easier in Iceland, because small boats are easier to turn than large vessels.

H:

I am grateful for critical communication, it is too scarce.

I might be in denial, or brain fog, but I truly don't experience this as any sort of privilege. It is serious how seldom we really face up to just how small this society is, how wide-ranging it still needs to be and what inhumane demands there are on everybody's capabilities for participation. Of course one often suspects that people are not fit for their jobs, and it is sad how fear, anxiety and an inferiority complex leads to people not expressing themselves clearly. I think that the problem linked with the equation I just mentioned puts this situation in an even more exaggerated context. Everybody acts as if they've got IT but then nobody dares pulling down their pants. If somebody would start, I am sure everything would collapse to a more truthful state and people might give up and let go of their illusions. But this demands such courage, people need to give in - in fact I think this is happening as we speak. There are stimuli and pressures on people throughout society now. The demand for flexibility and participation is, seriously Arna, quite ludicrous.

The problem is also that we have so few role models and mentors, and are still developing as an urban society. Old cliché, but embarrassingly obvious nevertheless.

A:

You are saying that someone who is very effective in their job can appear to others as somebody unfit for doing their job. In any case the lack of organisation must be a real drawback. I know it well from my own experience being an Icelander abroad, working with foreigners only. Everything is so much more organised over here (in Norway). Plans are made in advance and they are followed, while I (the Icelander) straddle along driven by passion and spontaneity... making me look like a complete idiot at times, but occasionally like a superwoman.

H:
Exactly, it is very resource-craving to plan
well, for that one needs an understanding
and abstraction that the Icelandic context, by
definition, has not reached yet, that's my feeling.
In any case it is obvious, considering that it is
never possible to plan anything ahead here, be
it due to fluctuating currency rates or natural
disasters. Today for instance, the country is
paralysed because of the weather - all activity
has been cancelled and the police seriously
suggested on the radio this morning that
people should read a good book or call a friend.

A:
That probably means you have a complete
snowstorm with zero visibility (not just 6 cm of
winter wonderland, which would make them
close the tube in London)? And the men kept
drowning by numbers… what a place to survive!

H:
Between us Arna, I personally suspect that
through the ages certain genes have been
bred forward through natural choice and that
in this country you will find a complete nation
with ADHD (attention deficit hyperactivity
disorder)… which actually rhymes quite
beautifully, in the context of alcoholism diluting
every little cell here.

A:
I liked the new Icelandic definition/translation
for ADHD:[4] "Víðhygli"… "wide scope" "wide
tension", as in attention. Meaning someone who
has a special ability to look at things untradition-
ally, knowing what they find interesting and what
not, as opposed to buying someone else's ideas
about everything, and being creative with it.

H:
Exactly, there you have the schizophrenic
Siamese twin character which Icelandic society
cannot survive without. Impulsivity and interest
in apparently stringy stuff is of course the
hallmark of the creative, abstract thinker…like
autistic people, who only envelope themselves
in their own interests.

A:
A propos electing somebody whom everybody
knows has ADHD for the Mayor of Reykjavík
after the crash, despite him making no
promises, except to have a polar bear in the zoo
(which he didn't).The only thing people knew
about him was that he was creative and funny,
and now he has published his biography 'The
Pirate', recording his troubled adolescence.

H:
For surviving in harsh conditions it is necessary
to have the ability to act quickly, not to have too

175

much long-term memory or a desire for qualities based on meticulousness.

In fact I think it is about time, since we now have electricity and phone connections, to reconsider the priorities - too much stress has rendered every other child handicapped with anxiety and neglect. We have cultivated a big urge for implementing stuff. It surely lies in the small degenerate island's genes; thank god for the drowned men that made a space for the odd foreigner so we did not have to just sit on the hillside and play the langspil (a historic Icelandic instrument). And when we start to take this equation seriously, people don't have to drink themselves to oblivion 24/7 because of their impotence alone...for not coping well enough (who could in this little country anyway) and continuously letting everybody down and being impossible, and we would start to make plans, taking into account that we are a semi-crazy opportunistic population with all types of people...which we in fact are!

A:
Plans are useful for saving time and money. People are forced to work within restrictions of time and money. For an Icelander, plans might sound boring and even perverse, rendering the ones that work on the systems and rules being considered "boring" by definition. And the others are losers, except for that little moment of brilliance when, in wild inspiration, they write something immortal. In permaculture, if it is boring it is not sustainable. Making planning fun could be the answer. Is it possible to recycle and retrofit the system and make it more fun?

H:
Precisely - boring doesn't have to be that boring if the premises make sense, but one has to see it to want to go with that flow - and work within a system that offers the possibility! All human communications are essentially systems in some ways. As far as I can tell, I do agree with those who claim that systems are practical methods of human agency to get to common conclusions...

Of course systems are always essentially pragmatic or practical, even bad unreliable systems, since they are predictable and thus reliable to a certain extent. Still what post-structuralism and modernism teach us, through the theories of people like Foucault, Derrida and Deleuze, is that systems are surely necessary but always in a context and to a certain degree, and then they start to exist only for themselves.

And I think that humanity does to a large extent have a built-in wish for making consensuses, forming societies and social structures. These structures just don't need to aim at the lowest common denominator.

Anarchism is in fact a very developed and appropriate form: 'I am trusted to look for consensuses and logic that suits my context, nothing is universal and works for everybody, and nobody should be able to take top-down responsibility on my behalf, without my consent.'

A:
Would anarchism secure participation by everybody?

H:
Hmmm, are we talking about "social" anarchism, that is to say NOT the neo-liberal attitude masked as a geek - "you leave me alone and I let you alone" or data nerds calling themselves anarchists? Those who shout loud on social media, or choose pink instead of blue Dell laptops, making them feel they are active in democracy...failing to see that nobody is listening? With the exception of the market of course.

A:
I was talking about intentional communities... based on the will for real community offline, physical proximity and cooperation with daily life, where those who spend their days in online alternative universes, and fail to share on the ground, get ignored. When in some contexts people get punished for participating, in this context one is socially marginalised for not participating.

H:
My bottom line is that by sharing and communicating in caution and mutual respect, people will slowly but surely find out with whom they share interests - and from thereon, social structures and consensuses follow -

Well...The wolves have started howling, I'd better feed my herd.
Over and out for now.

1 Interview with Saskia Sassen, 'Vi lever i en tid som skaper brutalitet', *Aftenposten,* Oslo, 2012 http://www. aftenposten.no/kultur/--Vi-lever-i-en-tid-som-skaper-brutalitet-6949265.html

2 Mouffe, Chantal. *The Democratic Paradox.* London/New York: Verso, 2005.
3 Schumacher, Patrik. *The Autopoiesis of Architecture.* West Sussex: John Wiley & Sons, 2011.

4 On Arna Valsdóttir's theory: *Hvað er „viðhygli"?* Verkmenntaskólinn á Akureyri, 2010 http://www.vma.is/is/skolinn/ymsar-upplysingar/frettasafn/hvad-er-vidhygli

"If life were not founded on community there wouldn't be any ecosystems... The ecosystem is Nature's economy."

Guðmundur Páll Ólafsson (in Viðsjá 2013, http://www.ruv.is/sarpurinn/vidsja/13122013-0)

4.

Scenarios into the future

Urban Design and Ecology

Sybrand Tjallingii

Introduction: what is ecology?

Arriving there for the first time in my life, it was Iceland's overwhelming nature, rather than any human presence, that struck me. Although I knew about the historic role of man in changing the Icelandic landscape, the first impression is of small urban and man-made islands in a sea of nature. Ecology is all. How different from the situation in The Netherlands, when I first came to the Delft School of Architecture in 1975. In the years after the war, an unprecedented urban growth had changed a green landscape with red islands into a red-coloured landscape with green islands. And this process was in full swing at the time. I was arriving from Utrecht University, where I had studied vegetation and soil science, and the dominant discourse among my fellow biology students, and within the nature conservation movement in general, was about urban development as the enemy that destroyed nature. Ecology was conservation, something found outside cities. Now I had passed over to the other side. But the 'enemies', the architects and urban designers, showed a lively interest in ecology. I joined the Department of Landscape and Ecology that played a key role in the school, and it became clear to me that the biological specialists, followed by policy makers and public opinion, had taken ecology into their own conservation corner.

I had arrived in a different world. Ecology as a science was defined as the discipline that studied the interactions between living organisms and their environment. It is a scientific discipline that seeks to explain the world. In the context of design, however, ecology became a set of ideas and tools to improve the world. At least, that was my first impression. At the school, ecology was hot in the 1970s. If you broadcast that you intended to teach on that subject, lecture halls would fill up with students. Rachel Carson's *Silent Spring*, the Club of Rome's report *Limits to Growth*, and a bunch of other publications, had caused an ecological awakening that coincided with a growing critique of the modernist rational approach to

building and construction that had dominated post-war years. A new generation of architects and urban designers started exploring fresh approaches, and ecology became a central theme. My own role, as teacher and in study projects, focused on landscape ecological potentialities and urban design decisions. My aim was to examine the relationship between design and the maintenance of green spaces. In so doing, I could follow in the footsteps of pioneers such as Ian McHarg, whose *Design with Nature* (1971)[1] paved the way for a new generation of urban designers including Michael Hough (*City Form and Natural Process*, 1984)[2] and Ann Spirn (*The Granite Garden*, 1984).[3]

In the early 1980s, however, ecology was suddenly ousted. Leading designers protested against the ecology-driven messy form. They detested what they called 'cauliflower urbanism' and they returned to the grid and other geometric forms that recalled the modernists. Ecology remained a source of inspiration for a relatively small undercurrent of people, but mainstream urban design returned to smooth, straight and tidy as the key elements of urban form. In hindsight, organic form turned out to be the main driver behind designers being interested in ecology. Designers, too, had taken ecology to their own corner, to a place where aesthetics and form were the dominant issues.

The Ecological Conditions approach

At the Landscape and Ecology Department we decided to go back to basics, to ecological processes as indispensable forces in the design of buildings and streets, parks and squares. Thus, we focused more on how urban environments create carrying conditions for working with water and climate, soils, energy and material flows. In doing so, we tried to learn about ingredients and structures that were able to create conditions for different forms and a variety of human activities. We came to the conclusion that the heart of the problem lay in sectors, departments, specialists or companies taking issues into their own corners, and that the search for synergism, whether with nature or between activities, was part of the solution. These ideas were later further developed into the *Ecological Conditions* approach.[4]

Instead of taking ecological, social and economic issues to their own corners, the specialists are invited to use their disciplinary knowledge and experience to look at the whole plan. The three angles generate questions about the territorial coherence of area-bound processes, the synergy of flows and the coop-eration of actors. The focus of an ecological approach to spatial planning and design is brought about by these three action perspec-tives: actors, flows and areas.

First we ask the question, who is playing which role? The second, how do we adjust input and output of activities, and their position upstream and downstream in flows? The third, how do we locate, and spatially organise, activities? Working with natural processes, and synergism of activities, need to be the guiding principles. The three little diagrams at the corners are examples of guiding models, which promise planning strategies to guide the making of detailed local plans. In the area corner is the two networks strategy[5] which treats the networks of water and traffic as carrying structures for multifunctional landuse zoning. In the flows corner, the 'ecodevice' guiding model directing us to recycling and cascading strategies to work with flows inside systems, and taking responsibility for input and output. In the third corner, for actors, is the forum-piloted project strategy which promotes shared learning – integrated solutions learned from practical projects.

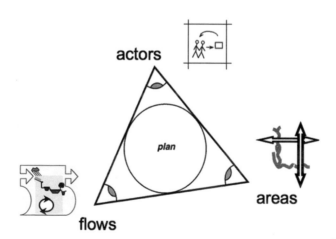

1 Ecological conditions: the triangle indicates the key elements of the approach.

Ecological issues and challenges
in the Reykjavik situation

Concentrating on the opportunities and challenges in the Reykjavik situation, one can use the general *Ecological Conditions* triangle to generate questions that may be relevant in the making of scenarios, spatial designs and pilot projects. Of course detailed analysis is required between the questions and real plans.

Flows

The usual questions of course arise, regarding wind and solar energy options in the built environment, and apparently there is no reason not to go down that path. However, to tackle Iceland's overall energy issue, it might be more important to first take a look at the rapid one-sided car-based urban growth of Reykjavik, and the resulting increased dependency on imported oil in the last decade. What are the options available for a switch to electric cars? Especially within the Reykjavik agglomeration, where the distances are limited, there seem to be ample opportunities to use electricity that is generated by geothermic plants.

It will not be easy to change the the the car-based traffic system of a city that is designed for the car, and that has a self-evident role for the car in the cultural tradition. However, leaving aside the energy debate, there are young and old people who cannot use cars, and there is city centre space that could be better adopted for densification, shopping and cultural life rather than car parks. What are the options available for giving public transport and bicycles a more significant role?

The low density of the residential districts is an argument against bus routes to and from the suburbs, but densification with affordable housing and student accommodation close to bus stops, might warrant some attention. The recently constructed wide asphalt main roads are only used by a few cars, so they offer an opportunity for special bus lanes. In the city centre and within the suburban centres there is a need for developing a more attractive and improved bicycle network.

The empty fields, left in half-finished suburban developments since the crisis, create a special problem. But, at the same time, they represent special opportunities, related to food flows for example. Iceland seems to be extremely dependent on imported food. What options are available for the empty fields to

be utilised for urban agriculture? Local food production may be possible, especially in urban developments that sprang up on former agricultural land with relatively good soils. Greenhouses with artificial substrate may also be possible, as the Iceland situation provides such easy access to hot water.

There is no scarcity of drinking water but there are problems related to other water flows. The sewage of Reykjavik is pumped to the sea by nicely designed buildings along the coast. Valsson calls them 'temples of the goddess Fecalia'.[6] Increased paved surfaces in urban developments cause erosion and, in some cases, pollution can affect groundwater quality. As there is plenty of open space in the new developments, an obvious question is: can we use green spaces for water drainage, infiltration and purification? Detailed designing, or redesigning, in the new developments might further elaborate the practical options.

Waste flows can be very important for the urban ecosystem, and recycling strategies are urgently needed to risks such as groundwater contamination. As with many other flows, the emphasis is on industrial ecology.

Areas

The emphasis shifts to landscape ecology, and it is important to take a close look at the ground layer – the ecological and cultural basis of the landscape that has developed over the centuries, through the interaction between nature and culture.

The key question for the Reykjavik landscape is how the ground layer can be used in the next round of planning and design. Will it be possible to develop a blue-green structure in the region that reflects the soils, the hydrographic network and the cultural history of the area? Following the two networks strategy, this blue-green network could be the carrying structure for a multifunctional set of activities (the slow lane) that together support the landscape and biodiversity. In order to make it work, disturbance by the traffic-based fast lane network should be avoided. Fig. 2 illustrates how water structure can carry the slow lane activities, such as recreation, water storage, urban agriculture and nature conservation. The traffic infrastructure carries the dynamic activities, and residential land use is an in-between zone. It follows from this that, with the Reykjavik area in mind, creative solutions should be developed in many valleys, where highways are part of the green structure and thereby create conflicts. Detailed designs may be the answer to controlling noise and pollution, and could bridge the barriers.

Trees and forests are a special case in the Reykjavik landscape. To what extent, and where, can (re)forestation be stimulated? Some Icelanders seem to feel that forests are not part of their country's characteristic landscape, but historic sources reveal that people who came to the island in the 8th century found extensive forests.[7] As a result of deforestation, extensive erosion shaped the present surface of Iceland. If lessons are learned from pilot projects at the eastern fringe of the city, reforestation is a real option. The goal is not to reconstruct a historic situation but to use trees and forests in the present landscape to provide shelter, and to ameliorate the diversity of landscape. Of course the above-mentioned green structure could be given shape in part by woodlands and trees.

In a planning and design process, once the flow options have been explored, and the ground layer and territorial options examined, an actor analysis should follow. Who are the key actors, what are their interests and conflicts, and what are the driving forces motivating them? For a design proposal to evolve into a full-blown scenario, we have to understand who will benefit, who can finance it and who is responsible for maintenance. Assessing the ecosystem services of green spaces may be useful in some cases. But in the context of design, we are comparing integrated action perspectives that should also include answers to uncertainties. Economic crisis and climate change, apart from anything else, involve many uncertainties. The vacant lands in Reykjavik's incomplete developments are a good illustration of this. Should they remain vacant until the property market is back to normal? Or can we launch temporary activities on these empty fields, as pilot projects involving rainwater storage and local food production. Learning from these pilots may change our ideas about the future of the city.

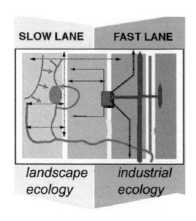

2 Two Networks strategy, activities model.

3 Citizens and politicians meeting on site.

1 McHarg, Ian L. *Design with Nature*. New York: Doubleday, 1971.
2 Hough, Michael. *City Form and Natural Process*. London & New York: Routledge, 1984.
3 Spirn, Anne Whiston. *The Granite Garden: Urban Nature and Human Design*. New York: Basic Books, 1984.
4 Tjallingii, Sybrand P. *Ecological Conditions. Strategies and Structures in Environmental Planning*. PhD Thesis, TU Delft, 1996.
5 Tjallingii, Sybrand P. *Carrying Structures, Urban Development Guided by Water and Traffic Networks* in: Hulsbergen, E.D., Klaasen, I. and Kriens, I. (ed). *Shifting Sense. Looking Back to the Future in Spatial Planning*. Amsterdam: Techne Press, 2005, p 355-369.
6 Valsson, Trausti. *Planning in Iceland*. Reykjavik: University of Iceland Press, 2003, p 336. http://bit.ly/1ezJNZ4
7 Diamond, Jared M. *Collapse: How Societies Choose to Fail or Succeed*. New York: Penguin Books, 2005, p 197.

Research by Design in the Reykajvík Capital Area (RCA)

Giambattista Zaccariotto and
Arna Mathiesen

In Reykjavik Capital Area (RCA) a new urban question has emerged, as a consequence of the unprecedented process of spatial upscaling that occurred during the first decade of the twentieth century. Bigger roads and new neighbourhoods on the outskirts of the city are the most visible evidence of the process. Less visible is the decline in liveability across the region, that began during the boom and became exacerbated during the crisis that followed. Paradoxically, despite the rhetoric of sustainability in planning and design, attempts to improve conditions typically only worsen them.

Locally, conflicts over goals and means among key actors such as urbanists, policy makers and investors, complicate the future planning of the built environment. Globally, changing socio-economic and climatic conditions further obscure the direction of future planning. Paradoxes, conflicts and dilemmas indicate the "need to formulate new questions" and to produce a fresh narrative that is not simply about the current critical situation and its possible counteraction.

Two workshops were organised in 2011 and 2012 as participative research actions. The design study made as its priorities an ecological framework and the concept of resiliency: to explore strategies that were based on the optimal use of local resources, physical and cultural, adapting to the conditions at hand. The construction of scenarios is an appropriate technique for such an investigation. A scenario is a "story about the future" prompted by a "what..if ?" question. A design scenario illustrates a future condition that may result from a hypothetical change related to selected elements of the present condition, such as habitation, water, food, mobility in the RCA study.

The two workshops focused on the same four case studies; four recent residential areas along the edge of the RCA, namely Úlfarsárdalur, Helgafellsland, Hafnarfjarðarhöfn and Vellir. All of the areas were unfinished at the time of the workshops, and each presented specific problems and opportunities. The workshops engaged participants, such as students, researchers and local agents, in a process of interaction and peer-to-peer learning that produced new knowledge.

The guiding principles of ecological rationality, such as reduce-reuse-recycle, steered the process; a miscellaneous palette of tools, including field visits, mapping, conceptual models and interviews, motivated "reflection-in-action" through cyclical operations of description (present situation), interpretation and prefiguration (possible future outcome). A coming and going of approximations and adjustments of the first hypothesis at the beginning of the workshop ("what... if"?) suggested cultural and physical potentials of the context at all scales.

1st workshop
At the Icelandic Academy of the Arts, undergraduate programme in Architecture.

Student participants: Hlynur Axelsson, Heiðdís Helgadóttir, Liesa Marie Hugler, Laufey Jakobsdóttir, Jón Valur Jónsson, Axel Kaaber, Helga B. Kjerúlf, María Kristín Kristjánsdóttir, Aron Freyr Leifsson, Arnheiður Ófeigsdóttir and Sigurlín Rós Steinbergsdóttir, all students at the Icelandic Academy of the Arts.
Instructors: Sigrún Birgisdóttir, Arna Mathiesen and Giambattista Zaccariotto.

2nd workshop
At the Agricultural University of Iceland, Master of Planning programme with guests from the post-professional European Master of Urbanism (EMU).

Student participants: Lucile Ado, French from the Universitat Politèchnica de Catalunya, Gunnar Ágústsson, Icelandic from LBHÍ, Luca Filippi, Italian from Universitá IUAV di Venezia, Perrine Frick, French from the Universitat Politèchnica de Catalunya, Carlos Salinas Gonzalez, Mexican from TU Delft, Sigurborg Haraldsdóttir, Icelandic from the Oslo School of Architecture, Johanna Jacob, Belgian from KU Leuven, Sam Khabir, Iranian from KU Leuven, Guo Mengdi, Chinese from TU Delft, Jón Hámundur Marinósson, Icelandic from LBHÍ, Zongkai Zhou, Chinese from KU Leuven, Sæunn Kolbrún Þórólfsdóttir, Icelandic from LBHÍ.
Instructors: Emanuel Giannotti, Sigríður Kristjánsdóttir, Arna Mathiesen, Sybrand Tjallingii, Paola Viganò and Giambattista Zaccariotto

Following the four design briefs, the results of the two workshops are presented as a coherent narrative; a contribution for an open and pluralistic "conversation" with the RCA situation.

WHAT IF: the urban landscape on the fringe of the capital leads the way for a new vision of Co-living, exploring new combinations of collective and individual spaces, including accommodation for the alternative tourist, one used to a slower pace?

What incentives could support such a scenario and what sort of processes would be suitable to develop them?

How does the intervention contribute to the economy as well as the comfort of the inhabitants?

Co-Living

Flexible spaces, alternative forms of co-habiting and hybrid uses make dwelling more robust

In the times of abundance the amount of housing units produced on the outskirts of the Reykjavik Capital Area (RCA) did not correspond with the population growth. Between 2000 and 2008, the number of dwellings in Iceland (including those under construction) increased by 26.8%, while the number of inhabitants grew by only 13%. Between 2002 and 2008, 313.4m^3 of living space in proportion to each new person got underway in the RCA.

Overzealous development, coupled with emigration and a population shift to other less expensive towns because of the recession, has meant that existing housing stock fails to meet present needs. There is an unfulfilled demand for particular kinds of housing in Reykjavik: affordable rental space for dwelling and tourist accommodation. This need has been brought about by unemployment, accumulation of household debt and the relatively low value of the local currency. Homeownership has taken precedence up until now, but financial problems make it simply impossible for many people to pay the mortgages. The fact that a whole generation (the young) now own much less than nothing (as a result of deep debt) renders the house ownership model a rather dubious part of the welfare system, of which it has long been considered part. Social housing is also scarce, and rent is expensive.

There is a need for more flexible household space, which could cater for entirely new and different needs and practices. Indeed as the habits and conventions established during the boom years are brought into question, so too the built environment must adjust to

reflect this. Currently, young people postpone starting their own households and stay with their parents, and some small businesses economise by moving from rented space to a working area at home. In general people have more time to spend at home and with their children, due to the scarcity of work since the economy slowed down. As more time is released, the opportunity arises for new living and accommodation practices.

Many buildings stand empty. This is especially noticeable on the outskirts where property, which could not be paid for by the inhabitants, has been taken over by loan institutions owned to a large degree by foreign creditors. The burst of the housing bubble left behind large developments of single family houses (often 300-400m^2) of which many remain unfinished. The other, very different, dominant typology is freestanding rectangular apartment blocks, containing considerably smaller units.

Developments on the outskirts mingle with leisure spaces traditionally located on the fringe, such as horse stalls and riding paths. These facilities remain largely unexplored in an urban setting with regard to the increasing tourism in the country, despite the fact that the Icelandic horse is an internationally renowned breed which is a huge attraction for visitors. The horse stalls under development during the economic boom (many of which are not completed) have large living spaces integrated within their complexes. In the present financial circumstances these might be thought a superfluous luxury, but in this scenario they could serve as a resource to be further explored, and possibly retrofitted.

Resources: Unnecessarily large homes, empty and unfinished buildings. Icelandic horses, riding paths, horse stalls, exotic nature, unused structures, new social practices, eccentric tourists.

WHAT IF: the urban landscape on the fringe of the capital had dwellings and workplaces integrated with nature, agriculture and horticulture?

What incentives could support such a scenario and what sort of processes would be suitable to develop them?

How does the intervention contribute to the economy as well as the comfort of the inhabitants?

You are what you eat

Growing your own food is like printing your own money

Historically, agricultural practices existed right within the urban fabric of Reykjavik. Post-war centralisation in bigger farms, and food imports, have pushed agriculture out of the city. After the meltdown, interest in growing herbs, vegetables and fruit trees has exploded, and organic farming has increased drastically in recent years. Farmers markets have also emerged.

In the three springs which followed the crash, around 2500 people registered on courses to learn about growing food, and this trend has continued; during the times of apparent abundance pre-crash, there was no market for this kind of teaching. The horticultural society and other agencies have become involved in projects with many inhabitants and the City of Reykjavik continues to support initiatives for food growing, among them one aimed at building greenhouses which can grow food in the public parks. This is especially pertinent due to the fact that greenhouse management in Iceland is relatively cheap owing to the hot springs and green energy which can provide extra light during the darkest months. Across the RCA, citizens can rent out land for allotment gardens, mostly on the fringe of the capital area.

These activities address the use of the natural urban environment to different degrees: from relatively small household self-consumption to organic local farming for inland consumption, and from the individual to the collective. Harvesting is carried out in kitchen windows, winter gardens, out on balconies and roofs, in private gardens and on land hired from the municipalities. There has been a surge of interest in growing on the premises of apartment blocks but this has proved difficult to realise, as all the owners would have to agree to adapting the use of the collective premises. Harvesting locally cuts the distance between the products and the consumer, and makes people less dependent on the mall and imported foods (which have become much more expensive after the crisis). This provides a certain level of satisfaction for consumers who care about the origin of their food, as well as giving them a chance to support local producers. Additionally it stimulates social cohesion and serves to educate children about food production. These practices can be enforced with planning and architectural intervention.

The Green Scarf, a multifunctional forest, is under construction in the territory of the Reykjavik Capital Area, and hedgerow-sheltered growing spaces and shelter woods may become some of the building blocks. Multi-functionality includes reducing the carbon footprint, providing recreation, producing wood for the building industry, preventing erosion and offering shelter from the wind on the heaths (that have been taken for development), while at the same time reinforcing the on-going green structure of the city.

The new suburban residential areas have copious open spaces between the buildings, particularly in areas where not all the planned buildings were erected. This decentralised urban structure represents a potential for better integration of dwellings, workplaces, and actors that work with nature and agriculture, than would be possible in the denser city centre. Climate change also presents an opportunity in Iceland in terms of growing food, since warmer weather makes it easier to grow a greater variety of species.

At the edges of the city there are several individuals who have been threatened by the new developments, regardless of the fact that they have been experimenting with practices involving local resources for decades: pioneers that are a great resource of knowledge and inspiration.

Resources: Soil, water, geothermal water brought to the site by ready-made infrastructure, renewable electro power, horse manure, road network, more spare time, labour.

WHAT IF: Reykjavík became the city of health, shifting towards more resilient water management where storage is a key concept; reducing, reusing and recycling, at all levels, starting from the bottom up?

What incentives could support such a scenario and what sort of processes would be suitable to develop them?

How does the intervention contribute to the economy as well as the comfort of the inhabitants?

Every Drop Counts

Water is essential to all life, and the quality of water is a pressing health issue
Water is vital for all ecosystems

Water has become a contested good, and issues surrounding water are used by researchers to reveal power structures (Political Ecology). It is clear that Iceland has its own treasure: the largest quantity of renewable freshwater per person in Europe. The freshwater resources are estimated to be around 170,000 million m^3 and the reserves are the most secure in the world because rainfall averages 2000 mm per year, the population is scarce and there is a low level of water stress, (European Environmental Agency 2010; Icenews 2010). Water offers many benefits, in swimming pools or greenhouses, for salmon breeding, fishing, recreational water courses and as lakes.

Water is a sensitive resource, and it can be in short supply even in some areas in Iceland where it may appear to be abundant - for example Reykholt, Akureyri and Bláfjöll. Droughts, flooding and pollution all present a threat to the ecological, social and economic foundations of any region.

The new housing areas on the fringe of the capital area negotiate the conservation space of the natural water resources, i.e. Gvendarbrunnar. Despite there being several half-built industrial areas with ready-made infrastructures in the RCA, the city of Reykjavík is planning new industrial areas on Hólmsheiði heath, near the water resource.

Water is instrumental in carrying heat from the geothermal reservoir to the surface. There was extensive drilling for geothermal steam in the vicinity of the RCA, during the last few years before the meltdown. However, even though geothermal power is marketed as green sustainable energy, it poses problems for the built environment and for habitation. Airborne pollution from the plant in the RCA is hazardous to health, and also damages electrical equipment. Furthermore, there are local problems with waterborne surface pollution, even in the Þingvellir National Park: new boreholes have to

be drilled when older boreholes are emptied, as it takes an estimated 200 years to refill them.

The drilling causes fractures in the rock, which can then generate earthquakes felt within a 45 kilometre (28 mile) radius, putting a strain on built structures and causing anxiety among the population. An escalation of the drilling activity in the Reykjanes peninsula is currently being planned, as part of the upscaling of aluminium production in the vicinity. Foreign businessmen are encouraged to participate in the processes, the idea being that investment from abroad will save Iceland from economic ruin.

In new residential areas piping infrastructures have been implemented. In order to service the few scattered inhabited dwellings, the system has to function at full pressure, as though it were servicing the larger number of buildings originally intended for the whole area. Along with other resource-intensive ventures, this has pushed the energy company to the brink of bankruptcy.

Recent global modifications exacerbate the pressure on water resources around the world as climate change brings shifts in precipitation and evaporation patterns. Global land use intensifies as the population expands, and when the water supply demand goes up as a result, there is an increase in the discharge of pollutants – an excessive input of nutrients and pesticides from agriculture, as well as industrial pollutants. These trends make fresh water increasingly valuable, as evidenced by the rising number of conflicts over the control of water, triggering global migration in the search for a better supply.

The abundance of water resources in Iceland makes it a highly attractive location for metal smelters; this is because energy from hydroelectric and geothermal power is considered renewable, and the energy prices are kept low and steady, as opposed to the price fluctuations associated with fossil fuels.

Resources: infrastructure, housing, land, water, energy.

WHAT IF: a slow network of high connectivity could take over as a main source of transport in the Reykjavík Capital Area?

What incentives could support such a scenario, and what sort of processes would be suitable to develop them?

How does the intervention contribute to the economy as well as the comfort of the inhabitants?

Slow Network

The traffic network links human activities and exchange of goods

In past decades, the planning of transport infrastructure has been guided by the principle of concentrating transport into large road corridors for high dynamic traffic: a fast network.

Urban highways have connected high dynamic uses, such as businesses, offices and mass recreation. The corridors have become bigger and more difficult to cross.

The bulk of new commercial space, which in the Capital Area expanded by 36% from 2002 to 2008, is lined up along the main road corridors. These spaces are surrounded with large asphalt surfaces (designed for parking), and many of them are not in use due to lack of business.

New residential areas were initially planned to be equipped with some local services, schools in particular, but many of them have not come about because of the meltdown. This makes it necessary for residents to seek these services elsewhere, and as they are dispersed, it is difficult to do so without a car – the result is energy-intensive, expensive, time-consuming and polluting.

The issues embedded in this transport system, and the deadlock of the unplanned meltdown, penetrate the dynamic within the home and might impact upon gender roles. Far-fetched as it may sound, careers can be defined by who has priority over use of the car, and who has to spend long hours collecting goods, ferrying children to and from schools, or other activities; the further apart the facilities are spread, the more time has to be spent reaching them.

A local discussion is ongoing, about the proposal to increase the diversity of transport corridors by further improving the connectivity. This would involve trains, underground transport, or trams that might have a fair chance of competing with motorised traffic, and integrating into the existing bus network. Reduction of CO_2 is at the heart of the debate, and it has become more urgent because of the high cost of imported fossil fuel, combined with a shortage of current alternatives to individual car transport. However, it is not likely to come to fruition in the near future for a number of reasons: the present economic situation, the buses being driven with methane, and a political regime in Reykjavik that has a greater interest in developing projects in the old city centre than finding solutions to problems in more remote parts of town and neighbouring municipalities.

Main roads in the capital area, built between 2002 and 2008, run for 60.8 kilometres (37.7 miles), minor roads for over 163 kilometres (101.2 miles), and nine highway interchanges were completed. There are currently only 1.5 kilometres of paths built exclusively for bicycle riding. Some money has recently been allocated in the budget, but it is to cover pedestrian use as well.

A call for the distribution of individual transport in all sorts of low dynamic transport corridors might encompass bicycle or riding paths, pedestrian tracks, children's trails, facilities for small boats, and a form of bike lift (similar to those for skiing) to transport them up hills. This sort of infrastructure is cheap to implement and use, and encourages a more flexible, healthy lifestyle, both in terms of exercise and mental well-being.

The slow network could go alongside fine grain and land uses, for example the protected areas, the green corridors, collective ecological gardens, streams and gently sloping sheltered areas.

Mainstream use of a slow network will demand more workplaces close to, or inside, the residential areas.

Resources: Existing mobility network, water network, energy network, open areas.

Helgafellsland

on fertile soil

Google Digital Globe

2002

Google Digital Globe

2008

Existing Situation

Helgafellsland residential area (about 44 hectares in size), in the municipality of Mosfellsbær,
is located on the northeast edge of the
Reykjavík Capital Area, where a rural and
urban system merge into a hybrid. The whole
area is built on south facing farmland under
Helgafell hill, which was an important point of
reference in the Saga Age, and in translation
means Holy Mountain.

Helgafellsland interacts with a woodland
corridor which goes by the name of The Green
Scarf, and which is planned, and partly realised, along the edge of the Capital Area.

Streams run alongside the site, one of which
has geothermal water and a lovely waterfall.
The water was important for one of the densest
(although small) urban developments in the
country, of its time; Álafoss, an industrial
settlement, was established here in 1896 and it
draws its name from the waterfall.

The water was essential for the manufacture
of textiles, as it was used to drive the factory
wheels and to wash the wool from the Icelandic
sheep. The river used to be warm because
of the hotsprings nearby, hence the name
Varmá (warm river). A dam was built over the
waterfall to facilitate recreational activities for
the workers - swimming and diving. Nowadays
the river has a cooler temperature, as the
warm water is channelled elsewhere to heat
up buildings. Once the textile industries had
closed down in 1990, plans were afoot to tear
down the old buildings, but this was avoided
as some creative minds saw the potential of
the building mass, and argued the case for it to
become a resource for Mosfellsbær community
as a whole.

Helgafellsland residential area lies on the
other side of the river, immediately north of
Álafoss. There are horse riding paths across
interesting landscapes in all directions from
the site, out to the sea, over wetlands, up to
the hills and to parts with impressive natural
water features.

Fig.1-2: Technical infrastructures in the unfinished area;
drinking water and waste water.

Fig. 3: Existing activities near the unfinished area: old
family farm, workshops and a café, rehabilitation centre and
workplaces.

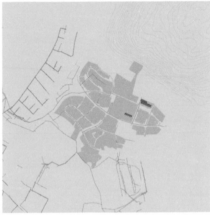

1

2

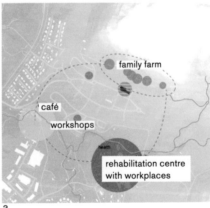

family farm

café

workshops

rehabilitation centre
with workplaces

3

Problems and Potentials

As in similar, recently planned residential settlements, the transition from an overheated housing market to the collapse of the building sector, triggered a series of problems. In the case of Helgafell, very little house building had been started but a considerable amount of infrastructure had been put in place: asphalted roads, street lights, water and energy networks. Complete systems needed to be instigated to serve just a handful of buildings in the area. Several excavations into the fertile soil were undertaken at the start of foundations for buildings that never materialised. The birds have found a use for these water-filled pits.

It is difficult for the local people to carry on building what had been started, if they lack the financial means to do so.

Taking a longer view, The Green Scarf will provide a number of services for the study area; they will include the provision of wind shelters, increased soil fertility, erosion prevention, timber harvesting and leisure opportunities.

The old industrial buildings in Álafoss were built with their facades directly lined up with the road (rarely seen in Iceland) and this creates an intimate atmosphere. Many artists have chosen to establish their work or living spaces there, and locally produced handicrafts are displayed on the ground floor. Outdoors, a café with parking space, and a fountain for horses makes the place a suitable stop-off point for those out on a pleasant stroll or a horse ride. Musicians flock here to make recordings in the studios of the world-famous band Sigur Rós, converted from an old indoor swimming pool. Even though there may be poor spatial connection between Helgafellsland and the immediately adjacent existing community in Álafoss, a contribution to the area as a whole is already being made towards it becoming a vibrant and multifunctional metropolitan edge. The factory in Álafoss, related to construction matters, can also go on to be a beneficial resource for further developments.

Fig 4: A designed synergy of land uses and actors creates a new coherent urban landscape.

4

Scenario

What if the area of Helgafell was retrofitted for becoming a coherent part of The Green Scarf; a park corridor for ecological living and producing? Forms and functions of diverse spaces could fit into a coherent new urban landscape mosaic.

The Green Scarf could be treated, not as a separate area of woodland but, as an integrated part, where synergies of different patches such as deciduous and coniferous woods, agricultural fields and playing fields, greenhouses and settlements, can all blossom. The green belt could, closely linked to Álafoss, turn into a park for living and working, in which the attractive environmental features may play a part in activating new social and economic possibilities.

Helgafellsland has some useful environmental features: fertile soil, good sun exposure and protection from strong winds. These features, if combined with the Álafoss street and urban infrastructures that are not in use, would provide win-win conditions for agricultural functions, as well as an interesting living environment. Suitable environmental conditions for agriculture are limited in Iceland but in this area there are several farms, greenhouses, places for horse breeding, a rehabilitation centre and zero km farmers markets. They could all be redesigned into an agropark. The expanse would become more appealing for habitation purposes, and the spatial attractions in the area could also be improved.

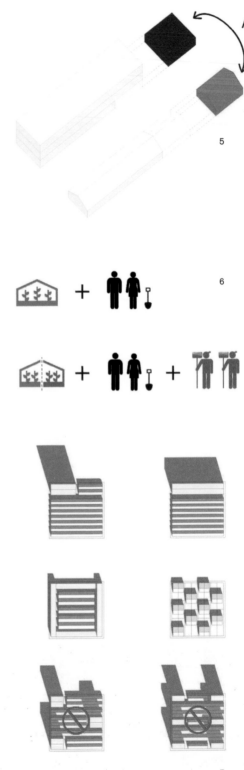

5

6

7

Fig 5: Residential and agricultural spaces are combined in a local economic model.

Fig 6: Local residents and farmers can cooperate in a local greenhouse management model.

Fig 7: The integration of greenhouse and dwelling types is shown on the shadow patterns.

Fig 8: In the upstream portion of the Varma river valley interesting win-win combinations may result from the specialisation and synergism of local spaces, such as the old industrial village and the residential area (a, c) the recent industrial platform facilities (b), the hospital (d), the dwelling-greenhouses (e) and the unfinished residential area (f).

Fig 9: In the downstream portion of the Úlfarsá and Varmá river valleys, interesting win-win combinations may result from the specialisation and synergism of local spaces such as residential areas (a,b), rural golf courses and other sports facilities (c), and pastures along the coast.

8 VISUAL CONCEPT
Investigating the spatial and social impli-
cations of the conceptual framework of the
Varmá valley as a productive landscape

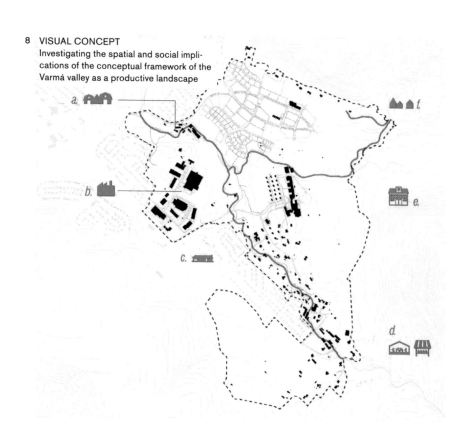

9 VISUAL CONCEPT
Investigating the spatial and social implications of golf courses and urban pastures on
the outskirts of the RCA

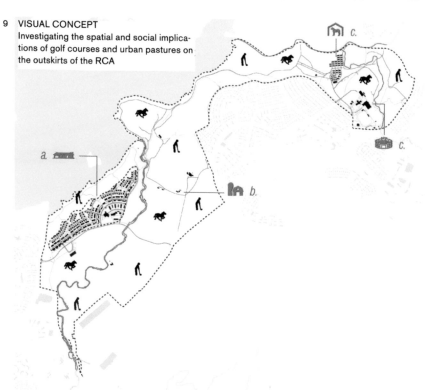

The leftover plots may be retrofitted as coherent elements of the food park, where dwellings and small-scale agricultural activities could integrate for mutual benefit. The original programme for the area comprised 60 new houses for families of four or five people, occupying 755 m² each, and seven apartment blocks, intended for approximately 1000 inhabitants. Two kindergartens and one primary school were also envisaged. What remains today, apart from the completed infrastructures, is just a few scattered, and mostly unfinished, buildings.

The design process investigates a model that combines dwellings and greenhouses on available plots. The revenues from agricultural production can be used as assurance for the bank loans that are necessary to complete the development. For comparison, the restructuring of the greenhouse business in Hveragerði (another geothermal area close by) has been driven by an increased demand for locally produced vegetables and flowers.

The inhabitants can choose between themselves working in their own greenhouse, or sharing the work with a farmers' coop, depending on their different lifestyles. Community Supported Agriculture, CSA, (sometimes referred to as Community Shared Agriculture) is already a successful model in many places around the world.

The concept could be expanded to include the pavilion-like settlements along the coast. These could in turn be linked up with golf courses nearby, a gradual transformation commenced and the project managed carefully so as to enhance biodiversity. This would be a winning situation for all concerned, stakeholders and wildlife. The same approach can be applied along Mosfellsbær's northern border, where a range of sport facilities are concentrated.

The excess water resulting from drilling activity (for geothermal water) could be channelled back to the river. The connection between Álafoss and the new region would be enhanced by this, and a pleasant meeting spot recreated.

Fig 10 : Models of integration between a residential space (red) and a greenhouse (green).

Fig 11 : Water management models for greenhouses: rain (rw) and purified waste (ww) are recycled to reduce consumption of drinking water (dw) and make the water visible.

Fig 12 : Water management testing in a section of the unfinished residential area.

Fig 13 : Greenhouses and residential blocks of flats.

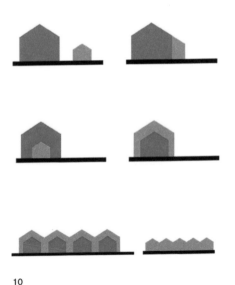

10

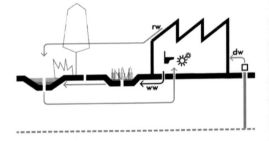

11

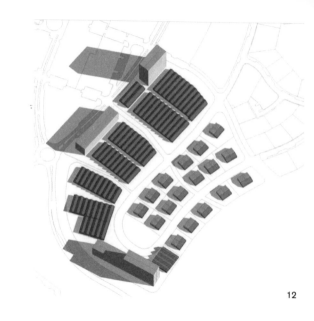

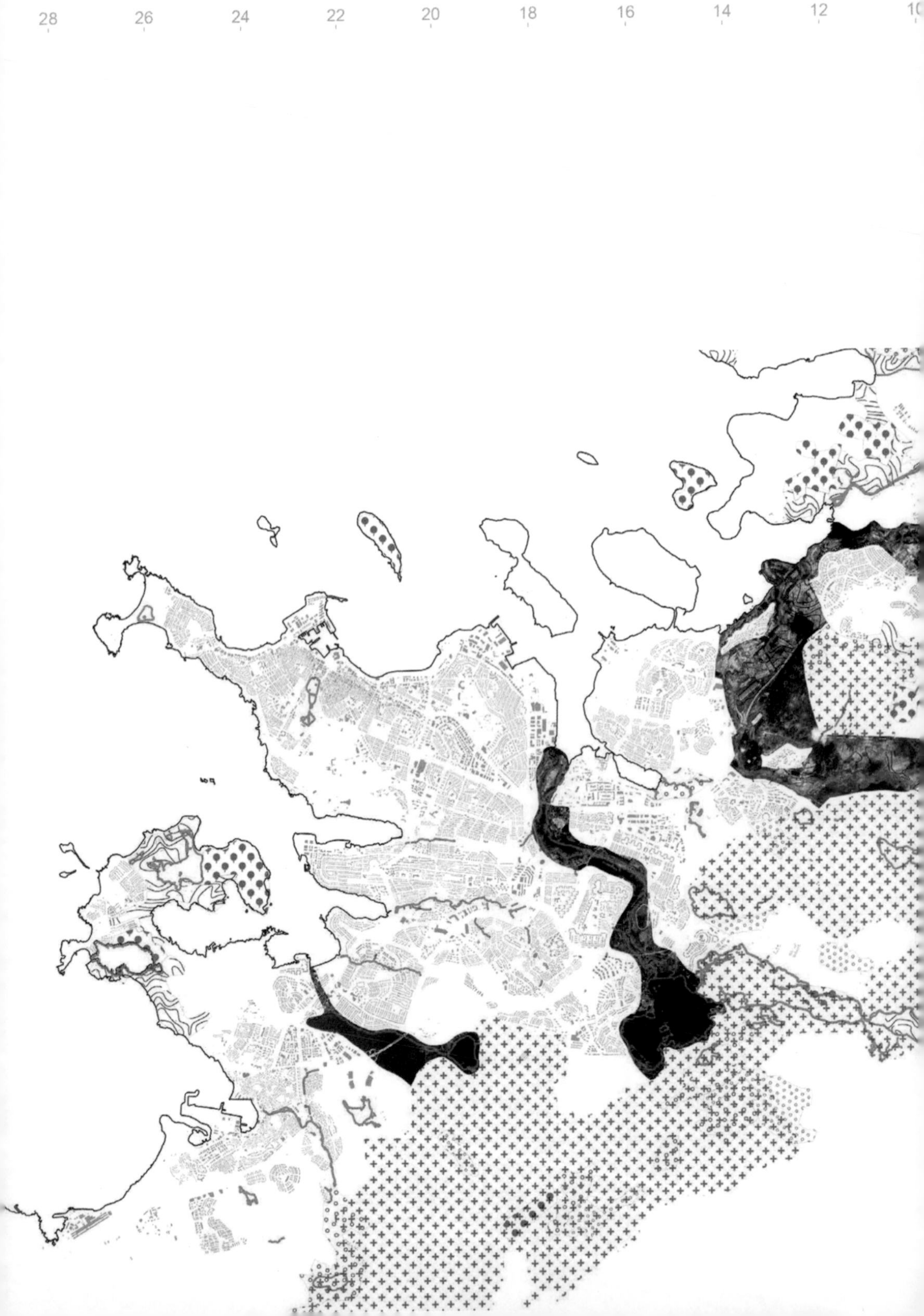
28
26
24
22
20
18
16
14
12

Reykjavík Capital Area and the future

Combining agricultural patches such as grasslands, pastures and greenhouses as part of a coherent strategy for settlement restructuring in Mosfellsbær, may strengthen the multifunctional nature of the green belt system. Low maintenance costs, and a high level of attractiveness based on the understanding of specific environmental features, may play a part in activating and supporting new social and economic possibilities.

From a wider perspective, Mosfellsbær can be seen as a piece in a larger mosaic of the metropolitan Green Scarf; an ecological park corridor that will stretch from fertile soils in the north, under mountain Esja, to lava fields down to the south of Hafnarfjörður. Benefits such as wind sheltering, soil fertility, erosion prevention, water protection and timber harvesting will be derived from this greenway, wild edibles can flourish, and jobs and leisure opportunities will arise. It therefore follows that The Green Scarf will be a basic infrastructure for future healthy, attractive and resilient living and working, on the edge of Greater Reykjavik.

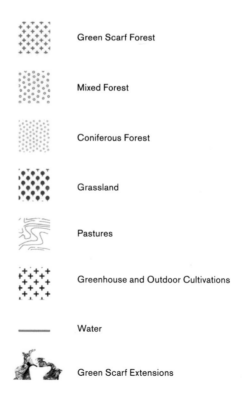

Green Scarf Forest

Mixed Forest

Coniferous Forest

Grassland

Pastures

Greenhouse and Outdoor Cultivations

Water

Green Scarf Extensions

14

Úlfarsárdalur

on tundra

Google Digital Globe

2002

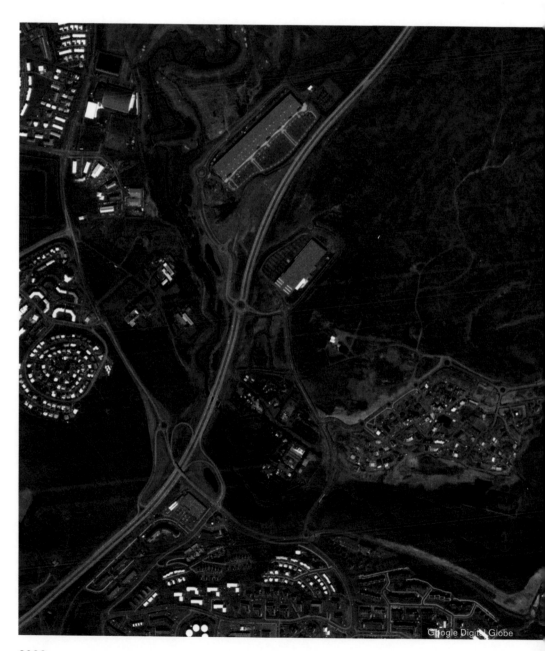

Google Digital Globe

2008

Existing situation

Úlfarsárdalur residential area (about 33 hectares in size) lies on a south-facing and windy slope on the eastern fringe of Reykjavík city. Nearby, on each side of the motorway, shopping malls have been built during the boom. The size of the malls, and the Icelandic climate, makes it reasonable to drive from one shop to another within the same mall. The age of eligibility for a driving licence is 17 in Iceland, and in 2011 there were 646 cars for every 1000 people (Statistics Iceland). Most adults in the neighbourhood own cars.

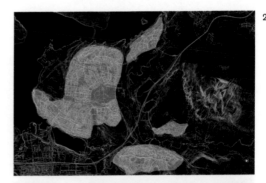

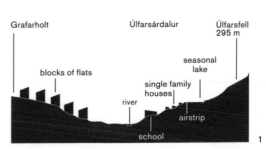

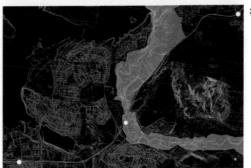

Fig 1 : Simplified section of the Úlfarsá river valley.

Fig 2 : Existing settlements (grey) on ridges, and the related transport network (red) for fast vehicular accessibility along valleys.

Fig 3 : The crossing of the Úlfarsá river valley (green) with the existing parkway is vital for a new system of accessibility in the area.

Problems and Potentials

Empty streets, abandoned plots and half-built houses characterise the neighbourhood of Úlfarsárdalur. People that were lured by the promise of living in a sustainable and attractive community suddenly found themselves living with virtually no neighbours, and far away from the city. It doesn't even make sense to walk to the nearby shopping malls, as it is rather too far for carrying any kind of shopping, and there is no pedestrian access except across a rocky and windy tundra. Only a handful of owners managed to complete the construction of their houses before the crisis hit. It may seem something of a contradiction that the people who did finish their houses are now generally worse off than those who are living in the half-finished buildings; it is because they took on such substantial mortgages, and after the crash those have become a big burden. The cost of having a car has been increasing, and as oil continues to become more scarce the culture of the private car will involve more expense. Families that have incurred a large amount of debt find themselves here in an urban context which only adds to their vulnerability. The future that lies ahead of them is an uncertain one.

After getting firsthand experience of the difficulties encountered in moving around the city without a car (the workshops were held close to this area and it took nearly an hour to get there by public transport, as opposed to ten minutes by car) we concluded that a carless person in this city is basically facing exclusion.

4

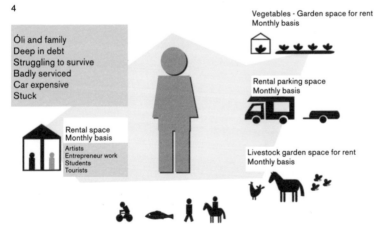

Óli and family
Deep in debt
Struggling to survive
Badly serviced
Car expensive
Stuck

Rental space
Monthly basis
Artists
Entrepreneur work
Students
Tourists

Vegetables - Garden space for rent
Monthly basis

Rental parking space
Monthly basis

Livestock garden space for rent
Monthly basis

Fig 4 : The constraints and opportunities of living on the urban edge.

Fig 5-6 : Úlfarsá river valley is a mosaic of diverse patches that stretch from the source, the Hafravatn lake, to the mouth, the Leiruvogur: aquatic areas, natural riparian areas and upland agricultural fields.

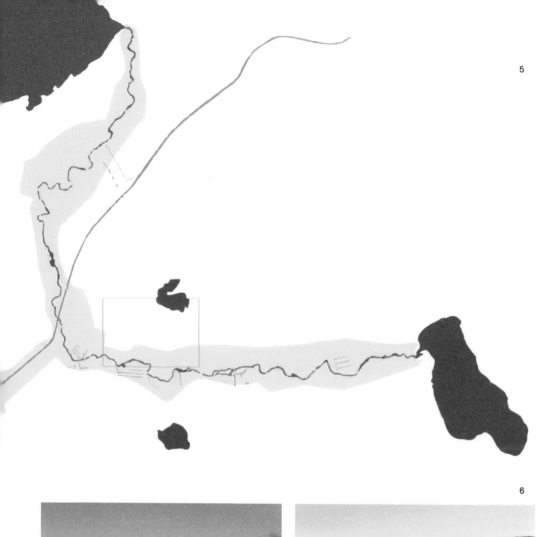

Scenario

What if the semi-finished urban tissue of the place could be assisted towards integration with neighbouring areas, by improving the mobility conditions locally, as well as in the metropolitan area of Reykjavik?

What if the space taken up by existing over-sized main roads in Reykjavik was to be used in a different way: what spatial implications would this shift in emphasis bring to the city? What new types of urban living could emerge on the outskirts?

The proposal radically restructures the network of arterial roads in the city, by implementing a system of Bus Rapid Transit (BRT), with very regular services operating along two fast corridors that cross the capital area from north to south, and from east to west. The new BRT system makes use of existing spaces and integrates them into the motorway; this way it allocates the two central lanes, and the ridge of the highway, to public transport. In that sense, the investment could be optimised. The construction of transit nodes (points where two or more transit routes intersect) would only be required where stops are located, and where links exist to connect them to the neighbouring streets.

Public transport nodes show signs of great potential in cities to induce a process of polarization of social and economic activities; accordingly, in Reykjavík the new nodes are conceptualised as urban platforms that are spatially integrated to the BRT stations. Urban

Fig 7 : New centres centralise high-dynamic activities with spatial and functional diversity, linked to both the fast and slow networks.v

Fig 8 : A bus rapid transit station is a key feature of the new centres.

Fig 9 : High-speed routes, existing parkways, are combined with high-dynamic activities concentrated in new centres; slow-speed routes along water landscapes, such as the river valley and the ocean coast, are combined with low-dynamic activities such as urban agriculture, water storage, recreation and nature conservation.

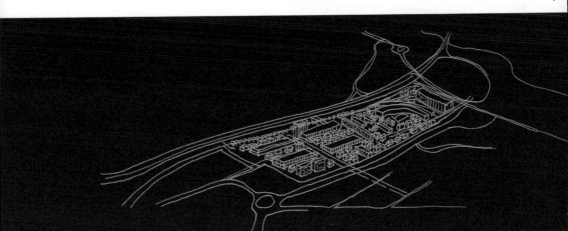

platforms promote intermodal integration between the BRT high frequency system operating at the metropolitan scale, and the local neighbourhood buses. Intensification of mixed-use programmes is encouraged, which engenders a more condensed form of urban life, rather than the sprawling nature of the city on the edge.

The platform is conceived as a public space that will set a framework to unify, and give continuity to, the node, and that allows space for the incremental developing and intensification of the city according to its future needs.

In the context of Úlfarsadalur, the location of the platform is determined by the specific landscape conditions of the area - a river valley that connects the sea with a lake upstream.

The landscape qualities are used as a tool for providing both recreational and natural landscape features to the residents of the area, and become part of a soft mobility corridor in which a variety of walking paths, cycle lanes and tracks for horses play a role in the mobility strategy.

Reacting to uncertainty, we proposed that if new constructions are to be built in the area, priority should be given to the river valley, letting it benefit from its relatively close location to the other complementary neighbourhoods, and to the slow mobility network. Inside the area, a flexible legal framework should give the existing inhabitants of the site permission to make temporary use of the empty plots for activities that could give them an income, such as using small greenhouses or workshops.

In terms of the future, undeveloped plots should be re-evaluated to cope with higher population densities so that maximum use could be made of the infrastructures, and so that the areas could become more of an attractive proposition for businesses, and the inhabitants less dependent on commuting.

10

Fig 10 : Diverse landform conditions, from river valley to hill peaks, together with slow-speed routes, offer excellent possibilities for slow-dynamic practices such as urban agriculture and outdoor sports.

Fig 11-12 : Leisure, husbandry and hospitality.

11

12

Reykjavik Capital Area and the future

On the scale of the metropolitan area of Reykjavík, the proposed system of platforms will provide easier access to services. Better connections between the slow, local scale of the neighbourhood and the high-speed corridors connecting the neighbourhood with other places in the metropolitan area, will create synergies across the scales. It is good for the economy, and more socially inclusive, if everybody can easily get to where they want or have to go in the city, for work and other purposes, without the need of a car.

Re-evaluation of what the neighbourhoods can become, together with the improvement of mobility with the incremental development of the platforms across the metropolitan of Reykjavik, will lay the groundwork for a more inclusive and well-rounded urban environment for the future.

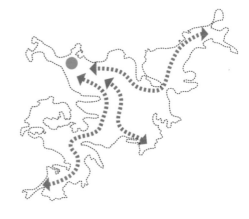

13

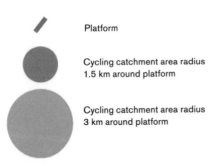

Platform

Cycling catchment area radius
1.5 km around platform

Cycling catchment area radius
3 km around platform

Fig 13 : The existing centralised traffic flow pattern along existing parkways: commuting from municipalities on the edge to the centre of Reykjavik.

Fig 14 : Distribution of bus rapid transit nodes along the main parkways that cross the great capital area in N-S and E-W directions.

Fig 15 : The distribution pattern for new centres follows existing patterns but increases their connectivity and accessibility.

Fig 16 : The metropolitan transport network: new centres as transit nodes and cycling catchment areas, in relation to existing neighbourhoods.

16

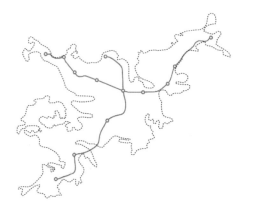

14

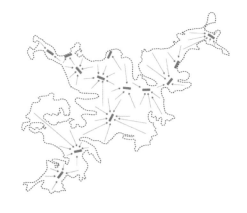

15

Hafnarfjarðarhöfn

on landfill

2002

Google Digital Globe

2008

Existing Situation

Hafnarfjörður (the fjord with a harbour) is located at the southern part of the Reykjavík Capital Area and is first mentioned in the literature of the 14th century. It has grown from fishing and trading, and is today the only municipality in the capital area which still bases a large part of its industry on fishing and related enterprise. Owing to the nature of its commerce, it has spread out from the harbour and into the hills, and today the waterfront constitutes the town centre, holding almost all the official buildings, restaurants, shops and institutions. It remains largely defined by a substantial road running along the waterfront, and the enormous number of parking spaces in the town centre. The whole of the present harbour (about 39 hectares in size) is a landfill site that took over 30 years in the making. The harbour activities include fishing, importing and exporting, boat building, the making of nets, and other related work. It is also home to a few artists' studios, a restaurant and some offices.

Only a section of the harbour is open to the public and they tend to use it for jig fishing – not much else happens there. Part of the explanation lies in the fact that only a small area has been developed, while the rest has been left empty; it's used as a dumping ground for all kinds of stuff people want to dispose of.

The harbour infrastructure consists of a simple network of streets, a single footpath, hot and cold water, power and a sewage system that was recently renewed. Sewage is sent to a treatment plant and, after a mechanical cleaning stage, waste water is pumped 5km out into the fjord. The solid residuals are brought to a landfill site. The harbour is well-connected to a rather poor public transportation system. Two buses run all the way through the area, with three stops. From the central bus station, 900 metres away, bus connections span out across the whole capital area. Where the urban fabric touches the waterfront, everywhere there is landfill. Where town and ocean meet, large stone revetments are in place to prevent land erosion. At selected spots around the harbour edge, a pier makes contact with ships possible. Right outside the town of Hafnarfjörður, at both ends, the edge transforms back into a natural sandy beach. All over the capital area this is what one finds: large stone revetments preventing contact with the Atlantic Ocean, at the very place where the urban fabric, with its inhabitants, meets the sea.

1

Fig 1: The radical spatial change of Hafnarfjörður bay over the last century: the platform, approximately 40 ha, is the result of an incremental process of filling in the natural bay.

Problems and Potentials

The type of edge found in Hafnafjörður ruptures any contact between the sea and the people, and makes it virtually impossible to experience any visual appreciation of the tides.

Seeing the harbour of Hafnarfjörður in the context of the other harbours in the capital area reveals that all the municipalities planned the extension of the harbours in the same manner in the same period. It seems that each municipality wanted their harbour to be the main one for the whole capital area – for fishing, import and export trade – and this went hand in hand with the need to dispose of debris produced from other ongoing urban transformations. During the planning process, there seems to have been no consultation between the various authorities, with the result that there are too many oversized harbours in different places.

There is an abundance of hot and cold water, cheap and clean power and recently a renewed sewage system in the area.

One of the reasons people dump rubbish at the harbour is precisely because they cannot be seen doing it – the area is so vast, and no-one is there to watch them.

The municipal plans were aimed at developing harbours that worked for extremely large industries, and the size and scale of the plot was out of proportion with the size of the town of Hafnarfjörður. There are limits to how much sewage can be dumped into the fjord without harming ecosystems. The sewage can, with appropriate treatment, become a resource for future scenarios with focus on ecological cycles. The abundance of space on the site would be a useful resource in such scenarios.

Fig 2 : Existing constraints and potentials in the area (clockwise from top left): wind conditions, hot water network, drinking water network, the extent of the built on area, a fenced off area, and a soft natural edge vs. hard edge.

Fig 3 : Unused cars, building cranes and other items stored behind the fence, protecting the inaccessible part of the harbour.

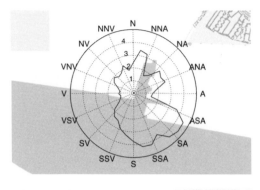

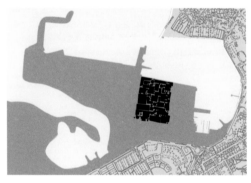

2

Scenario

What if the existing infrastructure could have an alternative mix and synergy of uses? We suggest using it – and that includes streets, footpaths, hot and cold water pipes, power cords and sewage systems – as an overlaying grid into which new projects can be placed.

The new projects differ from the old plans. They are a step towards a more sustainable and resilient future, and contribute to food security, recreation, the development of tourism, through camping for example, and the establishment of small businesses such as fishing. It is accomplished by means of a large variety of playing fields and greenhouses, and the flat terrain of the harbour is well-suited for these functions. The glasshouses have an all year-round multipurpose use, for indoor sports, events, markets, as greenhouses and so forth. Although their usage is multifunctional, the main focus is on food production, with relation to existing fishing businesses and access to plentiful pure water, as well as clean and low-cost energy in Iceland. Consequently, the greenhouses can foster food production on a grand scale, at the same time as housing food and fish markets, and food-related enterprises. This can become a pedagogic tool for a future generation; a generation more aware of where food originates and how it can be safely produced locally.

4

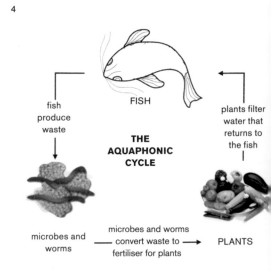

5

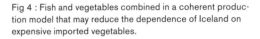

6

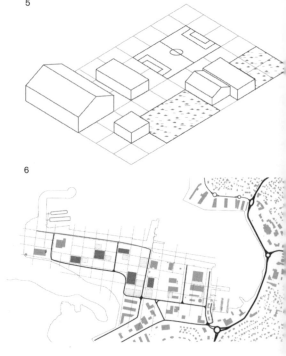

Fig 4 : Fish and vegetables combined in a coherent production model that may reduce the dependence of Iceland on expensive imported vegetables.

Figs 5-6 : The spatial restructuring of the harbour, from industrial space to a multifunctional park that combines harbour facilities with urban agriculture and recreation, is based on a flexible parcellisation to control the incremental process of change.

Fig 7 : Availability of wide open and sheltered spaces, and easy water and land connectivity, makes the existing platform a suitable expanse for markets and for displaying goods produced locally.

Fig 8 : Low maintenance vegetation patches are established in a relatively short space of time, by guiding a process of vegetation colonisation that fits the ecological potential of the area, as well as using existing vacant spaces as a plant nursery.

Figs 9-10 : Plan and section of a possible stage in the process of restructuring the existing harbour platform; new production and harbouring facilities are combined with research and leisure facilities.

8

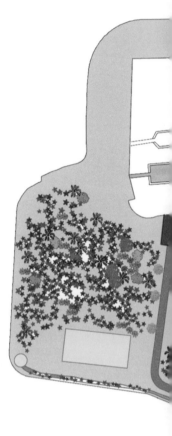

What if a new ecosystem was introduced to the site? One actually based on the extraordinary capabilities of the plant lupine, which has the power to transform sand into nutritious soil; it allows other pioneer species such as chervil to settle in, and gradually establishes an attractive habitat for larger shrubs and small trees. The new ecosystem develops in phases over time, and plays an important part in bringing local flora and fauna to the platform. A section of the large stone revetments along the southern edge is transformed into a soft sand and gravel border, which appears and disappears with the rhythm of the tides.

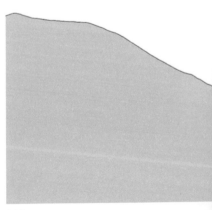

9-10

Reykjavik Capital Area and the future

The nuisance of the harbour can be seen as an opportunity for alternative scenarios as displayed in this exercise. It shows that the Hafnarfjörður harbour can become something different from the other harbours in the RCA; something that has more meaning for the local people and their survival. It also shows alternatives in building up businesses, in making food and in combining sports, tourism and nature for a more resilient urbanity.

Gufunes

Bryggjuhverfið

Sundahöfn

Reykjavíkurhöfn

Nauthólsvík

Kópavogshöfn

Hafnafjarðarhöfn

Straumsvík

Figs 11-13 : Existing harbours at the capital area level; the incremental restructuring of harbours, to improve their spatial and functional integration with the residential districts nearby, may be combined with a new system of metropolitan connectivity and accessibility.

224

12

13

Vellir

on lava

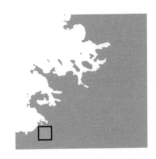

Google Digital Globe

2002

Google Digital Globe

2008

Existing Situation

Vellir is the newest residential area of Hafnarfjörður (about 200 hectares in size) and is located on the outskirts of the municipality, halfway between the airport and the centre of the capital area. In Vellir less than half of the planned constructions had been completed at the time the crisis hit. Today an estimated 4,323 people live in Vellir, the majority between 21 and 40 years old. The number includes 737 children of primary school age, and 660 in pre-school (calculated autumn 2011). There are two kindergartens, a big new swimming pool, and a sports field in the area.There may be no surface water up above, where the top layer is a young porous lava field, but large rivers run underground. Despite the presence of this water, which is of drinking quality, Hafnarfjörður municipality is serviced by water that has been pumped up and transported in big pipes from several places quite far away. In 1975 Hitaveita Reykjavíkur (Reykjavik Energy) became the company in charge of this water system, and the warm water and energy is sourced from the geothermal power plant that they own and operate in Hellisheiði. Hafnarfjörður has two main geological rock formations: glacier impacted basalt and modern lava. There has been a massive amount of volcanic activity in the last 10,000 years, and the most recent lava is about one thousand years old. A lava valley extends to the sea, through Vellir and all over the vast majority of Hafnarfjörður municipality. The region is well known for its horse riding tours, and there are also pedestrian paths winding through the impressive and unusual landscapes on the Reykjavík peninsula; its shape has been dictated by the close proximity to the active volcanic area, between the peninsula and the glacier Langjökull. Several quite prominent hills rise up from the lava. The overall landscape is diverse and uneven, with numerous fissures penetrating deep down.

Not far away from Vellir, on the oldest lava, it is possible to see the rapid evolution of vegetation on the type of soil that develops over time on such a surface. The prominent plants are lava moss, crowberry and several primitive species. Hot groundwater in Iceland is loaded with heavy minerals. The famous Blue Lagoon, a constructed lake that makes use of excess water from a geothermal plant, shows that it is possible to saturate a water course to the extent that the minerals form a carpet at the bottom of the depression, and then block the pores of the basaltic rock. The wind drives the fertile soil into ravines in the lava field and there the biggest plants can grow.

1

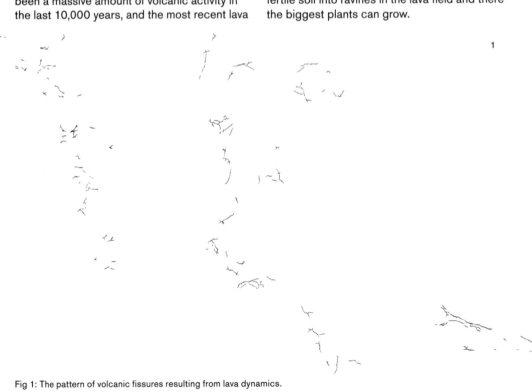

Fig 1: The pattern of volcanic fissures resulting from lava dynamics.

Problems and Potentials

Vellir has the feeling of a strange landscape, where there are wide roads, built and equipped with lighting and public utilities, leading to deserted fields of concrete. The area is exposed to polluting fumes that are carried across on prevailing winds from the southwest where there is an aluminium plant; the power lines to the plant frame the site on the east side.

The planning documents for Vellir state that the main focus should be on the good quality of the neighbourhood, a high standard of architecture, well-connected services and transport, road safety, and a thoughtful relationship with the natural surroundings, which should include protection of the site's lava landscape. However, none of it feels as though it was accomplished. Issues creating problems in the neighbourhood are varied. First of all, there are financial and social aspects, with many families living in unfinished houses. Sometimes they are crammed into a single room, sometimes they live in temporary buildings adjacent to their unfinished house. Owing to the lack of space, and money needed to finish the job, teenagers study in temporary barracks. A young mother commented: 'There are many families with very young children here, and this place is not at all suitable for children.' A new centre, planned for development between the residential area and the highway, is now a wasteland of a parking lot, scattered with big unused and empty buildings, some of them half-finished. Nobody knows when, or even if, the plan will be completed or whether it will work. There are very few social services, no local shop and the urban sprawl covers a wide area. The population density is very low in the capital area and it is virtually impossible to attend a social occasion without the use of a car.

Vellir is less than 5 km from the centre of Hafnarfjörður and well connected to Reykjavik and the airport by means of a motorway. Public transport, however, is scarce. The infrastructure is oversized and designed for an endless queue of private cars.

Building on a lava field brings with it the real risk of being stuck in a new lava stream at some point.

The geological conditions at Hafnarfjörður, in the rainy southwest corner of the country, with an abundance of water so close at hand yet invisible, throw up questions concerning the sensible use of local water sources and why this region should be so dependent on water from far away.

Fig 2: The existing landscape matrix is a mosaic of lava fields, golf courses, wetlands and tundra areas that consist of lichen, moss, grass and shrubs.

Fig 3: The high porosity of the top layer of lava results in dry land with a scant amount of water on the surface and a large underground water flow, as shown by the red arrows within the black box.

2

3

Scenario

What if the unfinished infrastructures of the neighbourhood were to become the carrying structures for a new water scheme, thereby reducing water consumption and boosting vegetation succession? What if the unfinished, abandoned buildings were recycled for innovative uses that increase the diversity of activities in the neighbourhood? What if the qualities of the lava landscape were highlighted?

With the houses in mind, rainwater could be stored and used for water-intensive activities that do not require top quality drinking water, such as car washing. On a larger neighbourhood scale, runoff water, canalized along the roads, could be delivered to selected areas in the barren lava fields; the very special ground

5

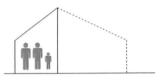

4

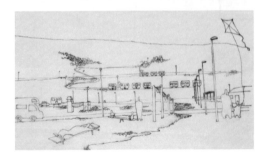

Fig 4 : Suitable spaces for tourist accommodation.

Fig 5 : Conceptual models for unfinished or partially finished houses, showing the integration of guest rooms and greenhouses.

Figs 6-7 : Section and plan of a conceptual model for a new local water cycle to reduce water consumption, protect groundwater, and carry a process of vegetation colonisation that fits the local ecological potentials; better living conditions are restored and small tourism-related and family-based enterprises can be sustained.

6

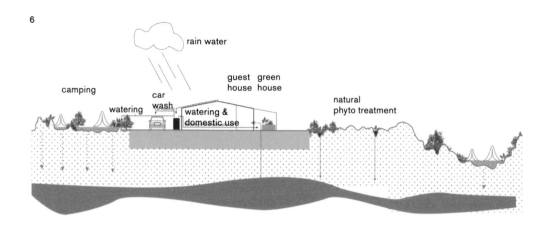

camping   watering   car wash   guest green house house   rain water   natural phyto treatment   watering & domestic use

7

there, with its micro cracks and depressions, has interesting potential for vegetation management. Releasing stormwater into land depressions, lined in advance with a thin layer of fertile soil, could go hand in hand with speeding up the ecological succession of vegetation as well as cleaning runoff water. We can envisage new functions for the plot bringing economic value to those living there. As the area is located close to the airport, Reykjavik and some important touristic attractions such as the Blue Lagoon, tourist accommodation in Vellir might be a good proposition. Accessibility to the pedestrian and horse riding paths, and the close proximity to equestrian centres, are useful selling points in terms of a more sustainable type of tourism. Unfinished houses could be put to good use as guesthouses, shared spaces, camping areas or 'Green Boxes'. One of the large unused buildings along the road could be transformed into a lava museum, displaying the sections of lava layers down to groundwater level. An educational approach could be taken, to value, preserve and throw a spotlight on the unique qualities of the fragile lava landscape.

The slow means of getting around, and inaccessibility of the area by public transport, could both be improved by connecting it to the main centres around Reykjavik on a fast bus route. The bus stop could be at the entrance to the whole area. A good pedestrian path and bicycle lane could link Vellir to the city centre, and small shops and services could be set up within the unused buildings.

8

Fig 8 : Conceptual model showing two centres connected, Vellir and Hafnarfjörður.

Figs 9-10 : Conceptual models for retrofitting a commercial building in the area as a visiting centre dedicated to lava landscapes.

Fig 11 : A new landscape mosaic: in addition to lava fields, rural golf courses, wetlands and tundra areas, a corridor of public spaces is integrated to connect Vellir with Hafnarfjörður, and the renewed harbour; Vellir's planned centre will be the central point of a diverse range of activities and the node for a new fast bus transit metropolitan system. The residential area, unfinished but complete with infrastructures, is retrofitted as a camping area.

9

10

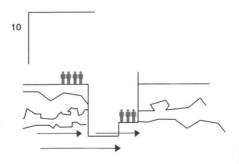

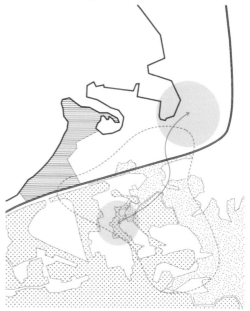

11

Reykjavik Capital Area and the future

Tourism has grown dramatically since the crash, bringing foreign revenue into the economy. Iceland can be seen as a victim of its own success. Maintaining this flow might be dependent on keeping Icelandic prices and salaries down, which would perpetuate the debt problems of many households. Increased tourism can also be very harmful to wildlife, and relatively new and sensitive rock formations. To minimise the impact on the natural environment, the main attractions can be framed and concentrated in specific locations. The best-known tourist track being the so called Golden Circle in south Iceland. Unfortunately, that is now swamped, and landmarks such as Geysir hot spring area are starting to look shabby. What if a more sustainable type of tourism was developed?

Accommodation which offered more interaction with the public than the traditional hotel trade, a business managed by relatively few (and large) operators. Guesthouses, bed and breakfast facilities, and other services would make the sleepy residential areas more lively. Why not build campsites on the abandoned area where there is, after all, already electricity and a water supply? South of Vellir, it is possible to imagine a thematic tourist course, focused around the natural water structures in the vicinity - lakes, geysers, a blue lagoon, rivers. The course could be designed to promote a slower type of tourism, one which utilises the existing pedestrian paths and leads visitors into the landscape on horseback, by bike or simply by walking.

Fig 12 : The local mosaic of Vellir's open spaces is part of the planned green scarf, a metropolitan forest corridor that has the potential to be utilised for multiple services, from wind sheltering and groundwater protection, to food and wood production and leisure, supporting the local communities.

Fig 13 : Vellir's lava fields could be integrated in the existing tourist route that includes part of the peninsula of Reykanes. This Blue Circle could be an addition to the well-established Golden Circle in the east, inland from Reykjavik.

13

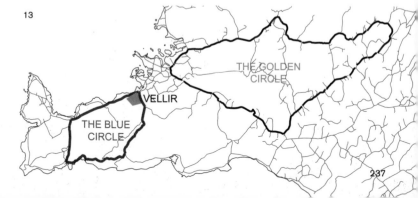

Conclusions

The building boom in Iceland exacerbated the already detrimental conditions of greenhouse gas emissions, energy consumption, construction waste and the exploitation of raw materials, which were to a large extent imported from overseas. Planning and architecture during the boom upheld old models of design that failed to accommodate ecological planning principles and that, albeit unintentionally, produced social and spatial exclusion. An enormous amount of resources was wasted on an irrational environment.

Design impacts both people and the culture at large through the orchestration of a complex system of forces - space, light, texture, distribution of functions, integration of city and nature, infrastructures, material assemblies, et cetera. Policymakers sometimes fail to grasp the complexity of design and, consequently, to recognise the importance of architecture and planning in the critical process of building engaged societies and sustaining healthy citizens. Design is too often associated with luxury, which implies that it is reserved for conditions in which material wealth is abundant. In fact, design is a powerful tool that, at all scales and in all states of economic abundance and scarcity, solves problems and also prevents new ones from emerging in the first place. As such, it should be proactive, not reactive.

Architects and urbanists are educated to spot opportunities where others see only problems, and they are trained to coordinate multiple disciplines that may mobilise change in the built environment in obvious as well as subtle ways. They therefore have a special responsibility to participate in the economic and political venues that affect the built environment. Many designers in Iceland, even before the building boom, understood the value of design principles in the service of resilient environments, and responsible development could have been projected and realised…
Why, then, did it not happen?

The motives behind conventional development do not necessarily promote the needs of the people who would be using the resulting spaces. The private interests of those with capital steer what gets built and what does not, despite laws (mostly unenforced) that mandate sustainable solutions. Election cycles, furthermore, motivate politicians to strive for short-term gains and to ignore the long-term health of buildings, infrastructure, and overall well-being. Incentives are necessary.

As a way forward, it is important to question whether the abundant resources expended during the boom were wasted on projects that benefitted the few rather than the whole. However, the main focus must be on the future, and the opportunities open to those looking at the field with fresh eyes. The practices and tools of the design professions, based on ecological approaches, are ready and waiting to explore the potential of the RCA and other regions around the globe.

Every period has the option of interpreting the territory inherited from its past as a gift - a resource to use and to adapt, through labour, to contemporary needs. The student projects presented here suggest how design may better explore scenarios for setting the agenda, and steer the political discourses. The workshops address critical questions. How may one envision a progressive and responsible adaptation strategy for the contemporary Reykjavík Capital Area? How may one construct conditions that cope with future uncertainty and risk, while sustaining the essential activities of society? What has to be conserved, modified, and substituted?

The workshops were fuelled by a passionate belief in design as a form of action. They were run, in just a few days, with limited funds and on the energy of a handful of dedicated individuals. Just imagine how much a whole profession could achieve if its resources were exploited to their full potential. This book calls for policies that can stimulate more reflection of this kind.

The editors

The Authors

Valur Antonsson is an Icelandic poet, writer and philosopher. He has spent most of his life abroad, growing up in Sweden, then living in France, Spain and America.

The Art Nurses (Listhjúkkur) investigate the possibilities, boundaries and the potential that art holds as a mechanism for dialogue and social change. The Art Nurses is an ongoing collaboration since 2003, between the artists Ósk Vilhjálmsdóttir and Anna Hallin. Vilhjálmsdóttir´s art is generally political; she seeks to disclose certain aspects of contemporary society, to examine them and often invites the viewer into the work for participation. Hallin, born in Sweden and now living in Iceland, employs more subtle methods in her work, but with an undertone that points in a similar direction. It could be said that she works with the subconscious elements of society, but her imagery derives from household equipment such as plumbing, as well as categorisation methods and interior spaces.

Ásmundur Ásmundsson graduated from the Icelandic College of Arts and Crafts (multimedia department) in 1993, and holds a master's degree from the School of Visual Arts in New York, where he graduated in 1996. He has held 21 solo exhibitions since 1993, has participated in over 50 group exhibitions and executed five dozen performances and art interventions. Ásmundsson is actively engaged in the public debate and has written numerous articles for magazines and newspapers, and worked for Icelandic National Broadcasting Service, radio and television. He has sat on the board of the Reykjavik's Sculpture Guild, the Association of Icelandic Visual Artists, the Richard Serra Grant (for young sculptors in Iceland) and The Living Art Museum in Reykjavik. Performance art and interventions are a major part of his work and work processes, but also sculptures, installations, collages and drawings.

Ásmundsson has curated six exhibitions, either in partnership with other curators or independently.

Bryndís Björnsdóttir is an artist and critic. She works on a socio-political research basis, by means of interventions, performances and publications. Björnsdóttir holds a BA in both Art Theory and Visual Arts. Since 2009 Bryndís has co-managed Útúrdúr, an art bookshop and publishing house in Iceland. She is also involved in the interdisciplinary art-based research at the former NATO base on Reykjanes Peninsula.

Margrét H. Blöndal studied art in Iceland and North America. She has been active as an international artist, as well as inventing and developing her teaching approach on all levels of the education system, from primary school to university level. She has shone a special light on the disabled by turning their lack of abilities into a creative source for new potentials. Her poetic approach to installing her works has led her to question the ways we differentiate between space and artworks, between sense and nonsense, normality and abnormality. Margrét H. Blöndal's drawings, writings, installations and intensively sensual sculptures have become a source of inspiration across a very broad spectrum.

Dr. Lúðvík Elíasson received a Ph.D. in economics from the University of Washington, Seattle, in 2001. Dr. Elíasson is an economist at the Central Bank of Iceland and was previously chief economist at MP Bank in Iceland (2009-2011). From 2005 to 2009 he was an economist in the research department of Landsbanki. He has also worked for the Icelandic parliament's (Alþingi) Special Investigation Commission, looking into the causes of internal and external misalignments in the Icelandic economy leading up to the 2008 crisis, with particular emphasis on economic policy, including housing. Dr. Elíasson has written numerous reports on various aspects of the Icelandic economy. His research has been published in the *Journal of Environmental Economics and Management* and in *Housing Studies.*

Thomas Forget is an Assistant Professor and Undergraduate Programme Coordinator in the School of Architecture at the University of North Carolina at Charlotte. His design practice, Ciotat Studio, is based in New York City and addresses multiple scales of the built environment, from media installations to urban design. The primary focus of his practice, teaching, and research is the evolving nature of the public realm of the contemporary city, in particular the crisis of public space posed by new technologies of communication. In 2007 he was the leader of a design team that was short-listed as a finalist in the international competition for the redevelopment of central Reykjavik. Since that time, he has lectured on the competition and its aftermath in the wake of the economic crisis. His contribution to this book synthesises these lectures into an analysis of the culture of abundance that preceded the crisis, as well as a critical survey of recent urban projects in New York City that resonate with the ethic of scarcity that emerged in Reykjavik after the crisis. His essay considers the condition of Iceland as emblematic of recent developments in the United States.

Dr. Emanuel Giannotti is an architect and has a PhD in Urbanism. He is currently undertaking post-doctoral research about the popular neighbourhoods of Santiago de Chile. Since spring 2012 he has been part of the teaching staff of the European postgraduate Masters in Urbanism (IUAV University of Venice). For some years he collaborated with the studio of Paola Viganò and Bernardo Secchi, based in Milan, following urban projects in Belgium, France and Spain.

His recent research is focused on the social dynamics at the heart of urban transformations, in order to evaluate the multiple interactions between actors and stakeholders, the role of the technicians and how they respond to a specific social and political context and the influence of those dynamics in the creation of urban forms.

Dr. Tinna Grétarsdóttir is an anthropologist, and lives and works in Iceland. Her research focuses on art, cultural politics and competing discourses of creativity in the neoliberal regime. She is currently working on multidisciplinary art-based research at the former NATO base on Reykjanes Peninsula, examining how histories of the Cold War, militarised landscapes, social crisis and concepts such as ecology, creative labour, and alternative economies unfold. Dr. Grétarsdóttir has published her research in books, journals and exhibition catalogues. She has been involved in curatorial works: *Koddu* (*Come along*), 2011 and *Haltu kjafti og vertu þæg* (*Shut up and be nice*), 2009. Dr. Grétarsdóttir has also taught at the University of Iceland and the Iceland Academy of the Arts.

Magnús Jensson is an architect in Reykjavik. He is a radical rethinker, who lectures about dwelling, the city, transport, gender, musical composition etcetera.

Salvör Jónsdóttir, a geographer and planner, she earned her BS degree in geography from the University of Iceland where she finished her graduate studies with some research into the environmental history of Reykjavik in the 19th century. Her M.Sc. in Urban and Regional Planning is from the University of Wisconsin, Madison. She has worked as the planning director for the city of Reykjavik and a planning consultant in Iceland, taught at universities in Iceland, and been involved in planning consultations and teaching at the University of

Wisconsin-Extension. She has also served on several committees related to environmental issues and historic preservation in Iceland.

Dr. Sigríður Kristjánsdóttir holds a B.Sc. in geography from the University of Iceland. She received a master's degree in urban planning at the University of Washington, Seattle, in 2000 and a Ph.D. degree from the University of Birmingham, UK, in 2007, specialising in urban morphology. Dr. Kristjánsdóttir is director of the masters programme in planning at the Agricultural University of Iceland where she has been an assistant professor since 2004. Her research has focused on the formation and development of urban areas as a part of a wider territory, including the urban fringe, and the interactions between the business cycle, planning regulations and the urban landscape. Dr. Kristjánsdóttir is an active contributor to international research projects, particularly collaboration between the Nordic countries.

Hannes Lárusson studied arts and philosophy in Iceland, Italy, Canada and America. Since 1977 he has exhibited extensively, internationally and in Iceland, with one-man shows, group exhibitions and performances. Through teaching and writing broadly, Lárusson has added critical understanding to Icelandic art and culture, and several books have been written about his projects. His ongoing project on the Icelandic farmhouse is of great importance in the context of the built environment, and will contribute significantly towards the knowledge of future potentials for habitation in Iceland.

Arna Mathiesen grew up on the outskirts of the Reykajvík Capital Area, where the intersection between the urban and the wild was her playground. She spent a year studying philosophy and art history in her native Iceland, before embarking on her architectural

education elsewhere, as it was not available in her home country at that time. She received a BA in architecture at Kingston Polytechnic in the UK, studied architecture and sculpture in Oslo for a year and then a MArch from Princeton University in 1996. Mathiesen is one of two founding partners of April Arkitekter AS, an architectural practice and research unit based in Oslo, with projects ranging from furniture to large housing estates and urban developments. She recently led a case study on the Reykajvik Capital Area before and after the financial meltdown, for The Oslo School of Architecture and Design.

Dr Kristín Vala Ragnarsdóttir is a Professor of Sustainability Science at the Institute of Earth Sciences and Institute for Sustainable Development at the University of Iceland. She is an Honorary Fellow of the Schumacher Institute for Sustainable Systems in Bristol. Prior to moving to the University of Iceland in 2008 as Dean of Engineering and Natural Sciences she was Professor of Environmental Sustainability in the Department of Earth Sciences, University of Bristol. Dr Ragnarsdóttir received a BSc in geochemistry and petrology at the University of Iceland, and MS and PhD in geochemistry at Northwestern University, Evanston, Illinois, specialising in geothermal systems. Dr Ragnarsdottir's transdisciplinary studies include determining sustainability indicators and ecosystem services for soil, as well as developing frameworks, processes and indicators for sustainable communities with food security at the centre. She is currently undertaking worldwide evaluations of natural resources.

Massimo Santanicchia is an architect and urbanist, teaching at Iceland Academy of the Arts of Iceland. He has conducted extensive research on the relationship between social, political, cultural factors and the city, focusing mainly on the cities of Reykjavik, Istanbul and Bogota. Santanicchia is working as a freelance architect and urban consultant for the city of Reykjavik. After winning a public competition, in the summer of 2012 he worked on the construction of small urban interventions to reactivate the public spaces of Reykjavik. Santanicchia has published and lectured extensively on the subject of sustainability: at the University of Venice (IUAV), the Architectural Association (AA) in London, the University of Perugia, The Oslo School of Architecture and Design (AHO), the Technological Education Institute of Athens (TEI), and in Zurich and Riga.

Silliness (Kjánska) is a collaborative collective founded by artists Anna Björk Einarsdóttir, Magnús Þór Snæbjörnsson and Steinunn Gunnlaugsdóttir in the autumn of 2006. The collective has sought to intervene in a society characterised by a booming economy at the height of the banking bubble, with inspiration from the broad tradition of committed art in the 20th century – both anarchist and Marxist-inspired theories and politics.

Hildigunnur Sverrisdóttir is an Adjoint Lecturer and Programme Director of Architecture at the Iceland Academy of the Arts. During the past decade, she has taught in various academic settings, mainly within architecture and design, but also in dramaturgy and various transdisciplinary programmes. Her work and teaching focuses primarily on the social, political and ontological relevance of architecture. She studied architecture in Paris and Copenhagen, graduating from The Royal Danish Academy of Fine Arts in 2004. Alongside her academic career, she has pursued traditional architectural practice, participated in competition teams with agencies in Iceland and abroad, and worked as a consultant to the Reykjavík building and planning authorities. Sverrisdóttir has initiated social, theoretical and critical activities within the local design field, earning her a nomination to an annual architectural prize, as well as a government artist's salary. She regularly appears as a cultural commentator on Radio 1.

Ásdís Hlökk Theodórsdóttir took over as director of the National Planning Agency in Iceland in 2013. Prior to that she was programme director in transport and urban planning at Reykjavik University. She has wide experience in planning and envi-

ronmental assessment, ranging from work for local and national government to consultancy, teaching and research. Her main areas of specialisation are planning systems and planning processes, strategic environmental assessment, environmental impact assessment, sustainable planning and the relationship between urban design, land use and transportation planning. In 2010-2012 Theodórsdóttir led a research project dealing with planning and development in the greater capital region of Iceland. The aim of the study was to analyse the role municipal planning has played in the construction boom of the first decade of this century, and to examine how municipal plans for the greater capital region guide and support a balanced and sustainable future development of the area.

Jeremy Till is an architect, educator and writer. Since 2012 he has been Head of Central Saint Martins College of Arts and Design, and Pro Vice-Chancellor, University of the Arts London. His extensive written work includes *Flexible Housing* (with Tatjana Schneider, 2007), *Architecture Depends* (2009) and *Spatial Agency* (with Nishat Awan and Tatjana Schneider, 2011). All three of these won the RIBA President's Award for Outstanding Research, an unprecedented sequence of success in this prestigious prize. As an architect, he worked with Sarah Wigglesworth Architects on their pioneering building, 9 Stock Orchard Street, which won the RIBA Sustainability Prize. He curated the British Pavilion at the 2006 Venice Architecture Biennale.

Dr. Sybrand Tjallingii is an urban and regional planner who graduated from Utrecht University (1969) in landscape ecology and took his PhD at Delft University of Technology (1996). His thesis, *Ecological Conditions,* analyses the role of ecology in urban planning. From 1975 to 1990, he worked with the Urban Design and Environment Group at the School of Architecture of Delft University of Technology. From 1990 to 2002, he was part of the planning department of Alterra, the research institute of Wageningen University, and worked as a senior researcher on practical planning studies related to the role of green areas in urban planning, commissioned by local and regional governments, and the EU. In 2002 he returned to the Design and

Environment Group at Delft to work as associate professor in teaching and research. After retirement in 2006, he carried on as a guest lecturer and researcher at Delft University of Technology. Present research projects include assignments from the Ministry of Spatial Planning and the Development Agency for Rural Areas. From 2008 to 2012, he lectured in the European postgraduate Masters in Urbanism courses at the University of Venice (IUAV).

Dr. Giambattista Zaccariotto is an architect and educator. He studied architecture and urbanism at the University of Venice (IUAV) and at Delft University of Technology. He has recently completed a design-driven PhD study, which focused on the development of spatial-functional models to integrate water at all spatial scales of urban landscapes. He is currently teaching in design masters courses at The Oslo School of Architecture and Design (AHO) and also works as an independent landscape architect. He has previously worked with West 8 Urban Design & Landscape Architecture in Rotterdam, and Studio Secchi-Viganò Architecture & Urbanism in Milan. As lecturer and critic, he has been a guest at graduate and postgraduate design universities: IUAV in Venice, TU Delft, European Institute of Design in Milan, University of Agricultural Sciences in Vienna and KU Leuven. As a researcher, he participated in design-driven projects, including Restructuring Cultural Landscapes and Water and Asphalt (2006), the Project of Isotropy for the metropolitan region of Venice (2008), and SCIBE Scarcity and Creativity in the Built Environment (2011), while working at April Arkitekter in Oslo.

Ursula Zuehlke graduated in electrical and information engineering from Darmstadt Technical University. Having always been passionate about Iceland, she moved there from Germany in 2001 and worked at the University of Iceland, in high schools and in an engineering consulting firm. Through this work, she became even more interested in the sustainable use of natural resources. She enrolled in the Environment and Natural Resources programme at the University of Iceland, and is currently working on her masters thesis on impervious surfaces in Reykjavík.

Illustration Credits

Acknowledgements

It would have been impossible to compile the materials in this book without the knowledge, efforts, cooperation and support of so many people. It has been a pleasure to work with all who have contributed to this comprehensive effort to analyse and reflect upon matters of scarcity, excess and creativity. The book results from a long process, yet it provides only a glimpse of an ongoing struggle to raise questions and devise solutions.

Thanks to all the authors of this book, and to all those who generously contributed imagery and other materials and insights into both the local and the global situation. In addition to those with official credits in the book, others deserve thanks: our interview subjects, all those who gave feedback on different contributions in various stages of completion, and bloggers who discovered, publically exposed and analysed the idiosyncrasies of the financial meltdown. My co-editors Giambattista Zaccariotto and Thomas Forget have been instrumental throughout the process of collecting the materials, and determining the scope of the project and its many details.

Thanks are also due to a research group conducting a broad inquiry into scarcity and creativity in the built environment (SCIBE), which was founded at the time of the financial meltdown that shattered so many preconceptions about architecture and urbanism. The serendipitous collision between the theoretical research and a real-life crisis steered SCIBE in unexpected ways. No one could have envisioned this book at the start of the crisis and the editors and many of the contributors were not even aware of each other then, but the insights from the collective research of SCIBE acted as a unifying force, for which I am deeply grateful.

I am predominantly grateful to Jeremy Till for initially inviting me to participate in the SCIBE project. Special thanks go to the leader of the SCIBE team in Oslo, Christian Hermansen, who has been supportive from the very start. Discussions with other members, Deljana Iossifova, Edward Robbins and Barbara Ascher in particular, have been very helpful.

Thanks to Karl Otto Ellefsen, the Dean of The Oslo School of Architecture, for giving April Arkitekter the opportunity to be responsible for the SCIBE-Reykjavík case study on behalf of the school. And thanks to HERA (Humanities in the European Research Area) for financing SCIBE, which later contributed some of the financial support necessary for the publication of the book.

Appreciation goes to Professor Paola Viganò for leading the effort to bring students from the European Post-master in Urbanism (EMU) and for contributing so much energy and insight during the workshops, and for her leadership in steering the panel discussions at the Nordic House on the final presentations of the workshops. Gratitude also goes to all of the students who participated and contributed their amazing work within such a tight schedule. Special mention should be made of the participants in the workshops who are not mentioned elsewhere in the book. Professor Trausti Valsson from the University of Iceland, Þorsteinn R. Hermannsson from

Mannvit Engineering, research scientist Hlynur Óskarsson from the Agricultural University of Iceland, Daði Þorbjörnsson from the Iceland Geosurvey and Einar Sveinbjörnsson from Veðurvaktin, provided excellent insights through their lectures.

I am grateful to Ólöf Örvarsdóttir, the planning director for the city of Reykjavík, for her support of the SCIBE project before HERA dedicated funds to it, as well as to Hjálmar Sveinsson, an activist-turned-politician in Reykjavík, for his support and helpful discussions at the outset.

Thanks to Sigrún Birgisdóttir, the director of the design programme at the Iceland Academy of the Arts, and to Sigríður Kristjánsdóttir, the director of the master's programme in planning at the Agricultural University of Iceland, for generously hosting the workshops. Their cooperation was critical to our process.

Several agencies contributed with materials that were a real asset for the mapping of the site: The municipalities in the Reykjavík Capital Area, National Land Survey of Iceland, National Energy Authority of Iceland and the Icelandic Met Office.

The financial support of the Icelandic National Planning Agency towards a seminar organised at the Icelandic Farm in September 2012 was a real encouragement, as were the preparations with Hannes Lárusson and Kristín Magnúsdóttir on the farm.

On-site food, accommodation and close relations with the local spirit were essentials not to be underestimated. Here friends and family in Iceland played a more important role than they might think. My warmest thanks go to them.

Language was a huge obstacle for the book project, as most of the authors are not native speakers of English, which is the language of publication. Philippa Thomson edited the text with great care and effort. Her kindness, grace, and professionalism have helped to steer this project through its challenging deadlines.

We were blessed to have the helping eye of book artist Brynja Baldursdóttir. Her contribution to the book design has been priceless, as she helped to maximise the visual impact of the book's themes.

Actar, the publisher of the book, has been an excellent partner, thanks to Ricardo Devesa and Núria Saban for their help.

Eyjólfur Kjalar Emilsson contributed to translations and (more importantly) has been by my side throughout the process, functioning not only as my personal dictionary on a daily basis, but also as an endlessly encouraging force in so many other ways.

Employees of April Arkitekter who have contributed to the project, and are not mentioned elsewhere, are Laufey Björg Sigurðardóttir, Lene Marie Grennes, Borghildur Indriðadóttir and Kristín Anna Eyjólfsdóttir.

Finally, Kjersti Hembre, my partner in April Arkitekter in Oslo and a member of the SCIBE team, has been the most fervent supporter of the project from the beginning, and she cannot be honoured enough for her many types of input, and for making space within our architectural practice for this project.

Arna Mathiesen
April Arkitekter

Published by
Actar Publishers, New York, 2014

Book concept:
April Arkitekter

Editorial director:
Arna Mathiesen

Co-editors:
Giambattista Zaccariotto
Thomas Forget

Text editor:
Philippa Thomson

Book design:
Arna Mathiesen
Brynja Baldursdóttir
Giambattista Zaccariotto

Production:
Núria Saban

Printed in:
Grafos S.A.

Distribution

ActarD
New York
www.actar-d.com

151 Grand Street, 5th floor
New York, NY 10013, USA
T +1 212 966 2207
F +1 212 966 2214
salesnewyork@actar.com

ISBN 978-1-940291-32-1

A CIP catalogue record for this book is available
from the Library of Congress, Washington D.C.,
USA.